The Practicing Stoic

THE
PRACTICING
STOIC

by WARD FARNSWORTH

 DAVID R. GODINE · *Publisher · Boston*

First published in 2018 by
DAVID R. GODINE · *Publisher*
Boston, Massachusetts
www.godine.com

LIBRARY OF CONGRESS
CATALOGING-IN-PUBLICATION DATA

Names: Farnsworth, Ward, 1967– author.
Title: The practicing stoic : a philosophical user's manual / Ward Farnsworth.
Description: Jaffrey : David R. Godine, Publisher, 2018.
Identifiers: LCCN 2017053581 | ISBN 9781567926118 (alk. paper)
Subjects: LCSH: Stoics.
Classification: LCC B528 .F37 2018 | DDC 188–dc23
LC record available at https://lccn.loc.gov/2017053581

SIXTH PRINTING 2021
Printed in the United States of America

CONTENTS

PREFACE

This is a book about human nature and its management. The wisest students of that subject in ancient times, and perhaps of all time, were known as the Stoics. Their recommendations about how to think and live do not resemble the grim lack of feeling we associate with the word "Stoic" in English today. The original Stoics were philosophers and psychologists of the most ingenious kind, and also highly practical; they offered solutions to the problems of everyday life, and advice about how to overcome our irrationalities, that are still relevant and helpful now. The chapters that follow explain the most useful of their teachings in twelve lessons.

That was a brief statement of the book's purpose. The reader who finds it enough can proceed to Chapter 1. For those wanting a fuller account of the rationale for what follows, here is a more complete statement.

1. The body of ideas known as Stoicism contains some of the finest and most durable wisdom of any age. The Stoics were deep students of desire, fear, status, emotion, and much else that bedeviled the human race thousands of years ago and bedevils it still. They were philosophers of a down-to-earth sort, seeking by force of their insights to free ordinary people from their sufferings and illusions. The Stoics had their limitations, of course; they held some beliefs that very few people do anymore. But in other ways they were far ahead of their times. They said a number of the best things that anyone ever has.

The teachings of the Stoics are as interesting and valuable now as when first written – maybe more so, since the passage of two millennia has confirmed so much of what they said. The idiocies, miseries, and other discouragements of our era tend to seem novel or modern; hearing them described in a classical dialogue reminds us that they are nothing new. This itself was a claim of the Stoics: that the stories and problems of humanity don't change, but just put on new masks. The same can be said for the remedies. The most productive advice anyone offers nowadays, casually or in a bestseller, often amounts to a restatement or rediscovery of something the Stoics said with more economy, intelligence, and wit long ago. The reader does better by going straight to the sages.

2. The Stoicism in this book is a set of ideas developed by philosophers in Ancient Greece and Rome. To repeat what was mentioned at the outset – for it cannot be said enough – Stoicism did not mean for them what the word now means to us. Stoicism usually refers in current English to suffering without complaint. Our subject is something else and more; philosophical Stoics don't do much complaining, but for them that is a small point. (A Stoic would probably be glad to complain if it helped anything.) "Stoic" also is sometimes thought to mean *grim*, which is likewise inaccurate. A Stoic is more likely to be distinguished by mild humor in the face of things regarded as grim by others. Or some imagine that Stoics seek to remove themselves from the world – that it is a philosophy of retreat into oneself. Again, the opposite is true. Stoics are supposed to involve themselves in public affairs. The result of all this confusion is a minor nuisance for the student of our subject: most people don't know what Stoicism is, but they don't know that they don't know.

Stoicism got its name because Zeno of Citium (c. 334–c. 262 BC), the founder of the school, did his teaching in a public colonnade or porch ("stoa") overlooking the Agora of Athens. Stoicism was known on this account as the Philosophy of the Porch, as opposed to the Philosophy of the Garden (that of Epicurus), or the Philosophy of the Academy (that of Plato), or the Philosophy of the Lyceum (that of Aristotle), with each name referring to the place where the teachings of the school were imparted. So if "Stoicism" sounds too forbidding because of the word's popular meaning, you could try telling your family that you are studying the philosophy of the porch. They might like that. More probably, readers who take an interest in our subject will also have to get used to explaining that when they refer to Stoicism, they mean the old kind.

3. Many books about the Stoics have been written already. I should say a word about why another one seemed worthwhile, and what this book does that others don't.

Stoicism has come to us largely through the works of three philosophers who lived in the first two centuries A D: Seneca, Epictetus, and Marcus Aurelius. Seneca and Marcus Aurelius were Romans; Epictetus was Greek, but he, too, lived and taught for part of his life in Rome. The works they left behind tend to be miscellaneous in character. Often they consist of notes written without much order, or sorted in ways no longer meaningful to most readers. Nor are their writings cross-referenced. As a result, what any one of the Stoics taught about a given subject, let alone what they all said, cannot easily be found in one place. Seneca's comments on a topic might be spread over three letters and an essay; the same issue might be addressed at the start and end of the discourses attributed to Epictetus, or at a few different places in the journals of Marcus Aurelius. This arrangement can have its advantages (sometimes unsystematic is better), but it is inconvenient for the student of Stoic thought who wants to see it as a whole, or to gain a sense of one writer's views, or the views of all of them, on a particular topic.

This book is a response to the state of affairs just set forth. It has three main features. First, it seeks to organize the ideas of the Stoics in a logical manner that might be described as progressive. Foundational principles come first, then their applications. I've tried to put the applications into a sequence that builds naturally, and, where relevant, that follows their growth in complexity. This approach is roughly reflected in the order of the chapters, in the order of the headings within each chapter, and in the order of the discussions under each heading. Those who don't care about the progression can roam around at random; the chapters are self-contained, so you don't need to read one to understand the next. But having a framework may still make the relationships between different parts of the philosophy easier to see.

Second, the book aims to draw together the most important points that the different Stoics made about each subject and each division of it. Sometimes they spoke to different aspects of an issue; Seneca addresses one part of it, Epictetus takes another. In other cases the same topic was discussed by all the Stoics. In that event it is interesting to compare what they said and how they said it. The format lets them talk to each other.

Third, this book mostly presents the teachings of the Stoics in their own words – or, more precisely, in the translated words of the writers who stated them best. The introduction that comes after this preface, and then the introductions to each chapter, provide summaries for those who want them, and the first chapter contains more exposition than the others because it is the beginning. But the reader can skip all this with no harm done. Those who prefer restatements of Stoicism have other books to read, including some fine recent entries. The goal of this one is to concisely present what the Stoics themselves said. There is a distinct pleasure to be had, for those with a taste for it, in receiving these lessons from their original sources. An observation about our world that seems sharp and accurate gains a different kind of force when we see it expressed twenty centuries ago. The truth improves with age.

4. Carving up long works into excerpts, as is done here, necessarily means a sacrifice of context. Isolated sentences from a letter that Seneca sent to Lucilius can't capture the larger purpose for which his point was offered, for example, let alone the full thrust of the letter or the place of it in the series that Seneca wrote. Nuances inevitably are lost. More generally, selecting and editing and arranging the words of different writers can't help but affect the way the reader takes their meaning. The same is true of the book's organization. It presents Stoicism under a series of headings meant to be intuitive – for us. It is not the organization that any of the Greeks or Romans would have used (in any event, none did).

In short, the choices this book makes about what to include, and in what order, amount to an interpretation of Stoicism. That will be plain enough to anyone familiar with the primary sources. I emphasize the point for the sake of those who are not. My hope is that readers who like what follows and haven't yet read the originals will do that next.

5. This book means to offer a short course on Stoicism taught princi- pally by the Stoics. In the living version of the class that I now and again imagine, though, we might have guest speakers as well. Mon-

taigne, for instance, would make a lively visitor. So we also will hear from him and some others who might be regarded as intellectual descendants of the Stoics because they were strongly and visibly influenced by them. The descendants typically depart from Stoicism on certain matters of theory but agree on points more germane to this book. They give memorable expression to Stoic tenets and offer variations on them; sometimes they pilfer them outright. Their writings are instructive to read for their own sake, and because they let us see Stoicism as a tradition of thought that has lived beyond its classical origins.

We sometimes will hear as well from Greek and Roman writers who were not Stoics themselves but agreed with them in ways that will interest us. It is usually the same story: philosophers of nearby schools dispute the answers to questions about the purpose of life or the nature of the universe or comparably large matters; but they have some of the same views on more immediate questions, such as how to think about money or fame or hardship or death. They converge as they descend.

In sum, this book treats Epictetus, Seneca, and Marcus Aurelius as canonical sources. If they said it, I've been prepared to include it here and to regard it as a Stoic teaching, whether or not it follows from anything the Greeks are thought to have said earlier. (More on this in a moment.) And once a proposition is so identified, the book will frequently pause to show how other writers – cousins or descendants of the Stoics – have expressed the same point, or illustrated it, or elaborated on it.

The book preserves some redundancies in the writings of the Stoics and eliminates others. If different writers are shown to have said similar things, it is because their agreement is of interest. If one writer is shown to have made the same point in different ways, it is because each restatement offers a detail of possible value to the student of the idea. But those who find that they have had enough of a theme can move on to the next without penalty.

6. Stoicism originated in Ancient Greece. This book nevertheless gives little attention to the early Greek Stoics. It might seem unjust as well as unfortunate to leave out Zeno, Cleanthes, Chrysippus, and other charter members of the school while including the later writers just

mentioned. The difficulty is that only fragments from the Greeks have survived; while there are texts from Galen, Cicero, Plutarch, and others that talk about what the early Stoics said, we have no extended works in which they speak for themselves. The secondhand accounts we do have are enough to allow scholars to piece together many of the earliest Stoic ideas. But the results don't fit well in a book of this type.

The approach this book takes instead, in which the late Stoics are treated as canonical, is open to objection. Stoicism might better be defined by the oldest and most consistent precepts of the philosophy that we can make out, rather than by the views of writers who came later and who have sometimes been accused of heterodoxy. In the late Stoic writings we do find some departures from what the Greeks seem to have said, or tension with it, or digressions from it. Not everything a Stoic says is Stoicism, on this view, and some of the entries in this book shouldn't have qualified for inclusion because they don't hew closely enough to the core principles of the philosophy.

My view is that the late Stoicism of the Romans deserves its own attention and credit. It was not as theoretically subtle and original as what the Greeks developed, no doubt, but it has other strengths. The late Stoics were more than popularizers of what the earlier ones said; they were innovators in adapting it to ordinary life. Granted, we don't have much of what the Greeks wrote (or all that the Romans did). But what we do know suggests that the late edition of the philosophy was a more pragmatic enterprise than the early one, as Roman undertakings are apt to seem when set next to Greek examples of the same. The late Stoic writings thus hold up as a separate body of work with its own advantages and choices of emphasis, and can be read with profit and without apology for however it might differ from the Greek variety.

The most important example of this point should be stated directly: I include some positions of Seneca's, and call them Stoic, that some would say are departures from Stoicism. Seneca's views on certain subjects (especially involving emotion) are, in my judgment, more helpful and convincing than those of other Stoics. Readers who like what he had to say should not have to be described as "Senecaists" or some comparable deformity. Seneca was the most prolific Stoic writer whose work has survived. I think it makes best sense to treat his teachings, even where they occasionally departed from those of the

Greeks, as a version of Stoicism rather than a mix of fidelity and lapses from it. If the result must be named distinctly, let it be called Reform Stoicism or some such thing.

7. Stoicism covered many topics, so a comment is in order about which ones are discussed here and which are left out. This book is, first, about ethics. In casual current usage, "ethics" usually means rules about what behavior is right and wrong, particularly in how we treat other people. For philosophical purposes, though, the term also refers to larger questions about how to act and the meaning of the good life. Much of what follows belongs under that heading, though some of what the Stoics thought about ethics, including much of their theoretical apparatus, is not included.

The subject of the book can also be described as psychology, a topic we regard as separate from philosophy but that the Stoics did not distinguish from it. Most chapters take as their topic some aspect of human irrationality and how it might be tamed. These inquiries of the Stoics will appeal to some readers for the same reasons they find modern cognitive psychology appealing. Understanding our own minds helps us become conscious of our misjudgments – a little more perceptive, a little more self-aware, a little less stupid. In some respects cognitive psychologists, too, can be counted as successors of the Stoic philosophers, and the Stoics anticipated a number of their findings, as we shall see. But the Stoics, while less rigorous in their methods, are more ambitious in the questions that they try to answer. They propose a way of life.

The Stoicism of this book, then, amounts to a blend of philosophy and psychology, and is weighted toward the latter. It is so weighted because the Stoics, from where we now sit, are at times more enduring psychologists than philosophers. Some of the philosophical claims they regarded as most important – about what it means to live according to nature, for example, and why it matters – have not aged well. Their observations of how our thinking betrays us have more often stood the test of time. There admittedly can be a loss as well as a gain from this choice of emphasis. Some Stoic teachings might appear incomplete or unsatisfying unless they are joined to first principles of ethics or metaphysics of a kind largely avoided here. But I expect that readers will bring along their own first principles regardless, and will find the counsels of the Stoics compatible with a wide range of them.

Stoicism originally included much besides ethics and psychology. The ancients would have identified logic and physics as additional headings; within physics they would put theories that we might assign to cosmology and theology, including some that, as just noted, have few subscribers left. The Stoics believed that reason infuses the universe. They saw nature as intelligent, and events as expressing the will of a benevolent Providence. This book does not present any of those doctrines or show how the ideas discussed here relate to them. They would require a volume much longer than this, and meanwhile most readers today don't believe in Stoic theology and don't need it to learn from what else the Stoics said. Such is the argument of this book: that the writings of the Stoics have retained vitality not because their beliefs about the cosmos still have resonance but because their insights about human nature do.

I do not mean to suggest that the Stoics have nothing worthwhile to say about the largest problems of life. On the contrary, Stoicism is rewarding in part because it addresses some of the same questions about how to live that many religions do, and sometimes reaches similar conclusions, but it gets there by observation and reason alone. Or rather it *can*. The Stoics did have a theology, as I've said, but you may remove that pillar and the temple still stands; their analysis and advice hold up well enough without it. To put the point differently, the Stoics, when speaking in the manner shown here, will sometimes be found to arrive at the same summit as the followers of other philosophical or spiritual traditions, but they go up the mountain by a different face. Their way will be congenial to many modern readers. It is the path of logic, reflection, and knowledge of humanity.

8. The title of this book is open to more than one reading. The discussion just offered will suggest the intent behind it. I regard a practicing Stoic as someone who tries to remember the wisdom of the Stoics when dealing with life and thinking about thinking – one attracted to Stoicism not as a creed or theology but as valuable counsel and as a form of psychological hygiene. This book, in other words, is for those more interested in the practice of Stoicism than the theory of it. (Of course I

do not begrudge any others their love of the high theory of Stoicism, and they are entitled to books, too – but they already have them.)

The title also means to suggest humility. A practicing Stoic can be considered one who is trying to learn what the Stoics had to teach and not doing it well enough to yet claim success. The book is not *The Proficient Stoic* or *The Complete Stoic*, but merely *The Practicing Stoic*, which is no doubt the most that anyone should say. ("Are you a Stoic?" "No, no – just practicing.")

9. Stoicism has been subject to many criticisms over the years, and a reader of this book should know something about them. My interest here is not so much in the technical critiques of Stoicism made by academics or rival philosophers, many of which I would concede or leave to the specialists. I'm more interested in knocks the Stoics have taken in literary conversation, because those assessments strike closer to the teachings that are the subject of this book. Chapter 13 shows three of the most standard of those criticisms and makes comments on them. It is healthy for those getting to know the Stoics to see what people who don't like them have said, and to consider what might be said back.

I will offer here my general view that many critics of Stoicism treat it uncharitably. They seize on the most extreme things the Stoics said but don't account for ways in which those points were offset or qualified elsewhere. Or they judge the whole philosophy by its least appealing adherents or features or moments. That's too bad, not because it is unfair to the Stoics (they don't care), but because it distracts from all that they said that was better. But the criticisms still stick. Many of those who have a view about Stoicism base it on what they have heard, and what they have heard is calumny. Or they associate Stoicism with some single idea that seemed memorable when they heard it, probably because it was jarring. If you study the subject and talk about it with others who haven't, you quickly will see for yourself. Opinions about Stoicism outrun knowledge of it by a hundred to one.

The critic might reply that I make an opposite sort of mistake, displaying the more attractive parts of Stoicism and giving short shrift to the rest. That may be true. I have tried to fairly introduce, in a modest space, the applied ethics and psychology of the late Stoics. But if there are more and less reasonable versions of a teaching available, the book goes with the more reasonable one. I've sought to take the Stoics at their best and to present them that way – not for the sake of persuading anyone to think well of Stoicism, but for the sake of producing a useful book.

10. The concessions in the last few comments invite a specialist's criticism that I wish, finally, to anticipate: that this book isn't about Stoic philosophy after all – that what it contains isn't Stoicism *or* philosophy. It isn't Stoicism because it leaves out too much that the Stoics thought necessary. It isn't philosophy because it leaves out too much that is foundational. Maybe it's good advice, but then it's *just* advice.

Distinctions of this kind may be boring to lay readers, but they mean something to academic scholars, and as an academic I sympathize. In view of this project's purpose, though, they are of little consequence. I have attempted to create a book for those interested in what the Stoics had to say of lasting value about the challenges of being human. If leaving out deeper precepts, or including ideas that stray from them, makes the result something other than Stoicism or other than philosophy, our subject can just be described as the practical teachings of those once known as the Stoics. I waive claims to anything more.

Nobody should care much anyway about being called a Stoic or not a Stoic. There are no membership benefits that I am aware of. If we want to read our authors in the spirit in which they wrote, we do best to focus on the questions that they thought were of higher priority. They weren't principally seeking to raise the status of a philosophical school or decide who was entitled to join. They were trying to help people see more clearly, live more wisely, and bear the burdens of their lives with greater ease. Let us see how they did.

———

Dramatis personæ. Getting acquainted with the Stoic teachers for oneself is a distinct pleasure of the study of our subject. For the benefit of those not already familiar with them, here are short introductions to the writers who will appear most often in the pages to come.

1. *Major figures.* Three Stoic writers dominate this book. On some topics all of them comment; on others, one specializes more than the rest.

a. *Seneca the Younger* (Lucius Annæus Seneca) lived from about 4 BC to 65 AD. He was born in Spain; his father, who had the same name (and so is remembered as Seneca the Elder), was a teacher of rhetoric. The son – our Seneca – was taken to Rome when he was young. After a period spent in Egypt, an early career as a lawyer and politician, and a banishment to Corsica, he became a tutor and advisor to Nero, an emperor of odious reputation. Seneca also became very wealthy.

Seneca was accused in 65 AD of joining the Pisonian conspiracy, which had unsuccessfully plotted the murder of Nero. He was ordered by the emperor to commit suicide, which he did; he cut open his veins and sat in a hot bath, though they say it was the steam that finally did him in. The episode is the subject of a fine allusion in *The Godfather Part II*.

Seneca wrote letters, dialogues, and essays on philosophy, and also a number of plays. His writings are the most substantial surviving body of work on Stoicism and the largest source of material for this book. His wealth and political life have sometimes caused him to be condemned as a hypocrite whose life was inconsistent with his teachings; this issue is discussed in a brief essay in Chapter 13.

b. *Epictetus* lived from approximately 55 to 135 AD. He was born in the region we now know as Turkey, and spent most of the first half of his life in Rome. (On that account I sometimes refer to him as one of the Roman Stoics.) When philosophers were banished by the emperor Domitian, Epictetus moved to Greece and established a school there.

Epictetus left behind no writings. The words attributed to him are the notes of Arrian, a famous student in his school. From Arrian we have works known as the *Discourses* of Epictetus, as well as the *Enchiridion* (or handbook; Arrian wrote in Greek). We also have some fragments of less certain authenticity preserved by Stobæus (c. 500 AD). When you read Epictetus, it is best to imagine that you are seeing a rough transcript of what he said in class.

Epictetus led a life very different from those of our other principal writers. He had a crippled leg. He was born a slave, and his later liberation gave him a curious connection to Seneca. As noted a moment ago, Seneca was accused of joining a conspiracy to murder Nero. The conspiracy was revealed in part by Epaphroditos, a secretary to the emperor.

Epaphroditos was the owner of Epictetus and may have been responsible for freeing him, though this and much else in the life of Epictetus involves some conjecture. (Epaphroditos was later put to death for failing to prevent Nero's own suicide. It was an age of hardball.)

Epictetus studied in Rome under Musonius Rufus, another Stoic who left behind no writings of his own (but later we will see a couple of fragments from him, too). Musonius Rufus is probably best known now for teaching that women are as suitable for philosophical training as men.

c. *Marcus Aurelius* (in full, Marcus Aurelius Antoninus Augustus) (121–180 AD). In 138, the emperor Hadrian selected his own successor, Antoninus Pius, by adopting him. Hadrian also arranged for Antoninus to adopt Marcus Aurelius, who was then a teenager. Antoninus Pius ascended to the throne soon thereafter and was emperor for more than twenty years. Upon his death in 160, Marcus Aurelius became emperor and reigned for nearly twenty years more – for the first eight years in partnership with his adoptive brother, Lucius Verus, and during the last few years in partnership with his son, Commodus, of whom the less said the better. For a stretch of time in the middle, Marcus Aurelius was emperor by himself, an improbable moment in which the most powerful person in the world may have been the wisest.

Mostly while on military campaigns during the last decade of his life, Marcus Aurelius wrote philosophical notes to himself in Greek that we call his *Meditations*. He never described himself as a Stoic in his writings, but he was a devoted student of the philosophy and has long been treated as one of its defining authors.

As is apparent from these notes, our Roman Stoics lived overlapping lives, but just barely. The first died when the second was young, and the second died when the third was young. So far as we know, none of them had any contact with each other. Marcus Aurelius does thank one of his Stoic teachers, Junius Rusticus, for giving him a copy of the *Discourses* of Epictetus, and he occasionally quotes from that work.

2. *Supporting classical characters.* A few other classical writers – not quite Stoics, but friends or cousins of them – will appear less regularly.

a. *Epicurus* lived from 341 to 270 BC. He is associated, of course, with a philosophy of his own: Epicureanism. By reputation Epicureanism and Stoicism are opposites. The first is said to be a philosophy of sensual enjoyment and indulgence, the second a philosophy of austerity. Both reputations are misleading; the English word "Epicurean" nowadays gives an impression of Epicurus about as inaccurate as the word "Stoicism" does of the Stoics. The two schools of thought do differ in many significant ways, most prominently in the relationships they propose between virtue and happiness. Epicurus regarded pleasure as the only rational motive for mankind, whereas the Stoics thought that our sole rightful purpose is to act virtuously – to live by reason and to help others, from which happiness follows assuredly but incidentally. Despite these differences, however, the Epicurean and the Stoic agree on some important points in their analysis of judgment, desire, and other subjects.

Like many other Hellenistic philosophers, Epicurus produced books and essays that have not survived. But we do have a small set of his writings – mostly a few letters and some sets of quotations. One of the larger sets was found in a manuscript in the Vatican Library during the 19th century (the so-called "Vatican Sayings"). Epicurus is also quoted here and there in the writings of other classical authors. Indeed, a number of the entries from Epicurus in this book were preserved by Seneca himself, who saw it as no cause for embarrassment.

> I shall continue to heap quotations from Epicurus upon you, so that all persons who swear by the words of another, and put a value upon the speaker and not upon the thing spoken, may understand that the best ideas are common property.

Seneca, *Epistles* 12.11

This book will take the same liberty.

b. *Cicero* (Marcus Tullius Cicero) lived from 106 BC–43 BC. He was one of the leading statesmen and philosophers of Rome and the most eloquent of its orators. His life was spent largely in political activity as a lawyer, quæstor, prætor, and consul. After the assassination of Julius Cæsar he advocated the rescue of Rome as a republic; when Mark Ant-

ony secured his place as one of the dictators of the Second Triumvi-
rate, he ordered Cicero to be executed and mounted his head and
hands in the Forum.

Cicero turned to philosophical writing in the last phase of his life.
Though much of his aim and achievement was to preserve Greek philosophical learning, he also made contributions of his own. His philosophical books were, until recent times, among the most widely read
and influential of all ancient works. The extent to which Cicero can be
considered a Stoic has been subject to debate; he shared some of their
positions and rejected others. But he agreed with the Stoics on many
points of ethics, and described Stoic principles in ways that sometimes
are helpful to see.

c. *Plutarch* (Lucius Mestrius Plutarchus) (c. 46–120 AD) was a prolific
biographer and philosopher, and the author most notably of *Parallel
Lives* and his essays collected as *Moralia*. He was born in Greece and
lived most of his life there, though at some point he became a citizen
of Rome. He also was a priest at the Temple of Apollo at Delphi for his
last 25 years. In his philosophical writings he followed Plato and made
many direct criticisms of the Stoics; he probably would not have
wanted to appear in a book about them, though his feud seems mostly
to have been with the earlier Greeks and to have involved claims not
at issue here. At any rate, his ethics sometimes overlapped with those
found in late Stoicism, as we will see.

3. *Supporting modern characters.* This book sometimes offers passages
from more recent writers who, as explained earlier, might be regarded
as descendants of the Stoics. They can't be called Stoics themselves
because they parted company on too many questions. But they all
read the Stoic philosophers and all expressed Stoic views on some of
the topics in this book.

a. *Montaigne* (Michel Eyquem de Montaigne) (1533–1592) was a
French lawyer, statesman, and philosopher. His essays, written over a
22-year period after he mostly withdrew from public life, popularized
that format as a kind of literature. Their topics are wide-ranging and
often personal. He provides a more extensive discussion of certain

Stoic principles, and sometimes a more felicitous statement of them, than is found anywhere else. Montaigne was raised to speak Latin as his first language, and he retained a lifelong love of classical learning. At one point he was referred to as the French Seneca, and he openly acknowledged the debts he owed to Seneca and to Plutarch.

> When I transplant the reasoning and ideas of others   Montaigne, *Of Books*
> into my own soil and mix them with mine, I deliber-   (1580)
> ately conceal the names of the authors. I do this to
> rein in the temerity of those hasty criticisms thrown
> at every kind of writing, especially contemporary writings by
> living authors, and writings that use common language – lan-
> guage that invites anyone to be a critic, and that can make the
> conception and design of the book seem just as common. I want
> them to tweak Plutarch on my nose, and to burn themselves by
> insulting the Seneca in me.

The truth of this assessment will be seen in the pages ahead.

Montaigne also presents some challenges for our purposes because he was an endless fount of ideas, many of which were not Stoic. He was a skeptic, and so could not subscribe to the more theoretical claims the Stoics made. And some of his views changed over time; I will treat 1580 as the date of publication of his essays, but he wrote and revised them over two decades. So I have generally proceeded as explained earlier: by asking first whether a given claim is found in the ancient Stoic sources. If so, restatement or elaboration of it by Montaigne will sometimes be provided.

b. *Samuel Johnson* (1709–1784) was an English essayist, poet, critic, and producer of various other sorts of writings. He was author of the most celebrated and amusing of all English dictionaries, and subject of the most celebrated and amusing of all English biographies (Boswell's *Life of Johnson*). Though Johnson has occasionally been described as a Stoic, that label is best avoided. It is not a fit to his writings as a whole, some of which disparage Stoicism. In Johnson's writings on ethics, though, he agrees with the Stoics often and gives excellent form to many of their ideas. Johnson often wrote in a style that now seems grandiloquent; he liked to use fancy words. This makes his prose hard for most people now to enjoy in long stretches, but our doses of it will be modest.

c. *Adam Smith* (1723–1790) was a Scottish philosopher and economist who was a close reader of the Stoics and much influenced by them, though his own philosophy departed from Stoicism in many ways. He critiques it in detail in *The Theory of Moral Sentiments*, but agreed with the Stoics on some particulars.

Smith was a contemporary of Samuel Johnson's (and a professor of James Boswell's at Glasgow University), but it is not clear whether they met. A well-circulated anecdote describes Smith and Johnson as encountering each other for their first and only time at a party in Scotland and briefly exchanging insults, but it has been challenged (alas) as a fabrication.

d. *Arthur Schopenhauer* (1788–1860) was a pessimistic German philosopher and essayist. He wrote about a large range of topics, many of them far from the concerns of this book, but touched on a number of our themes in essays he wrote late in his life. He, too, did not accept Stoicism in full; he made criticisms of it and did not believe happiness could be achieved through reason. But as with all the others mentioned here, he read the Stoics carefully and had much in common with them on subsidiary points. He is good to have around in a book like this, because his interpretations of Stoic ideas have a different and more modern intellectual flavor than that of our other writers.

There will be appearances by some other writers as well, including Guillaume du Vair, a French contemporary of Montaigne's. He attempted explicitly to reconcile Stoicism with Christianity (a movement sometimes known as neostoicism). His interpretations are of occasional interest, as are those of various others who appear too infrequently in the book to introduce here.

As this book is meant for a general audience, I have not used endnotes. When explanatory comments have seemed worth including, they appear directly in the text. They consist mostly of brief notes on ancient characters who are referenced by the Stoics or their friends. Part of the fun of our topic is the chance to touch and learn a bit about the classical world, inexhaustibly fascinating ancestor of our own.

Translations. This book contains many passages not originally written in English. Translations of all the original texts exist in the public domain; when those versions were found suitable for our purposes, I have not hesitated to use them. This book is especially indebted to many venerable translations in the Loeb Classical Library, and the translations of Schopenhauer done by T. Bailey Saunders. In most cases, however, the translations have been revised or redone entirely to bring them into clearer modern English that remains faithful to the originals. I wish to thank Michael Gagarin, Karl Galinsky, Andrew Kull, and Ashley Voeks – magnificent colleagues, all of them – for their talent and generosity in helping with that aspect of the project.

There is at times some sexism in how the Stoics expressed themselves that I have not expunged, as my aim has been to show what they said as accurately as can be managed. I hope the reader will look past that issue. While the political thinking of the Stoics is mostly beyond our scope, they were notable for welcoming women to the practice of their philosophy and favoring equality for them in other ways as well, sometimes to a degree that was radical for their times.

For comments on the manuscript, my thanks to the colleagues mentioned above and to Anya Bidwell, Chelsea Bingham, Daniel Cantor, Robert Chesney, Alexandra Delp, Anne Farnsworth, Janet Farnsworth, Sam Farnsworth, David Greenwald, Aaron Gregg, Harris Kerr, Lucy Lyford, Brian Perez-Daple, Reid Powers, William Powers, Ion Ratiu, Christopher Roberts, Ted Skillman, and Brendon Walsh. Responsibility for errors is mine. I also wish to thank Carl W. Scarbrough, the best in the business, for designing the inside of the book and the cover.

INTRODUCTION

This introduction provides a brief and rough summary of the ideas that follow in the rest of the book. None of this is necessary; it is just a convenience for the reader who likes to have an overview.

1. We appear to go through life reacting directly to events and all else in the world. That appearance is an illusion. We react to our judgments and opinions – to our thoughts about things, not to things themselves. We usually aren't aware of this. Events come to us through lenses of judgment that are so familiar we forget we have them on. Stoics seek to become conscious of those judgments, to find the irrationality in them, and to choose them more carefully.

   This idea is foundational to Stoicism. Sometimes its truth can be seen by noticing that when we react to an event, we really are reacting to what we've said to ourselves about it. (Perhaps we can say something different.) But in other cases it's harder to see the role of judgments in producing a reaction because they are so ingrained that we take them for granted. The Stoics investigate those reactions – the ones that feel inevitable – by comparing them to the very different reactions that others have to the same things when their conditioning is different (or to the different reactions that *we* have when our circumstances are different). The Stoics infer from all this that our way of reacting to anything depends, indeed, on thoughts we think and beliefs we hold, however deeply buried they might be. Since those beliefs and thoughts belong to us, they should be possible to change, and so ought to be subject to more rational scrutiny than they usually get. Our experience of the world is our own doing, not the world's doing, and the Stoic means to take responsibility for it. (Chapter 1.)

2. We should stake our well-being on what we can control and let go of attachment to what we cannot. We generally can't control events, or

the opinions or behavior of others, or whatever else is outside ourselves. The Stoic thus considers money, fame, misfortunes and the like
to be "externals" and regards them with detachment. A Stoic still has
preferences about those things, and so would prefer to avoid adversity
and would rather have wealth than not have it. But *attachment* to those
desires or fears is considered a guarantee of anxiety, and a form of
enslavement to whoever controls the objects of them. In sum, it is
against Stoic policy to worry about things that you can't control. What
we can control, and should care about, are our own judgments and
actions. (Chapter 2.)

To put these first two points together: we get attached to things
beyond our control, and this brings us misery; we are oblivious to
features of our thinking that we *can* control and that, if managed better, would bring us peace. Stoicism tries to make us conscious of this
pattern and reverse it.

3. Having shown that our thoughts and judgments create our experience, the Stoics set out to change them. They use two kinds of strategies for the purpose, which we might describe as analytical and
intuitive. The analytical side consists of rational arguments – using
reason and evidence to show the futility of material desires, the needlessness of various fears, and so on. The intuitive approach consists of
looking at life from perspectives that are meant to have effects similar
to those produced by the arguments, but without the arguments. One
just sees things from a new angle and has a different reaction to them.
Equivalently, we might say the Stoics seek to persuade with words and
with pictures.

To begin with the intuitive side – that is, the pictures: we all have
an ordinary and automatic point of view. We peer out from inside
ourselves and see the world accordingly. This angle of observation
makes us captive to a long list of deceptions. The Stoic seeks freedom
from them by looking at events from a standpoint less obvious – comparing things or events to the scale of the world, or of time, or seeing
them as they would look from far away, or seeing your own actions
through the eyes of an onlooker, or regarding what happens to yourself as you would if it happened to someone else. Stoics gain skill at
viewing life from perspectives that encourage humility and virtue and

that dissolve the misjudgments we live by. (Chapter 3 and elsewhere.)

The Stoic also works not only to overcome the fear of death but to treat mortality as another source of perspective and inspiration. Being mindful that existence has an end puts daily life into a new and ennobling light, in much the same way as contemplation of the scale of the universe or of time. (Chapter 4.) Stoics also practice thinking about comparisons that make us less neurotic than the envious ones with which we ordinarily harass ourselves. (Chapter 5.) These all can be considered more examples of seeking wisdom through adjustment of one's point of view.

4. Turning to the analytical side of the project: the Stoics dissect the stuff of our inner lives – desires, fears, emotions, vanities, and the rest. Those states are shown to be products of how we think and to mostly amount to mistakes; the judgments that lie behind them are found on inspection to be false or idiotic. The Stoic remedies broadly amount to applications of the first two points above. We react not to things but to our judgments about them, and those judgments typically consist of scripts that follow convention or are otherwise foolish or fictitious. The Stoics try to dismantle the scripts and give us better ways to talk to ourselves about the subjects of them.

The more specific Stoic analysis of desire, fear, and perception consumes the middle of the book, and it can't all be summarized here. Much of it involves observing human nature very exactly and taking notes on the irrationality found in it. For example: we desire whatever we don't have, we are contemptuous of whatever we do have, and we judge our state and our success by comparisons that are arbitrary and pointless. We chase money and pleasure in ways that can bring no real satisfaction; we pursue reputation in the eyes of others that can do us no real good. We torment ourselves with fear of things that are more easily endured than worried about. We constantly overlook the present moment because we are preoccupied with future states that will in turn be overlooked when they arrive. There is more, but this suggests the flavor of the Stoic diagnosis. In short, we vex ourselves with beliefs, mostly half-conscious, that came from nowhere we can name and that tend to make us unhappy and ridiculous. Thinking better and harder about the workings of our minds can free us from many subtle insanities.

It might seem doubtful that analysis of the kind just sketched could change the way one feels about anything; you might suppose that people can't be talked out of habits and feelings that they weren't talked into. But sometimes they can. Besides, the point of Stoicism is that, without realizing it, we often *were* talked into our feelings – by our culture, and by ourselves. (Chapters 5–9.)

5. Stoics take a different view of adversity than is conventional. They don't seek out pain or hardship, but they seek a mindset that isn't thrown into disarray by those things and that is able to turn them to good. It is an unavoidable and important part of life to meet with what we don't want; and unwanted developments produce great achievements, strong characters, and other things we *do* want. Stoicism therefore means applying one's imagination to developments that seem unwelcome and using them as a kind of building material. The Stoic takes whatever happens and puts it to use. (Chapter 10.)

6. Some of the Stoic analysis just reviewed has a rich but negative character. It amounts to the reasoned annihilation of false beliefs that serve us badly. As a Stoic sees it, though, none of this should lead to despair. Quite the contrary: we can find more durable and satisfying pleasures in wisdom, and less anguish, than we ever did in our illusions. The Stoics propose an escape to reality, so to speak, not away from it. Seeing the world clearly, understanding life rightly, and being free from the fictions that drive most people crazy – this they regard as the good life. (Chapters 6 and 11.)

Stoics also advocate enjoyment of pleasures that are natural, as opposed to the ones we invent to keep ourselves going on the hamster wheel. The usual Stoic goal is to enjoy or react or do most else in the world with moderation and a sense of detachment. (Chapter 6.) The detachment doesn't mean a lack of attention or interest. It is better considered an aspect of moderation – moderation, that is, in our relationships to external things. Stoics avoid getting elated or crushed or otherwise worked up about them. A large share of Stoicism might be viewed, in effect, as interpretation of two famous inscriptions above the entrance to the Temple of Apollo at Delphi: know thyself; nothing in excess. The Stoics turn those maxims into a detailed philosophical practice.

7. Stoicism also offers a strong affirmative vision of what life is for: the pursuit of virtue. Living virtuously means living by reason, and the Stoics regard reason as calling for honesty, kindness, humility, and devotion to the greater good. It also calls for involvement in public affairs – that is, in the work of helping others in whatever ways are available. Instead of living to satisfy desires, Stoics regard themselves as meant to function as parts of a whole. There is great joy to be had in this, though it is not the variety that comes from the acquisition of things or approval from others. The happiness the Stoic seeks is *eudaimonia* – the good life, or well-being. Virtues bring about that type of happiness as a byproduct, and Stoics regard this as the only reliable path by which happiness can be secured. (Chapter 11.)

8. Stoicism is meant to be a practice, not a set of claims to admire. It is hard work, because many of our judgments, and the fears and desires that follow from them, are habitual and hard to change or set aside, and they are constantly reinforced by our surroundings and conventions. Taming the mind through reason takes the same kind of commitment that we associate with martial arts or other demanding physical disciplines. In return, Stoicism offers happiness, equanimity, and sanity. (Chapter 12.)

9. Stoicism has been criticized for advocating a lack of feeling or compassion, for asking the impossible of its students, and (because it is impossible) for making hypocrites out of those who claim to follow it. Chapter 13 offers some replies to those criticisms. To summarize:

a. Stoics can be viewed as using reason as a substitute for time and experience. They try to respond to temptations and hardships in about the way they might if they were experiencing them for the thousandth time; the recommended Stoic reaction to most things is the natural reaction of the veteran. This way of looking at Stoicism makes it less otherworldly. The philosophy can be considered an effort to help us toward the state of mind we might reach on our own with more time, rather than as an effort to make us less human. Looking at Stoicism this way also makes clear that the practicing Stoic isn't unfeeling or uncaring. The Stoic responds to the suffering of others like a good doctor who has seen it all before: with activity and compassion, though probably without much emotion.

b. Perfect Stoicism is no doubt impossible. The "wise man" held up as an example by the Stoics is best viewed as an ideal. It is meant to provide a direction rather than a destination. This shouldn't be alarming. Many philosophical and religious traditions call on their aspirants to work toward an ideal that nobody quite attains. The question is not whether anyone gets to the end. It is whether we are helped by trying.

c. Claims of Stoic hypocrisy usually arise from a misunderstanding of what Stoicism is for. Its purpose is to help those who use it, not to give them a basis for judgment of others. The exhortations of Stoic teachers sometimes create a different impression, but explaining Stoicism and practicing Stoicism are different activities. Stoicism may have to be taught if it is to be learned, but the practice of it involves thinking and acting, not preaching. If Stoicism inspires claims of hypocrisy against its students, the students are probably bad Stoics – not because their actions are impure, but because they are talking too much.

The order of the chapters in this book mostly follows the order of the discussion above. Many discussions of Stoicism start instead with the definition and place of virtue in the philosophy. In this book that comes later – not because it is less important than what comes earlier, but because it is (I suggest) easier to follow once one understands the Stoic view of what reason means and requires, which is a theme developed in the earlier chapters. I say this so the reader will feel free to take what follows in whatever order is of interest, and not treat the sequence of topics as an argument of the Stoics or as an argument of mine. The order is proposed as useful, not at all as essential.

The Practicing Stoic

Chapter One

JUDGMENT

The first principle of practical Stoicism is this: we don't react to events; we react to our judgments about them, and the judgments are up to us. We will see the Stoics develop that idea in the pages to come, but this expression of it is typical:

> If any external thing causes you distress, it is not the thing itself that troubles you, but your own judgment about it. And this you have the power to eliminate now.

Marcus Aurelius, *Meditations* 8.47

The Stoic claim, in other words, is that our pleasures, griefs, desires and fears all involve three stages rather than two: not just an event and a reaction, but an event, then a judgment or opinion about it, and *then* a reaction (to the judgment or opinion). Our task is to notice the middle step, to understand its frequent irrationality, and to control it through the patient use of reason. This chapter starts with the noticing. Later chapters will talk about the irrationality and offer advice about control. We begin here because the point is foundational. Most of the rest of what the Stoics say depends on it. Soon we will hear from them about "externals," desires, virtues, and much else. But it all begins with the idea that we construct our experience of the world through our beliefs, opinions, and thinking about it – in a word, through our judgments – and that they are up to us.

For many students of Stoic philosophy, this first principle starts as counterintuitive, gradually becomes convincing, and finally seems obviously true – and then the cycle may be repeated, because the mind constantly gives us an opposite impression that appears convincing in its own right. Our reactions to whatever happens usually feel direct and spontaneous. They don't seem to involve judgment at all, or at least no judgment that could ever be otherwise. The Stoics consider all this an illusion. The work of dispelling it is hard because the mind is an unreliable narrator of where our reactions come from. It tells us that we respond to externals – to things out there, not to the mind itself. It has to learn to see and describe its own role more accurately. Stoicism means to help us think better about our thinking, to teach the mind to understand the mind, to make the fish more aware of the water.

The truth of the Stoic claim is easiest to see when we react to an offense given strictly to the mind. Suppose someone insults you. The insult is meaningless apart from what you make of it. If you are bothered, it must be because you care: a judgment. Instead you could decide not to care, and that would be the end of the insult for you. All irritations can be viewed the same way – the noisy neighbor, the bad weather, the traffic jam. If you are riled up by these things, you are riled up by the judgments you make about them: that they are bad, that they are important, that one should get riled up about them. The events don't force you to think any of this; only you can do it. The same then goes for bigger setbacks, and for desires, fears, and all the rest of our mental events. We always feel as though we react to things in the world; in fact we react to things in ourselves. And sometimes changing ourselves will be more effective and sensible than trying to change the world.

When we feel physical pain or pleasure, the role of the mind in forming our reaction is harder to see. Pains and pleasures seem like immovable facts that owe nothing to our thinking. But even then the Stoics insist that our judgments about those feelings produce our experience of them. Yes, pain is pain: a sensation that exists no matter what we think about it. But how much bother it causes, how much attention we pay to it, what it means to us – these are judgments, and all ours to determine. Pains and pleasures are made bigger or smaller by the way we talk to ourselves about them, or by judgments that are too deep to articulate but are nevertheless our own. We underrate the power of these judgments because we barely notice them. Stoics notice them. (For more discussion of pain in particular, see Chapter 10, Section 11.)

The idea that our reactions depend on our judgments can seem especially strange if "judgments" are all imagined to be conscious and rational. But a judgment can take many forms. You conclude that spiders aren't dangerous yet still are afraid of them; does this show that your fear is separate from any opinion you hold about spiders? No, it just means you have conflicting judgments – that spiders are safe and that they aren't. The second will take time to uproot even after you decide it's wrong. Put differently, some judgments are just things we say to ourselves, and those are the easier ones to fix. Others are ingrained and nonverbal. The Stoics will sometimes include under "judgments" everything that we bring to the world when we meet it – the appetite that we have or don't have that makes a plate of food look better or worse, or a lifetime of conditioning that produces the same effect. These may not be easy to change. Here, then, is another reason why Stoicism is hard, and why nobody gets to perfection. Some reactions may belong to us and yet not quite be up to us. Or they are up to us in theory but we don't have the psychological strength to change them.

More broadly, the Stoics didn't distinguish in their thinking as we now might between all the forms that our judgments can take – conscious opinions, unconscious attitudes, conditioned responses, chemical predispositions, genetic tendencies, and so on – and how some of those can be changed more easily than others. They do make a few such acknowledgments. The Stoics say that some reactions have a physical basis we can't control.

(See Chapter 9, Section 1.) And Seneca concedes that we are born with some temperamental features that can't be changed. (See Chapter 10, Section 10.) But our ordinary reactions to things – our reactions at rest – are viewed mostly just as ours to control with practice. Anyone can see how difficult this idea would be to carry out in full; just think of your own strongest likes and dislikes, and how hard it would be to reverse them with any amount of thinking. But fortunately, and importantly, Stoicism doesn't care what our tastes are, and doesn't call for reversal of our aversions and desires. It calls for detachment from them. That isn't easy, either, but it is far more often feasible.

We may consider it the Stoic goal, in any event, to become conscious of our judgments and take control of them as far as we can. One's ability to do this may be limited in ways that we now understand better than the ancients did; a psychiatric patient would not be well-served by a helping of Epictetus alone. But even after making allowances of that kind, the Stoics would say that our ability to change our experience by changing our thinking about it is much greater than we usually suppose. Many of the judgments they urge us to notice and to reconsider aren't so deeply rooted. They're just habits and conventions.

The Stoics don't expect these claims to be taken on faith. They support them with arguments. Sometimes they use easy examples, such as the insults already discussed – things that anyone can see are a big deal only if we decide they are. For reactions that more stubbornly seem to be inevitable, though, the Stoics often use comparisons to make their point. They look at the different ways that people react to the same events in different circumstances, times, and places. What some people fear (and can't imagine *not* fearing), others don't; what some are ready to die for, to others is nothing. The pain or grief that seems a brute fact to us is experienced very differently in other conditions and cultures. Evidently our reactions aren't inevitable after all. They somehow must be our doing, and depend on judgments that we hold and thus might be able to change.

1. *The general principle*. Stoicism starts with the idea that our experience of the world – our reactions, fears, desires, all of it – is not produced by the world. It is produced by what the Stoics call our judgments, or opinions.

> Everything depends on opinion. Ambition, luxury, greed, all look back to opinion; it is according to opinion that we suffer. Each man is as wretched as he has convinced himself he is.

Seneca, *Epistles* 78.13

Cicero's expression of the Stoic thesis:

> Grief, then, is a recent opinion of some present evil, about which it seems right to feel downcast and in low spirits. Joy is a recent opinion of a present good, in response to which it seems right to be elated. Fear is an opinion of an impending evil that seems unbearable. Lust is an opinion about a good to come – that it would be better if it were already here.

Cicero, *Tusculan Disputations* 4.7

How Epictetus put it:

> For what is weeping and wailing? Opinion. What is misfortune? Opinion. What is discord, disagreement, blame, accusation, impiety, foolishness? All these are opinions and nothing else.

Epictetus, *Discourses* 3.3.18–19

> Men are disturbed not by the things that happen but by their opinions about those things. For example, death is nothing terrible; for if it were, it would have seemed so even to Socrates. Rather, the opinion that death is terrible – *that* is the terrible thing. So when we are impeded or upset or aggrieved, let us never blame others, but ourselves – that is, our opinions.

Epictetus, *Enchiridion* 5

The first line of this last passage from Epictetus was a favorite of Montaigne's. He inscribed it in Greek into one of the beams in the ceiling of his study.

Montaigne, *That the Taste of Good and Evil Things Depends in Large Part on the Opinion We Have of Them* (1580)

An ancient Greek saying holds that we are tormented not by things themselves but by the opinions that we have of them. It would be a great victory for the relief of our miserable human condition if that claim could be proven always and everywhere true. For if evils have no means of entering us except through the judgments we make of them, it would then seem to be in our power to dismiss them or turn them to good.

Montaigne, *On Democritus and Heraclitusi* (1580)

Things in themselves may have their own weights, measures, and qualities; but once we take them into us, the soul forms them as she sees fit. Death is terrifying to Cicero, coveted by Cato, indifferent to Socrates. Health, conscience, authority, knowledge, riches, beauty, and their opposites all strip themselves bare when they enter us and receive a new robe, of a new color, from the soul.... Let us therefore find no excuses in the external qualities of things; what we make of them is up to us. Our good or bad depends on no one but ourselves.

Montaigne, *That the Taste of Good and Evil Things Depends in Large Part on the Opinion We Have of Them* (1580)

Comfort and poverty depend on the opinions we have of them; and riches, glory, and health have only as much beauty and pleasure as is attributed to them by their possessor. Each of us is as well or badly off as we believe. The happy are those who think they are, not those who are thought to be so by others; and in this way alone, belief makes itself real and true.

Or as Montaigne said elsewhere in the same essay: "That which gives value to a diamond is our having purchased it; to virtue, the difficulty of it; to devotion, our suffering; and to medicine, its bitterness." Compare:

HAMLET: ...There is nothing either good or bad, but thinking makes it so.

Shakespeare, *Hamlet*, 2, 2

It is not what things are objectively and in themselves, but what they are for us, in our way of looking at them, that makes us happy or the reverse.

Schopenhauer, *The Wisdom of Life* (1851)

2. *Stoic practice.* As stated so far, this first teaching might seem to be a way to understand the workings of the mind and where our reactions come from. It is that. But Stoicism differs from some other philosophical traditions because it is an activity, not just a theory. If we view the idea of this chapter in that way, it is an instruction to take more responsibility than usual for one's thinking – to treat how we talk to ourselves as a choice. If distress is caused by our thoughts about things rather than by the things themselves, we should try dropping those thoughts and using new ones.

That claim may sound so elementary, or perhaps so much easier said than done, as to barely be worth making at all. But it does have to be said, because treating thoughts and judgments as matters of choice is central to the practice of Stoicism but something that many people rarely do and some never do. It is more normal to take for granted whatever ideas and opinions pass through our minds, living them out with no more scrutiny than we give to the air we breathe. Stoics try to get enough separation from those mental events to control them – to notice the irrationality that drives much of what we say to ourselves and to replace it with something wiser. Sometimes this is indeed easier said than done, or even impossible. But sometimes, to the contrary, it is easier than it sounds. You stop saying one thing to yourself and say another instead. Later you work on judgments less verbal in form. Squashing a noxious and conventional thought is a wholesome source of Stoic satisfaction, and an ability that improves with practice.

Consider some examples of our first Stoic teaching

expressed this way by Marcus Aurelius – not just as an interesting idea to think about, but as a practice useful to try.

Marcus Aurelius, *Meditations* 4.7

Take away your opinion about it, and "I have been harmed" is taken away. Take away "I have been harmed," and the harm is taken away.

Marcus Aurelius, *Meditations* 5.2

How easy a thing it is to push away every thought that is disturbing or out of place, and to be at once in perfect peace.

Marcus Aurelius, *Meditations* 6.52

We can choose to have no opinion about a thing, and not to be troubled by it; for things themselves have no power of their own to affect our judgments.

An example from Seneca:

Seneca, *Natural Questions* 3 Pref. 15

What is important? To raise your life high above chance occurrences, and to remember that it is a human life – so that if you are fortunate, you know this will not last long; or if you are unfortunate, you know that you aren't really, if you don't think you are.

There is some risk that these passages, taken in isolation, could seem to encourage a kind of vacuity. The goal of the Stoic, though, is not to empty the mind, but to clear it of foolishness and misjudgment. Learning to identify foolishness and misjudgment will be the work of the chapters to come. In the meantime, we may recall that neither of the authors just shown was seeking a placid or retiring existence, or a mind free from complexity. Each of them, in their times, was among the most powerful people on earth.

3. *Comparisons.* The Stoics claim that our reactions to all things are created by the thoughts or subtler judgments that we have about them. They seek to show this, first, by

asking us to look at ourselves more carefully. Some of our reactions, when viewed in a dispassionate mood, seem obviously to be the results of our own sensitivities.

> When pleasures have corrupted both mind and body, nothing seems to be tolerable – not because the suffering is hard, but because the sufferer is soft. For why are we thrown into a rage by somebody's cough or sneeze, by negligence in chasing a fly away, by a dog that gets in the way, or by the dropping of a key that has slipped from the hands of a careless servant?

Seneca, *On Anger* 2.25.3

But sometimes the conclusion isn't so obvious, and in that case the Stoic's favorite way of proving the claim of this chapter is by use of comparisons. If a reaction that seems natural isn't found elsewhere, maybe it isn't so natural; perhaps it is up to us. The Stoics start by comparing our *own* reactions to similar things in different circumstances, thus demonstrating that the reactions aren't inevitable even in ourselves. They especially like to consider our strong but inconsistent responses to whatever we find annoying. The inconsistency shows that those responses reflect more on us than on the things we curse.

> These same eyes of yours – which at home won't even tolerate marble unless it is varied and recently polished … which don't want limestone on the floor unless the tiles are more precious than gold – once outside, those same eyes look calmly at the rough and muddy pathways and the filthy people they mostly meet, and at the walls of the tenement houses that are crumbled, cracked, and crooked. What is it, then, that doesn't offend your eyes in public but upsets them at home – other than your *opinion*, which in the one place is easygoing and tolerant, but at home is critical and always complaining?

Seneca, *On Anger* 3.35.5

Cicero's account of the Stoic view used the same general approach, comparing how the same people react to identical things in different ways when they bring different judgments to them.

Cicero, *On the Ends of Good and Evil* 3.13

The mere fact that men endure the same pain more easily when they voluntarily undergo it for the sake of their country than when they suffer it for some lesser cause, shows that the intensity of the pain depends on the state of mind of the sufferer, not on its own intrinsic nature.

Or as Montaigne put it more concretely:

Montaigne, *That the Taste of Good and Evil Things Depends in Large Part on the Opinion We Have of Them* (1580)

We are more sensitive to a cut made by a surgeon's scalpel than to ten wounds by sword in the heat of battle.

Next, the Stoics suggest that we think of others who react more strongly than we do to an event or any other provocation. From our vantage point, those others look hypersensitive. But we seem different to ourselves – not hypersensitive – only because we take our own sensitivities for granted. When everyone shares a weakness, it no longer looks like a weakness. It looks like the state of nature.

Seneca, *Epistles* 71.23

Those things with respect to which everyone is weak, we regard as hard and beyond endurance. We forget what a torment it is to many of us just to abstain from wine or be made to get up at daybreak. These things are not essentially difficult. It is we who are soft and slack.

Marcus Aurelius, *Meditations* 6.57

To someone with jaundice, honey tastes bitter; to one with rabies, water becomes terrifying; to small children a little ball is a wonderful thing. Why then am I angry? Do you suppose that mistaken thinking has any less effect on us than bile has in a man with jaundice, or than the poison has in someone bitten by a mad dog?

In the same way that studying is a torment to the lazy, so is abstinence from wine a torment to the drunkard, frugality a torment to the extravagant, and exercise a torment to the delicate and the idle; and so it is with all the rest. Things are not that difficult or painful in themselves. Our weakness and cowardice make them so.

Montaigne, *That the Taste of Good and Evil Things Depends in Large Part on the Opinion We Have of Them* (1580)

This style of thought can be applied not just to the sensitivities that others have to suffering and annoyance, but also to the behavior (and especially the extremes) to which their beliefs drive them—beliefs that may seem strange to us, but no stranger than ours would seem to them.

Any opinion can seem important enough for someone to die for. The first article of the fine oath the Greeks swore and defended in their war against the Medes was that everyone would sooner exchange life for death than their own laws for those of Persia. How many people, in the wars between the Turks and the Greeks, accept cruel deaths rather than reject circumcision for baptism!

Montaigne, *That the Taste of Good and Evil Things Depends in Large Part on the Opinion We Have of Them* (1580)

Or think about those who react *less* strongly than you do to something. If you see them putting up with things that you can't, it makes your reaction seem more clearly to be your own doing. Thus Seneca's conversation with his own pain, which he belittles by thinking of people who endure the same or worse without complaint:

In truth you are only pain – the same pain that is despised by that wretch who is ridden with gout, that the dyspeptic endures for his fancy foods, that a girl bears bravely in childbirth.

Seneca, *Epistles* 24.14

In this passage and others, the Stoics often are shown to speak of despising pain or other externals or as having contempt for them. In English the words "contempt" and "despise" are often used to suggest varieties of hatred. In this book they do not necessarily have that shading.

They usually suggest viewing a thing as small, as unimportant, as something to which we should rise superior; and one can have any or all of this without the overtones of vituperation and dislike.

Cicero, *Tusculan Disputations* 2.20

When you have seen children at Sparta, and young men at Olympia, and barbarians in the amphitheater, receive the severest wounds, and bear them in silence – will you, if some pain happens to brush against you, cry out[?].... Will you not rather bear it with resolution and constancy? – and not cry, "It's intolerable! Nature cannot bear it!" I hear what you say: boys bear this because they are led on by the wish for glory; others do it out of shame, many out of fear – and yet are we afraid that nature cannot bear what is borne by so many, and in such different circumstances?

Montaigne, *That the Taste of Good and Evil Things Depends in Large Part on the Opinion We Have of Them* (1580)

We cope with the pains of childbirth, deemed to be great by doctors and by God himself, through our many rituals; yet there are entire nations that make nothing of them. Never mind the Spartans; among the Swiss women who walk among our foot soldiers, what difference does childbirth make except that, as they trot after their husbands, they carry on their backs the infants that just the day before they carried in their bellies?

As these examples suggest, Stoics are known to engage in casual anthropology – sometimes very casual; the reader may not be impressed by the sophistication of their discussion of childbirth. But the important point is the spirit of these inquiries. Convention and habituation have a remarkable power to affect our judgments. What we are used to seeing others do, and what we are used to doing or feeling ourselves, can make anything seem normal or strange, inevitable or a matter of choice. And those forces tend to do their work invisibly. Once we take in a custom or habit, the judgments they produce feel as though they are strictly our own, not anything that was implanted and could be different. The spell of familiarity must be broken, and this is best done by looking at the great range of responses to the same things that have come to seem natural to people in different conditions.

4. *Food.* We don't need to look to Sparta or swordfights to find good topics for the types of comparisons just shown. As a case study, consider some ways the principle of this chapter can apply to food, a common subject of Stoic reflection. Reactions to what we eat feel unavoidable as we are having them, and seem to be brought about by the food rather than anything in ourselves; but those reactions often owe as much to us as they do to what is on the plate. The Stoics are close students of the appetites that produce our reactions to foods and all else.

> My baker is out of bread; but the overseer, or the steward, or my tenants all have some to offer. "Bad bread!" you say. Wait; it will become good. Hunger will make even that bread taste delicate and seem to be from the finest flour. For that reason we should not eat until hunger bids us; I will wait until I can get good bread or cease to be fussy about it.

Seneca, *Epistles* 123.2–3

> Who does not see that appetite is the best sauce? When Darius, in his flight from the enemy, had drunk some water which was muddy and fouled by cadavers, he declared that he had never drunk anything more pleasant; the fact was, he had never drunk before when he was thirsty.... Compare [to those who use moderation] those you see sweating and belching, being overfed like fatted oxen; then will you perceive that they who pursue pleasure most attain it least, and that the pleasure of eating lies in having an appetite, not in being glutted.

Cicero, *Tusculan Disputations* 5.97, 99–100

Our topic in this chapter is the role of our own judgments, or opinions, in producing our experience. An
appetite can be considered an example of such a judgment if judgments are understood to include all those
things within us that shape our reaction to what we meet
in the world. From a certain point of view this is obvious.
On the one hand, there is the food – an external thing;
on the other hand, there is how much we want it – a
judgment of our own. Still, it might seem surprising to
describe the appetite for food as a "judgment" in the
Stoic sense, because we feel it as a physical fact. Our hunger or thirst presents itself as a sensation of the body, not
as something in the mind that we might be able to
change with our thinking. But the Stoic would challenge
those impressions.

First, our appetites often *are* up to us – in advance. We
may have trouble changing them once they exist, but we
have a lot to say about whether and how they arise in the
first place. Stoics become more aware not just of how our
appetites affect our experience, but of how our choices
affect our appetites. We allow ourselves to get hungry, or
not; we tantalize ourselves with comparisons and other
thoughts that stir desire, or we don't. The management
of appetites – when and how to cultivate them, when
and how not – is part of Stoic practice. (Cultivation is
called for in cases like the one Seneca describes above, as
when learning how to take satisfaction from simple and
natural pleasures.) All this is an example of the reorienta-
tion the Stoics recommend in general: spending less
energy on getting or avoiding things, and more on
knowing why we want them (or don't) and how the way
we think might affect this. We will come back to these
points in later chapters.

Second, though, the Stoic wouldn't concede too
quickly that appetites, even once they exist, are physical
facts entirely beyond the reach of the mind. Of course
great hunger *may* be a hard fact of that sort, just like
other kinds of pains and sensations. But in this setting

and others, it is easy to forget how strongly our minds can influence the sensations that external things create for us. A food that looks delicious can become impossible to enjoy, and cause physical revulsion, if you hear something disgusting about how it was prepared. (You might say then that you've lost your appetite.) It is not much better – it may even be worse – if the mind makes such a discovery afterwards.

> Very often, when men have eaten fancy foods with great pleasure, if they perceive or learn afterwards that they have eaten something unclean or unlawful, not only is this discovery attended by grief and distress, but their bodies, revolted at the notion, are seized by violent vomiting and retching.

Plutarch, *On Moral Virtue* 4 (442f)

Montaigne gave a more picturesque illustration.

> I know a gentleman who, having entertained a large group of company at his house, a few days later boasted as a joke (for there was nothing to it) that he had fed them a pie made out of a cat. One of the young ladies in the party was so stricken with horror that she developed a violent stomach disorder and a fever. It was impossible to save her.

Montaigne, *On the Power of the Imagination* (1580)

Food interests the Stoic in another respect as well. It provides a useful source of analogies from the way the stomach works to the way the mind works.

> Just as the stomach, when it is impaired by disease, gathers bile, and, changing all the food that it receives, turns every sort of sustenance into a source of pain, so, in the case of the perverse mind, whatever you entrust to it becomes to it a burden and a source of disaster and wretchedness.

Seneca, *On Benefits* 5.12.6

Such comparisons were recurring themes for Plutarch, who wasn't a Stoic on the biggest questions but was with them on this and other more immediate issues.

Plutarch, *On Tranquility of Mind* 8 (468f–469a)

In a fever everything we eat seems bitter and unpleasant to the taste; but when we see others taking the same food and finding no displeasure in it, we stop blaming the food and drink. We blame ourselves and our malady. In the same way, we will stop blaming and being disgruntled with circumstances if we see others accepting the same events cheerfully and without offense.

Plutarch, *On Virtue and Vice* 4 (101c–d)

Have you never noticed how sick people turn against and spit out and refuse the daintiest and most expensive foods, though people offer them and almost force them down their throats – but at another time, when their condition is different, their respiration is good, their blood is in a healthy state, and their natural warmth is restored, they get up and enjoy a good meal of simple bread and cheese and cabbage? Such, also, is the effect of reason on the mind.

Dr. Johnson continued the idea, though reversing the facts of the illustration.

Johnson, *The Adventurer* no. 119 (1753)

What we believe ourselves to want, torments us not in proportion to its real value, but according to the estimation by which we have rated it in our own minds; in some diseases, the patient has been observed to long for food, which scarce any extremity of hunger would in health have compelled him to swallow; but while his organs were thus depraved, the craving was irresistible, nor could any rest be obtained till it was appeased by compliance. Of the same nature are the irregular appetites of the mind; though they are often excited by trifles, they are equally disquieting with real wants: the Roman, who wept at the death of his lamprey, felt the same degree of sorrow that extorts tears on other occasions.

Johnson refers to an anecdote told by Plutarch. Crassus and Domitius were Roman generals. Crassus was ridiculed by Domitius for weeping over the death of an eel-like fish that he owned; Crassus replied that the tears were more than Domitius had shed over his three late wives.

Food has been offered here just as an example of how Stoics might think about something familiar. Much of the stuff of daily life can be put through the same sort of analysis. Lest the reader think Plutarch was too preoccupied with food, for instance, here he opens a different field of application to which many of the points just made may be adapted:

> Another illustration is the banishment and retreat of our private parts, which stay calm without trembling in the presence of those beautiful women and boys whom neither reason nor law allows us to touch. This happens in particular to those who fall in love, then hear that they have unwittingly fallen in love with a sister or a daughter. Then desire cowers in fear as reason takes hold, and the body exhibits its parts in decent conformity to that judgment.

Plutarch, *On Moral Virtue* 4 (442e)

5. *Metaphors and analogies.* The Stoics offer a vision of the mind and the role it plays in turning objects and events into an experience felt by the self. We don't have good literal language for describing that role; the mechanisms of the mind aren't visible to us in a way that allows for exact depiction. So as we just saw, the Stoics resort at times to figurative comparisons and analogies that make their ideas easier to see. Some further examples:

> Like a bowl of water, so is the soul; like the light falling on the water, so are the impressions the soul receives. When the water is disturbed, the light also seems to be disturbed; yet it is not disturbed.

Epictetus, *Discourses* 3.4.20

Seneca, *Epistles* 71.24

It takes greatness of mind to judge great matters; otherwise they will seem to have defects that in truth belong to us. In the same way, certain objects that are perfectly straight will, when sunk in water, appear to the onlooker as bent or broken off. It is not so much what you see but how you see it that matters. When it comes to perceiving reality, our minds are in a fog.

From Plutarch:

Plutarch, *On Virtue and Vice* 1 (100b–100c)

Clothes seem to warm us, but not by throwing off heat themselves; for in itself every garment is cold, which is why people who are hot or have fevers frequently are constantly changing clothes. Rather, the clothes that wrap us keep in the heat that is thrown off by the body and don't allow it to be dissipated. A somewhat similar case is the idea that deceives the mass of mankind – that if they could live in big houses, and get together enough slaves and money, they would have a happy life. But a happy and cheerful life does not come from without. On the contrary, a man adds the pleasure and gratification to the things that surround him, his temperament being, as it were, the source of his feelings.

6. *Implications.* This chapter has introduced the most basic idea in the practice of Stoicism: that our reactions to all things are of our own making, even if they don't seem that way, and that we underrate our power to rid ourselves of the ones that serve us poorly. We can end the chapter with some reflections on the fundamental nature of this point. From Epictetus:

Epictetus, *Discourses* 2.11.13

Behold the beginning of philosophy! – perception of men's disagreement with one another, and a search for the origin of the disagreement; rejection and distrust of mere opinion, and inquiry to see whether an opinion is right or wrong; and the discovery of some standard for judgment – just as to deal with weights we discovered the balance, or for straight and crooked things, the ruler.

Epictetus's description, taken broadly, can indeed be viewed as an account of how Stoic philosophy came into being in general, and also of how it might begin for anyone who studies it. We see others talking or thinking or acting differently than we would, or differently than we had imagined anyone might – the disagreement to which Epictetus refers. This causes us to take our contrary thoughts and customs less for granted, and to see them as more dependent on choice and circumstance than we had supposed (the rejection and distrust of mere opinion). We are led to look harder at our own thinking, and to seek a more true and accurate basis for it – the acquisition of the balance and ruler. The result may not be our old opinion or the alternative that surprised us; it may be a perspective that accounts for both and in some way elevates our understanding. Run through that cycle a thousand times and you might reasonably end with the principle discussed in this chapter.

We have reviewed some specific examples of that cycle, but the point goes beyond any particular case. It isn't that our reaction to this or that is created by our own minds. It's that our experience of *everything* is, and that it is up to us to a greater extent than we usually know. The work of philosophy is to take responsibility for our own thinking, and in so doing to liberate ourselves from the attachments and misjudgments that otherwise dictate our experience.

Two more ways to summarize the point of this chapter:

Pay attention to your impressions, watch over them without sleeping, for what you guard is no small thing: self-respect and fidelity and self-pos-

Epictetus, *Discourses* 4.3.7

session, a mind free from emotion, pain, fear, disturbance – in a word, freedom.

Cicero, *Tusculan Disputations*
4.31

It seems to me that in this whole doctrine about mental disturbances, one thing sums up the matter: that they are all in our power, that they are all taken on as a matter of judgment, that they are all voluntary. This error, then, must be uprooted, this opinion stripped away; and just as things must be made tolerable in circumstances we regard as evil, so too in good ones, those things thought to be great and delightful should be taken more calmly.

We can find a good closing remark for this discussion in what Cicero said to close a related discussion of his own.

Cicero, *Tusculan Disputations*
4.38

Now that we have determined the cause of these disturbances of the mind – that they all arise from judgments based on opinion, and by choice – let there be an end to this discussion. Besides, now that the boundaries of good and evil have been discovered so far as they are discoverable by man, we ought to realize that nothing can be hoped from philosophy greater or more useful than what we have been discussing for the last four days. For besides instilling a proper contempt for death, and making pain bearable, we have added the calming of grief, as great as any evil known to mankind.... For there is one cure for grief and other ills, and it is the same. They are all matters of opinion, and taken up voluntarily because it seems right to do so. This error, as the root of all evils, philosophy promises to eradicate utterly. Let us therefore devote ourselves to its cultivation and submit to being cured; for so long as these evils possess us, not only can we not be happy, we cannot even be right in our minds.

Chapter Two

EXTERNALS

A great share of Stoicism amounts to the study of externals: what they are, how we misjudge them, and the ways that they tend to enslave us. An "external" can be defined as something outside ourselves or outside our power. Later chapters will talk about specific examples, such as money, fame, and calamity. Before we reach those cases, though, this chapter considers two sets of Stoic teachings about externals as such.

First, a principal aim of the Stoic is to regard externals without attachment. This has consequences, first, for the decisions and developments that one spends energy fussing about. If Stoics are distinguished by one policy as an everyday matter, it is a refusal to worry about things beyond their control or to otherwise get worked up about them. Detachment also means not letting happiness depend on getting or avoiding externals – wealth, for example, or the good opinion of others.

Now a qualification: of course everyone will have *preferences* about those externals just mentioned and many others. The Stoic would rather have wealth than not have it, and would prefer to do without adversity. But we have to distinguish between preferences and attachments. The difference between them can be seen most easily by comparing how you feel when they aren't satisfied. Imagine wanting one thing more than another and not getting it, but not being too upset as a result. That sort of wish is what we might call a (mere) preference. Having what you prefer is pleasing, and not having it is a disappointment, but it's no threat to your equanimity. And the same can be said when something happens that you would have preferred not happen. It is just spilled

milk, and Stoics try to look at all things they can't control in roughly that way. An attachment is different
because it makes your happiness depend on the object of
it. It pushes and pulls you. This distinction will be discussed more in later chapters. For now, we can just say
that Stoics try for an equilibrium based on the quality of
their thinking and their actions – one that doesn't
depend on anything beyond their control.

The second general Stoic teaching about externals is
that we have a hard time seeing them accurately. Externals fool us, or we fool ourselves about them. Stoicism
offers some ways to get past those deceits, as by taking a
literal view of an external that seems exciting or scary, or
by breaking it down into parts that one can see more
clearly than the whole. Stoics look this way at objects but
also at people, whose reputation or wealth (or lack
thereof) can cloud our judgments of them. The Stoic
tries to see things as they are.

The teachings of the first chapter can be linked to the
teachings of this one. The first chapter was about things
that are up to us. This chapter is about things that are not
up to us. To say it a little more fully: Chapter 1 showed
the claim that we are affected by our judgments about
events, not by events themselves. We therefore have more
control than we think over what we experience. This
chapter is the other side of the coin. We attach ourselves
to externals that we imagine we can control but really
can't, and deceive ourselves about them routinely – habits that make us unhappy and unfree. So in effect these
first chapters suggest a reversal. We waste our energy on
things that aren't up to us, and are barely conscious of
the things that *are* up to us. Stoicism is the effort to turn
that around and to move one's center of gravity to a
more useful location.

1. *Things not up to us*. The Stoics all have their specialties. This chapter belongs first to Epictetus, whose most

constant refrain was the urgency of renouncing desires and fears that depend on externals.

There are things up to us and things not up to us. Things up to us are our opinions, desires, aversions, and, in short, whatever is our own doing. Things not up to us are our bodies, possessions, reputations, offices, or, in short, whatever is not our own doing.

Epictetus, *Enchiridion* 1

There is only one road to happiness – let this rule be at hand morning, noon, and night: stay detached from things that are not up to you.

Epictetus, *Discourses* 4.4.39

Man's perplexity is all about externals; his impotence about externals. What will I do? how will it take place? how will it turn out? Let this not happen, or that! These are all the cries of people worried about things that aren't up to them. For who says, "How can I avoid agreeing to what is false? How can I not turn away from what is true?" If there is anyone whose nature is so fine that he is anxious about those things, I'll just remind him – "Why are you distressed? Rest assured, it's up to you."

Epictetus, *Discourses* 4.10.1

What do we admire? Externals. What do we spend our energies on? Externals. Is it any wonder, then, that we are in fear and distress? How else could it be, when we regard the events that are coming as evil? We can't fail to be afraid, we can't fail to be distressed. Then we say, "Lord God, let me not be distressed." Moron, don't you have hands? Didn't God make them for you? So are you going to sit down and pray that your nose will stop running? Better to wipe your nose and stop praying. What, then – has he given you nothing to help with your situation? Hasn't he given you endurance, hasn't he given you greatness of spirit, hasn't he given you courage?

Epictetus, *Discourses* 2.16.11–14

An aside for those who share my interest in the etymology of insults: "moron" comes from Greek, where the word (transliterated into English) was "mōros." It was an adjective, but Epictetus uses it as a noun, as one might do in English by saying "Now listen, stupid – " Returning to our theme, via Seneca:

Seneca, *Epistles* 23.2

> A man reaches the heights if he knows what makes him joyful, if he has not made his happiness depend on things not in his power. He will be troubled and unsure of himself so long as it is the hope of anything that spurs him on – even if it is not difficult to get, and even if his hopes have never disappointed him.

Marcus Aurelius:

Marcus Aurelius, *Meditations* 6.41

> Consider those things outside your control that you regard as good or bad. When the bad things happen, or the good ones don't, you inevitably will blame the gods and hate the people responsible (or who are suspected of it). We do great injustice through our disputes about these things. But if we judge as good and bad only what is in our power, there is no occasion left to accuse God or take a fighting stance toward men.

Some related comments:

Montaigne, *Of Presumption* (1580)

> Not being able to govern events, I govern myself, and if they will not adapt to me, I adapt to them.

Johnson, *The Rambler* no. 6 (1750)

> The fountain of content must spring up in the mind.... He, who has so little knowledge of human nature, as to seek happiness by changing any thing, but his own dispositions, will waste his life in fruitless efforts, and multiply the griefs which he purposes to remove.

Schopenhauer, *The Wisdom of Life* (1851)

> The ordinary man places his life's happiness in things external to him, in property, rank, wife and

children, friends, society, and the like, so that when he loses them or finds them disappointing, the foundation of his happiness is destroyed. In other words, his center of gravity is not in himself; it is constantly changing its place, with every wish and whim.

2. *Good and evil.* The Stoic analysis of externals implies an adjustment of what we call good and evil. The Stoics hold that those properties lie only in what is up to us – our use of judgment, as discussed in Chapter 1. Things and events, then, aren't good or evil. Our minds are.

> Let us say that the happy man is he who recognizes no good and evil other than a good and an evil mind.

Seneca, *On the Happy Life* 4.2

> Where is the good? In our choices. Where is the evil? In our choices. Where is neither of them? In those things we do not choose.

Epictetus, *Discourses* 2.16.1

The meaning of good and evil to the Stoic will become clearer in the course of the book. Generally the Stoics identify the good with the rightful use of reason, which in turn leads them to a life led for the benefit of the whole – that is, for others. More immediately it means avoiding vices such as greed, dishonesty, and excess. Those are viewed as errors that result from attachment to externals, and from treatment of externals as themselves good and evil. So dropping those attachments, in the way our authors have just suggested, is regarded by the Stoic as an essential first step toward virtue. Said differently, things in the world are (as the Stoics sometimes put it) "indifferent." We turn them to good or evil with our choices.

> "Is health good, and disease evil?" No, you can do better than that. "What then?" To use health well is good, to use it badly is evil.

Epictetus, *Discourses* 3.20.4

> We speak of a "sunny" room when the same room is perfectly dark at night. Day fills it with light;

Seneca, *Epistles* 82.14

night takes it away. So it is with those things we term "indifferent" or "middle," such as riches, strength, beauty, reputation, sovereignty – or their opposites: death, exile, ill-heath, pain, and all the others that we find more or less terrifying. It is wickedness or virtue that gives them the name of good or evil. By itself a lump of metal is neither hot nor cold: thrown into the furnace it gets hot, put back in the water it is cold.

This position allows Seneca an answer to the old question of why bad things happen to good people: they don't. Genuinely bad things occur only in the mind, and the mind of the good person is free from them.

Seneca, *On Providence* 6.1

"But why does God sometimes allow evil to befall good men?" Assuredly he does not. Evil of every sort he keeps far from them – shameful acts and crimes, evil counsel and schemes for greed, blind lust and avarice intent on another's goods. The good man himself he protects and delivers. Does anyone require of God that he should also guard the good man's luggage? No, the good man himself relieves God of this concern; he despises externals.

Marcus Aurelius turned that idea around and made it a test: nothing is good or evil if it can happen as easily to a good person as a bad one.

Marcus Aurelius, *Meditations* 2.11

Both death and life, honor and dishonor, pain and pleasure, wealth and poverty – all these things happen equally to good men and bad, being neither noble nor shameful. Therefore they are neither good nor evil.

Epictetus also discussed more directly what things we should consider good and therefore regard as sources of delight. Again, he discourages excitement about externals; we should be delighted, or not, with the quality of our understanding, not with the properties of things that aren't up to us.

> Don't be elated by a superiority that belongs to another. If the horse in its elation were to say "I am beautiful," one could endure it. But when you in your elation say, "I have a beautiful horse," be aware that you are elated by the good of the horse. What then is yours? Your way of handling impressions. When you are handing them in accordance with nature, that's when to be elated. For then you will be elated about a good of your own.

Epictetus, *Enchiridion* 6

3. *Externals and liberty*. Epictetus had been a slave. He and other Stoics often spoke of dependence on externals as itself a variety of slavery. Someone attached to externals is enslaved to whoever controls them; Stoic philosophy thus is a way to liberation. Epictetus regarded volition, or will, as one's true self, and as the only part of us that is free.

> Whoever then wishes to be free, let him neither wish for anything nor flee from anything that depends on others: otherwise he must be a slave.

Epictetus, *Enchiridion* 14

> If you gape after externals, you will inevitably be forced up and down according to the will of your master. And who is your master? Whoever has power over the things you are trying to gain or avoid.

Epictetus, *Discourses* 2.2.25

> Man is not the master of man, but death and life and pleasure and pain. Bring me Cæsar without these things and you'll see how calm I am. But when he comes with them, amid thunder and lightning, and I am afraid of them, what else do I do but acknowledge my master, like a runaway slave? So long as I have only a sort of truce with

Epictetus, *Discourses* 1.29.60

these things, I'm like a runaway slave standing in a theater; I bathe, I drink, I sing, I do everything in fear and suffering. But if I free myself from these slave-masters – that is, from those things by which these masters are fearsome – what more trouble do I have, what more master?

It was a lively feature of Epictetus's classroom style that those who worried or complained about externals would customarily be denounced as slaves.

Epictetus, *Discourses* 2.13.17

No good man grieves or groans, no one wails, no one turns pale and trembles and says, "How will he receive me, how will he listen to me?" Slave, he will act as *he* sees fit. Why do you care about other people's business?

Epictetus, *Discourses* 4.1.57

In short, if you hear him say, "Wretched me, the things I have to endure!" call him a slave. If you see him wailing, or complaining, or in misery, call him a slave – a slave in a toga with purple trim.

A toga with a purple border was the attire of Roman senators.

Epictetus, *Discourses* 4.1.55

When you see someone groveling before another man, or flattering him contrary to his own opinion, you can confidently say he is not free. And not only if he does this for a mere dinner, but also if it is for the sake of a prefecture or consulship. People who do these things for petty ends you can call petty slaves, while those who do them for grand purposes can be called mega slaves, as they deserve.

Seneca saw all of us as slaves in something like this way.

Seneca, *Epistles* 47.1

I was pleased to hear, through those who come from you, that you live on familiar terms with your slaves. This befits a sensible and well-educated man like yourself. "They are slaves." Nay, men. "They are slaves." No, comrades. "They are slaves." No, they are lowly friends. "They are slaves." No, they are rather our fellow-slaves, if one reflects that Fortune has the same rights over them and over us.

Show me who is not a slave. One is a slave to lust, another to avarice, another to ambition, and all are slaves to fear. I will name you an ex-consul who is slave to a little old woman, a millionaire who is slave to a serving-maid; I will show you youths of the noblest birth in serfdom to pantomime players! No servitude is more disgraceful than that which is self-imposed.

Seneca, Epistles 47.17

Pantomime players were not silent mimes. They were troupes of singers and dancers who would enact scenes from myth and legend. It was a popular form of entertainment in Rome, and the most successful of the players were celebrities.

If you would attain real freedom, you must be the slave of philosophy.

Epicurus, quoted in Seneca, Epistles 8.7

Compare Montaigne:

True and effective servitude is only a concern of those who willingly submit to it and those who try to acquire honor and wealth from the labors of others. One who is content to sit by the fireplace, and who knows how to manage a household without falling into quarrels and lawsuits, is as free as a Duke of Venice.

Montaigne, Of the Inequality Amongst Us (1580)

4. *Adding nothing to externals.* This chapter has been devoted so far mostly to a single Stoic aim: letting go of attachment to externals. A related set of teachings involves the problem of viewing externals clearly. We have trouble resisting externals because they seem appealing or frightening or otherwise impressive; but they seem that way because we haven't learned to see

them as they are. Seneca thought it worthwhile to look at our reactions the way we do at the reactions of children. The point as applied to externals we like:

Seneca, *Epistles* 115.8

> How contemptible are the things we admire – like children who regard every toy as a thing of value, who prefer a necklace bought for a few pennies to their own parents or their brothers. What, then, as Aristo says, is the difference between us and them, except that we elders go crazy over paintings and sculpture, making our folly more expensive?

Aristo of Chios was one of the early Greek Stoic philosophers, and a colleague of Zeno of Citium – the founder of the Stoic school. The same point as applied to externals we fear:

Seneca, *Epistles* 24.13–14

> So remember this above all, to strip away the disorder of things and to see what is in each of them: you will learn that nothing in them is frightening but the fear itself. What you see happening to boys, happens to us too (slightly bigger boys). Their friends – the ones they are accustomed to and play with – if they see them wearing masks, they are terrified. The mask needs to be removed not just from people but from things, and the true appearance of each restored.

To help with this removal of the mask, the Stoics offer two techniques general enough to discuss here (more specific advice will come in later chapters). First is the practice of adding nothing when an external presents itself. As soon as an event happens, we are quick to assign it a meaning. It is tagged as good news or bad news, as a reason for excitement or outrage, and so on. Or we give it a place in a story that we tell ourselves, long-running or new. Then we react to those labels and narratives and imaginings. Stoicism regards this process as a trap. The assignments of value or meaning that we attach to things are usually half-conscious, borrowed from convention, and false or unhelpful. They nevertheless determine how we feel and what we think and do next. So the Stoics say that our thinking should be slowed down, and imagination should be viewed with distrust – not imagination in its creative capacity, but imagination as "the enemy of men, the father of all terrors," as Joseph Conrad once called it. When confronted with a report or an event or an object, in short, the Stoic tries to just see it as it is. Any additions are made with care.

"His ship is lost." What has happened? His ship is lost. "He has been led off to prison." What has happened? He has been led off to prison. The notion that he fares badly, each man adds on his own.

Epictetus, *Discourses* 3.8.5

"I have a headache." Do not add "Alas!" "I have an earache." Do not add "Alas!" I'm not saying that you cannot groan, but don't groan inside.

Epictetus, *Discourses* 1.19.19

Say nothing more to yourself than what first appearances report. Suppose it is reported that a certain person is saying terrible things about you. This much is reported; but it is not reported that you have been hurt. I see that my child is sick. I see that much; but that he is in danger, I do not see. So always stay with first appearances, and add nothing from within yourself – nothing happens to you. Or rather add something, but do it like someone who knows of all that happens in the world.

Marcus Aurelius, *Meditations* 8.49

Guillaume du Vair noted a particular snare when interpreting events: creating false metaphors to describe them, and making other kinds of alarming and misleading comparisons.

Our opinions torment us more than things themselves, and are formed by the words we use when something surprising occurs; for we call one

du Vair, *The Moral Philosophy of the Stoics* (1585)

thing by the name of another, and imagine it to be like that other thing, and the image and idea stay there in our minds.

Another Stoic technique involves subtraction. It is used for externals that are already known to us, and that we have trouble seeing clearly because they are covered already with conventional meanings. One has to chip away at the romance or horror or other story that has been overlaid onto the thing, and to distinguish between what it is and what it is called. This is really a variation of the process shown a moment ago: seeing things as they are, not as we have been told they are, or as everyone pretends they are, or as we tell ourselves they are. But rather than adding nothing, one takes off what is already there.

A favorite Stoic method for the purpose involves viewing a subject in the most literal way possible, or breaking it down into parts that dissolve the formidable appearance it might have, whether of desirability or the reverse.

Epictetus, *Enchiridion* 3

With everything that is beguiling, or useful, or that you love, remember to say also *what sort it is* – starting with the smallest things. If you love a piece of pottery, say "it is a pot that I love" – and when it is shattered you will not be upset.

Marcus Aurelius, *Meditations* 6.13

The thought might occur to us, when eating fancy foods, that "this one is the corpse of a fish, this one the corpse of a bird or a pig"; or again, that "this fancy wine is the dribble of a bunch of grapes, and this purple robe is sheep hair dyed with shellfish blood"; or, about copulation, that "this is the rubbing of a little piece of entrail and, along with some convulsion, an excretion of mucus." Impressions like these are the ones that penetrate to the heart of things themselves and let us see what they really are. We should do the same in all areas of life, and, whenever things appear too highly valued, we should lay them bare in our minds, perceive their cheapness, and strip off the prestige they have traditionally been assigned.

You will disdain lovely singing and dancing, and martial arts, if you will cut up the musical phrase into separate notes, then ask yourself, about each one, if you are unable to resist it. You won't know how to answer. Do the same with dancing, for each movement or position; the same even with martial arts. To sum up: apart from virtue and the things that stem from it, remember to go over things piece by piece, and by separating them come to look down on them; and carry this over to your whole life.

Marcus Aurelius, *Meditations* 11.2

By "martial arts" he was referring to pankration, which was roughly what we would now call ultimate fighting or mixed martial arts. It was an Olympic event.

5. *Judging others.* The events and worldly goods just considered are the simplest and commonest examples of externals. But other people also amount to externals for Stoic purposes; we have as much trouble seeing them clearly as we do anything else. Again, Stoics try to strip away their disguises.

Just as the eyesight can be sharpened and cleared up by certain drugs, if we are willing to free our spiritual vision from impediments, we will be able to perceive virtue even when it is hidden within the body, even with poverty as an obstacle, even where insignificance and disgrace stand in the way. We shall see that beauty, I say, however much it may be covered in filth. Conversely, we will be able to perceive evil, and the sluggishness of a wretched mind, however much the view may be blocked by gleaming riches, or however strongly a false light – here of rank and position, there of great power – beats down on the beholder.

Seneca, *Epistles* 115.6

Seneca, *Epistles* 76.31–32

None of those who have been raised to a lofty height by riches and honors is really great. Why then does he seem great? Because you are measuring the pedestal along with the man. A dwarf is not tall, though he stands on a mountain; a Colossus will maintain its size even when standing in a well. This is the error under which we labor, and how we are deceived; we value no man by what he is, but add the trappings in which he is adorned.

Montaigne, *Of the Inequality Amongst Us* (1580)

The pedestal is no part of the statue. Measure him without his stilts; let him lay aside his wealth and his titles; let him present himself in his undershirt. Is his body healthy, active, and able to perform its functions? What sort of soul does he have? Is it beautiful and capable, and fortunate enough to have all of its parts intact? Is the soul rich in what is its own or rich in what it has borrowed? Has luck had nothing to do with it? Can it face the drawing of swords without flinching? Is it indifferent between a death by the expiration of breath or the slitting of the throat? Is it calm, unflustered, and content? This is what we must see; that is how the great differences between us should be judged.

And the same analysis might be turned on oneself.

Seneca, *Epistles* 80.10

Do you see that king of Scythia or Sarmatia, his head elegant with the badge of his office? If you wish to see what he amounts to, and to know his full worth, take off his headband; much evil lurks beneath it. But why do I speak of others? If you want to take your own measure, put aside your money, your estates, your honors, and look inside yourself. At present you are taking the word of others for what you are.

Scythia and Sarmatia were territories lying in the steppes north and east of the Black Sea. They were often at war with the Roman Empire, and their peoples were regarded by the Romans and Greeks as barbarians.

We saw in the previous section that Stoics sometimes look at worldly objects in a literal way; it is a technique for seeing things as they are and without romance or fear. The same general idea can be applied to people.

> What are they like when they're eating, sleeping, copulating, defecating, and so on? What are they like when they're being imperious and arrogant, or angrily scolding others from some position of superiority? A little while ago they were slaves, and doing all those things just named; and soon they will be again.

Marcus Aurelius, *Meditations* 10.19

6. *Knowing the difference*. The first question that Stoics typically ask about any apparent problem or prospect is whether it is up to them. If not, they don't agonize about it, because it wouldn't help if they did. Stoics therefore are very attentive to the difference between things within and beyond their control.

> Right from the start, then, practice saying to every harsh appearance, "You are just an appearance, and not at all what you appear." Then examine it, and test it by those rules you have – and by this first one especially, whether it has to do with things that are up to us or things that are not up to us. And if it has to do with something not up to us, let the thought be close at hand that "It is nothing to me."

Epictetus, *Enchiridion* 1.5

Of course there are mixed cases: situations where we have control over some aspects of a problem but not others, or the power to control it but perhaps not the right or responsibility. Those cases may call for hard analysis, and the Stoics do not spend as much time on them as one might have wished. But the basic approach is set forth by Epictetus.

Epictetus, *Discourses* 2.5.9

It is difficult to combine and bring together those things – the carefulness of one devoted to material things, and the steadiness of one who is indifferent to them – but it is not impossible; otherwise happiness would be impossible. It is like planning a sea voyage. What can I do? I can choose the captain, the sailors, the day, the right moment. Then a storm comes upon us. At this point, what concern is it of mine? My part is done. The problem belongs to another – the captain.

Detachment from externals should not be confused with withdrawal from the world. As the last part of Chapter 11 will illustrate, Stoicism calls for involvement in public life, not retreat from it. But in all circumstances one can draw lines between the decisions that are up to us and the ones that aren't.

Epictetus, *Discourses* 2.5.1–7

Material things are indifferent; how we use them is not. How then may a man maintain not only steadiness and calm, but also the state of mind that is careful and neither reckless nor negligent? He can act like people playing a board game. The game pieces are neither good nor bad, nor are the dice. How can I know what the next throw of the dice will be? But to use the throw carefully and skillfully, this belongs to me. In life, too, then, the principal task is this: to distinguish and separate things, and say: "Externals are outside my power: my choices are within my power. Where shall I seek the good and the bad? Within, in the things that are my own." But in what depends on others, call nothing either good or bad, benefit or harm, or anything else of the kind. "What then? Does this mean we shouldn't care how we use them?" By no means. That would be a wrongful use of our faculty of choice, and so contrary to nature. External things should be used with care, because their use can be good or bad. But at the same time you should keep your composure and your calm, because the things themselves are neither good nor bad.

The comparison to dice is anticipated in Book 10 of Plato's *Republic* (604c). Adam Smith elaborated on the Stoic comparison to the play of a game, and his account provides a good note on which to conclude this discussion.

Human life the Stoics appear to have considered as a game of great skill; in which, however, there was a mixture of chance, or of what is vulgarly understood to be chance.... If we placed our happiness in winning the stake, we placed it in what depended upon causes beyond our power, and out of our direction. We necessarily exposed ourselves to perpetual fear and uneasiness, and frequently to grievous and mortifying disappointments. If we placed it in playing well, in playing fairly, in playing wisely and skillfully; in the propriety of our own conduct in short; we placed it in what, by proper discipline, education, and attention, might be altogether in our own power, and under our own direction. Our happiness was perfectly secure, and beyond the reach of fortune.

Smith, *The Theory of Moral Sentiments* (1759)

Chapter Three

PERSPECTIVE

Marcus Aurelius thought two principles of Stoicism especially important.

Marcus Aurelius, *Meditations*

4.3.4

These are the two ideas you should keep at the very front of your mind and think about. One is that things in the world do not touch your spirit, but stand quietly external to it; that which disturbs us comes only from the opinions within us. Second, everything you see changes in a moment and will soon be gone. Keep in mind always how many of these changes you have already seen. The world is constant change; your life lies in your opinion.

One of these points – that our experience of the world depends on our judgments or opinions about it, rather than on externals themselves – was the subject of the first two chapters. His other principle is the subject of this one. The principle might be stated as mortality or perishability, but for our purposes it will be better to speak of those as parts of a larger topic: perspective.

The Stoics may be said, in general, to use two strategies to dissolve an illusion. One is analytical: using reason to take apart an external and show its true nature. The other is intuitive: looking at the world from a point of view that can produce an automatic change in how we see it. Viewing a problem, an adversary, or oneself from a certain perspective – seeing it from far away, or as part of a bigger picture – can sometimes detach us from an appetite or fear without need for analysis.

The Stoics use both methods throughout this book. Most of the chapters to come use analysis as the primary instrument of correction. Externals are taken up and scrutinized one by one. Time and space can be treated this way, for example, and receive some Stoic dissection in this chapter. To ourselves we seem exceedingly important, and the time and place where we live feels significant. The Stoic regards those impressions as mistakes. They arise because our ordinary perspective on the world, the one we use by default, is misleading. We look out from inside and see things in terms of ourselves; we are forgetful or unconscious of how puny and brief our allotments are. The Stoics rectify this by pointing out the facts about the scale of our existence and our mortality.

But the ideas in this chapter are also, and especially, meant to advance the intuitive side of Stoicism. By seeing how small our affairs look in the larger scheme of things, the Stoic means to induce a felt sense of humility and attraction to virtue. The method can be called intuitive because it isn't a matter of argument. It's more a question of showing and pointing, and expecting perceptions and adjustments to follow directly from a new point of view. Granted, by not using argument the Stoics sometimes open themselves to analytical criticism. The choice to look at a problem from one point of view rather than another can seem arbitrary. But in this respect, as in many others, the late Stoics may be classified as pragmatists. If a perspective has the consequence of freeing us from a bad psychological habit, they do not hesitate to recommend it.

A change in perspective can sometimes lead a viewer to more than one conclusion. The Stoics have specific ideas about which lessons are the right ones to draw. Staring at the small scale of our lives and concerns, for example, could seem nihilistic and dreary, but the Stoic has an opposite reaction. The long view is good for morale. If it is an affront to the ego, it is also an antidote to vanity, ambition, and greed. Our ultimate insignificance makes the case for living well in the present, for no other purpose survives. It also suggests the value of viewing oneself as part of a whole. If you wanted to convince ants to work together rather than obsess about individual glory, you might start by showing them how they look to us.

Nor should the long view lead to passivity. We have remarked already that two of our Stoic instructors were among the most significant statesmen of Rome, but the example of Marcus Aurelius is worth a moment of particular reflection. He was, as this chapter will show, the most persistent Stoic student of perspectives that make our affairs seem tiny. So far as our histories tell, though, none of this made him any less active or compassionate. Quite the contrary:

de Quincey, *The Cæsars* (1851)

> It must be remembered that Marcus Aurelius was by profession a Stoic; and that generally, as a theoretical philosopher, but still more as a Stoic philosopher, he might be supposed incapable of descending from these airy altitudes of speculation to the true needs, infirmities, and capacities of human nature. Yet strange it is, that he, of all the good emperors, was the most thoroughly human and practical.

Someone who rightly understands Stoicism shouldn't find that observation strange at all.

1. *Time.* We measure time by how much of it we have. A normal lifespan seems a long increment because it is the most that anyone knows of firsthand. The Stoic seeks to view time from the outside in, a point of view that creates a different sense of scale.

Marcus Aurelius, *Meditations* 9.32

> You can get rid of a great number of your annoyances because they lie entirely in your own head. You will clear ample space for yourself by comprehending the scale of the universe in your mind, by observing the infinity of time, and by studying carefully the rapid change of each part of each thing – how short the time is from birth to disso-

lution, the time before it an abyss, the time afterwards also endless.

Imagine the vast abyss of time, and think of the
entire universe; then compare what we call a
human lifetime to that immensity. You will see
how tiny a thing it is that we wish for and seek to
prolong.

Seneca, Epistles 99.10

We live for an instant, even less than an instant.
But nature adds mockery to even this trivial span
by giving it an appearance of longer extent – making one part infancy, another childhood, another
youth, another the gradual slope (so to speak)
from youth to old age, another old age itself. How
many steps for so short a climb!

Seneca, Epistles 49.3

You might name long-lived men, men of legend-
ary old age; you might count up a hundred and
ten years for each; but when you turn your mind
toward the whole of time, the difference between
the shortest and the longest life will be nothing –
if, having examined the intervals, you compare the
time each has lived with the time he has not lived.

Seneca, Consolation to Marcia
21.3

2. *Space.* The importance of our place is likewise determined, for us, by the scale we experience as we move
through it: what we can see, where we can go. The Stoic
views space (or sometimes time and space together)
from a perspective outside the observer.

Asia and Europe are corners of the universe; the
whole of the sea is a drop in the universe; Athos, a
tiny clod of dirt in the universe; all the present
time is one point in eternity. Everything is small,
easily changing, disappearing.

Marcus Aurelius, Meditations
6.36

Short-lived are both the praiser and the praised,
the rememberer and the remembered. And all this
in just one corner of this continent – and yet even
here we are not in accord with each other, nor

Marcus Aurelius, Meditations
8.21

with ourselves; and the whole of the earth, too, is a speck.

Seneca, *Consolation to Marcia* 21.2

This earth with its cities and peoples, its rivers and encircling sea, if measured by the universe, we may regard as a mere dot. Our life occupies a portion *smaller* than a dot, if it is compared with all of time, because the measure of eternity is greater than that of the world; the world recreates itself over and over within the bounds of time.

3. *Perishability.* The scale of time and space makes all human doings seem small. To this the Stoic adds that such doings are also highly perishable: all human works, and for that matter all works of nature, soon change and are gone. This perspective is a help toward the detachment from externals urged in Chapter 2. Marcus Aurelius:

Marcus Aurelius, *Meditations* 7.34

Consider that as the heaps of sand piled on one another hide the former sands, so in life the events which go before are soon covered by those which come after.

Marcus Aurelius, *Meditations* 5.23

Think often about how quickly everything that exists, and that is coming into being, is carried away and disappears. For substance is like a river that constantly flows on: the action is constantly changing, and the causes of it operate in endless variations; almost nothing is fixed. And next to us is the boundless abyss of what has passed by and what is about to be, into which all things are lost. How then is he not a fool, who gets worked up and carried away over these things, complaining as if they were enduring and troublesome?

Marcus Aurelius, *Meditations* 9.28

Soon the earth will cover us all. Then the earth itself will be changed; and whatever comes next will continue to be changed endlessly; then those things again, to infinity. Someone who contemplates these successive waves of change and alteration, and their speed, will look down upon all mortal things.

Seneca:

> The sage will say just what Marcus Cato would say, on thinking over his past life: "The whole human race, both that which is and that which is to be, is condemned to die. As for the cities that ever held sway over the world – and those that have been the splendid ornaments of empires not their own – someday people will ask where they were.... So why should I be angry or feel sorrow if I precede the fate common to all things by a tiny interval of time?"

Seneca, *Epistles* 71.15

That passage refers to Cato the Younger, a Stoic who had died about forty years before Seneca was born. Cato was a famously scrupulous statesman and an opponent of Julius Cæsar. When Cæsar prevailed over Pompey and his forces in the Roman civil war, Cato used a sword to take his own life rather than surrender and submit. He became part of the Stoic roster of heroes, and was sometimes cited as an example of the ideal wise man. We will see further references to him later in the book.

Seneca offered some more specific prophesies about the passing of human creations.

> The works of nature itself are under attack, so we ought to bear the destruction of cities with equilibrium. They stand but to fall! A common doom awaits them – whether by the explosion of some internal force, and blasts that are violent so long as their exit is blocked ... or whether age, from which nothing is safe, will wear them down bit by bit; or whether severity of climate will drive their people away, and neglect will destroy what they have abandoned. All the ways their fate may arrive

Seneca, *Epistles* 91.11–12

would be tedious to relate. But this one thing I know: all works of mortals are doomed to mortality. We live in the midst of things destined to die.

Seneca, *Consolation to Polybius*
1.1–2

The Seven Wonders of the World, and things far more wonderful than those, which (if such there be) the ambition of succeeding years has brought forth, will one day be seen leveled to the ground. So it is: nothing is everlasting, and few things are long lasting; different things perish in different ways, their endings may be varied, but whatever begins also ceases.... Let him go, he who would mourn departed spirits one by one, who would weep over the ashes of Carthage and Numantia and Corinth – and any place loftier that has fallen – when even this universe, which has no place to fall, is going to perish; let him go, too, he who would complain that Fate, which will one day dare so great a crime, has not spared him!

The Seven Wonders of the World were sites featured in ancient books telling the Hellenistic traveler where to visit and what to see, such as the Colossus of Rhodes and the Hanging Gardens of Babylon. From this list that Seneca had in mind, only the Great Pyramid of Giza now survives. Carthage (in modern Tunisia), Numantia (in modern Spain), and Corinth (in Greece) were cities that Rome had destroyed during conflicts in the second century BC.

Seneca noted, too, that the forces of dissolution usually work much faster than the forces of creation.

Seneca, *Epistles* 91.6

It would be some consolation for the feebleness of our selves and our works, if all things should perish as slowly as they come into being; but as it is, increases are of sluggish growth, but the way to ruin is rapid.

A variation on our general theme from Montaigne:

This great world, which some would say is only one species within a genus, is the mirror in which we must look to see ourselves from the right perspective.... So many revolutions, so many changes in the fates of nations, teach us to see our own fate as no cause for astonishment. So many names, so many victories and conquests buried in oblivion, make it ridiculous for us to hope to immortalize our names by capturing a bunch of soldiers and some chicken coop that is remembered only for being destroyed.

Montaigne, *Of the Education of Children* (1580)

As a way to bring home the perishability of human lives and works, Marcus Aurelius often would review examples of those that came before and passed on. If the cases he cites are no longer vivid to us, his claim is stronger still, but of course modern illustrations can readily be devised if one wants them.

Expressions that used to be familiar now require explanation. In the same way, the names of people who used to be heroes now need some explanation – Camillus, Cæso, Volesus, Leonnatus, a little later Scipio and Cato too, then also Augustus, then also Hadrian and Antoninus. For all things fade and become mere tales, and are buried soon thereafter in complete oblivion. And I'm speaking just of those who have shone in some way with great brilliance. As for the rest, they are gone and forgotten when they take their last breath. And what, after all, is even an everlasting remembrance? Completely empty.

Marcus Aurelius, *Meditations* 4.28

Picture in your mind, as an illustration, the times of Vespasian. You will see all these things: people marrying, raising children, getting sick, dying, making war, celebrating festivals, being merchants, being farmers, flattering others, being arrogant,

Marcus Aurelius, *Meditations* 4.32

being suspicious, plotting, wishing for some people to die, grumbling about the present, loving, laying up treasure, setting their hearts on consulships and kingdoms. Well, the life of those people no longer exists at all. Now pass ahead to the time of Trajan. It's all the same things again, and that life too is gone. Carefully view other eras and other nations the same way, and see how many, after strenuous exertion, soon fell and were resolved into the elements.

Vespasian had been Roman emperor from 69 to 79 AD, about a century before Marcus Aurelius.

4. *Applications to mortality.* The perspectives encouraged by the Stoics are a countermeasure against many deceptions, vices, and misjudgments, including the fear of death. That topic will be fully treated in the next chapter, but the use of our current ideas to address it can be shown briefly and generally here – that is, the application of the long view to reduce the fear of mortality.

Marcus Aurelius, *Meditations* 4.50

It is a simple but still useful help toward contempt of death to call to mind those who have clung tenaciously to life. What did they gain beyond those who died early? Regardless, they were all buried somewhere eventually – Cadicianus, Fabius, Julianus, Lepidus, anyone like that. They carried out many to be buried, then were carried out themselves.

Marcus Aurelius, *Meditations* 4.47

If one of the gods told you that you would die tomorrow, or the day after tomorrow at the latest, you wouldn't consider the choice between those days important unless you were very small-minded; for how much difference is there? Likewise, the difference between dying at a great age and dying tomorrow you should consider no great thing.

Compare:

"Do you think that a mind habituated to thoughts of grandeur and the contemplation of all time and all existence can deem this life of man a thing of great concern?" "Impossible," said he. "Hence such a man will not suppose death to be terrible?" "Least of all."

Plato, *Republic* Book VI (486a–b)

Aristotle tells us of little creatures on the river Hypanis that live for only a day. One that dies at eight in the morning dies young; one that dies at five in the evening dies of old age. Who would not laugh to see the difference between such momentary lifespans counted as happiness or unhappiness? Yet calling our own lives long or short, when they are compared with eternity, or even to the spans of mountains, rivers, stars, trees, and certain other animals, seems no less absurd.

Montaigne, *That to Study Philosophy is to Learn to Die* (1580)

Montaigne's reference is to Aristotle, *History of Animals* 5.17.14.

5. *Reduction*. We turn to a different Stoic use of perspective – of the microscope, perhaps, rather than the telescope. Chapter 2 looked at some Stoic methods for demystifying externals: viewing them literally or reducing them to smaller elements, thus making it easier to take them lightly. Marcus Aurelius applied the approach not just to particular externals but to human life and to the world in general.

The sort of thing that bathing appears to be, when you think about it – oil, sweat, filth, greasy water, everything revolting – such is every part of life, and everything that underlies it.

Marcus Aurelius, *Meditations* 8.24

To sum up: do not overlook how short are the lives of all mortal things, and how insignificant – yesterday a little blob of mucus, tomorrow a mummy or ashes.

Marcus Aurelius, *Meditations* 4.48

All this is foul smell and blood in a bag.

Marcus Aurelius, *Meditations* 8.37

Marcus Aurelius, *Meditations*
9.36

The rottenness of the matter that underlies everything! Water, dust, bone, stench – or again, as marble is only a stone in the earth, and gold and silver are only sediments, and clothing is only hair, and purple dye is only blood, and everything else is just as these are. The life breath in us is another similar thing and changes from this to that.

6. *Repetition.* Another Stoic maneuver of perspective observes the sameness of things that seem novel, thereby draining them of their power to provoke attachment.

Marcus Aurelius, *Meditations*
6.46

It is tiresome to go to the theater or other such places and see the same things over and over again; it makes watching them tedious. It is the same in the whole of life. For all things above and below are the same and from the same sources. How long then?

Marcus Aurelius, Meditations
7.1

So for everything that happens, keep this in mind: it is something you have seen many times before. Look up and down, in short, and you will find the same things that the histories are filled with – ancient histories, histories of the intervening years, histories of our times – and that fill the cities and the houses of today. Nothing is new; everything is both familiar and short-lived.

Marcus Aurelius, *Meditations*
7.49

Carefully consider the past – the countless changes of political regimes. You can also see future events in advance; they will be of entirely the same kind, for it is impossible to depart from the pattern of what is happening now. It follows that to have observed human life for forty years is the same as for ten thousand. For what more are you going to see?

Lest these perspectives seem excessively somber:

Seneca, *Epistles* 101.9

When a steadfast mind knows that there is no difference between a day and an age, whatever the days or events that may come, then it can look out from the heights and laugh as it reflects on the succession of the ages.

7. *The overhead view.* Some of the perspectives considered so far can be brought home at once with an imaginative exercise: viewing humanity from a sufficiently high perspective to see it all at once. The intended effect is to help us naturally reach some of the familiar Stoic conclusions, such as the repetitive character of human life and the perishability of it.

> The mind cannot despise colonnades, paneled ceilings gleaming with ivory, manicured shrubbery, and streams made to approach mansions, until it goes around the entire universe and looking down upon the earth from above (an earth limited and covered mostly by sea – while even the part out of the sea is squalid or parched and frozen) says to itself: "Is this the pinpoint that is divided by sword and fire among so many nations?"

Seneca, *Natural Questions* 1 Pref. 8

Marcus Aurelius returned often to this vantage point.

> This is a fine saying of Plato—that a person who is going to discuss human affairs should examine earthly things as if looking down from somewhere above: groups of men, armies, tilled fields, marriages, divorces, births, deaths, the noise of the law courts, the deserts, the patchwork of foreign peoples, festivals, mournings, markets, the whole mixture and the orderly arrangement of opposites.

Marcus Aurelius, *Meditations* 7.48

> Look down from above on the countless gatherings and countless ceremonies, and every sort of voyage in storm and calm, and the disputes between those being born, living together, and dying. Think also of the life that was lived by others long ago, and that will be lived after you, and that is being lived now in other countries; think

Marcus Aurelius, *Meditations* 9.30

of how many don't know your name at all, how many will quickly forget it, how many who – perhaps praising you now – will soon be finding fault. Realize that being remembered has no value, nor does your reputation, nor anything else at all.

Marcus Aurelius, *Meditations*
12.24

If being suddenly lifted up in mid-air you should examine human affairs and their variety from above, you will look down upon them.... And however often you are lifted up, you will see the same things, the same kind, their short duration. Vanity, on account of these things!

A similar theme is pursued in Cicero's "Dream of Scipio":

Cicero, *On the Republic*
6.19–20

Though marveling at these things, I was still turning my eyes back to earth from time to time. Then Africanus said: "I can tell that you are now contemplating man's dwelling and abode. If it appears as small to you as it really is, look always up to these celestial things, and down on those human ones. For what renown in men's mouths can you attain, what fame worth seeking?"

8. *Implications.* We arrive at the conclusion of Seneca:

Seneca, *Natural Questions* III, 1
Pref. 15

We believe these affairs of ours are great because we are small.

On the implications of human lowliness, Marcus Aurelius – the Stoic most preoccupied with the theme – had definite views. They were humble and benevolent: we should treat each other well and with good humor, for the things that distract us from those simple aims aren't worth worrying about.

Marcus Aurelius, *Meditations*
5.33

The things highly valued in life are empty and rotten and trivial; we are little dogs biting each other, quarrelsome children laughing and then crying.... Reputation, in such a world, is meaningless. What then? You graciously wait for death – for extinction, or for passage to another state. And until the time for that has arrived, what is enough? What else but to venerate and praise the gods, to do good to others, and to treat them with tolerance and restraint; and as for what is within the bounds of your body and your breath, to remember that it is neither yours nor up to you.

The empty pursuit of ceremony, plays on the stage, men with flocks of sheep, or in herds, or fighting with spears; a bone thrown to little dogs, a crumb into the fish ponds; the hard labors of burden-bearing ants, the scurrying of panicky little mice, tiny puppets moved by strings. Among all these things you must take your place, with good humor and without being haughty – understanding, however, that each man is worth just as much as the things he cares about.

Marcus Aurelius, *Meditations* 7.3

Progress in Stoicism, or temperamental aptitude for it, might be measured in part by one's ability to read the ideas in this chapter and come away in better humor rather than worse, and with greater purpose rather than less. Some would regard Marcus Aurelius as a notably poor motivational speaker. For the Stoic he is among the only kind tolerable.

Chapter Four

DEATH

Death has two kinds of significance for the Stoics. First it may be considered an external. It is out of our control; we can accelerate death and sometimes delay it, but its eventual arrival is not up to us. It is also the most frightening prospect the mind confronts. An external that is frightening makes a natural topic for Stoic analysis, so death gets their attention at length. Stoics consider death hard to see accurately, and they find the usual attitude toward it irrational; what death is like is unknown to anyone, but it appears to be a painless state that leaves us no worse off than we were before we were born. They also view death as similar to other changes that are familiar to all, and as a continuous process rather than a sudden one: we die every day as our time on earth passes behind us. They make various other arguments as well to drain the terror from mortality. Overcoming the fear of death is considered by the Stoics to be one of the most important of all philosophical achievements, and the gain of an important liberty.

But Stoicism treats death as more than just an external that needs to be laid bare. It is also a source of perspective and inspiration – a valuable aid, not just something to which we overreact. Mortality is the defining feature of our existence; Stoics want the imminence of it to inform their daily lives. The fact that we will soon be gone can induce some of the same changes in mindset as the perspectives considered in the previous chapter. Meditation on death is thus used by the Stoic to stimulate humility, fearlessness, moderation, and other virtues.

1. *Fear of death*. Before setting out to cure a fear or desire, the Stoics typically analyze the ordinary attitude toward it. They are especially dedicated analysts of the fear of death.

> No one doubts that death has in it something that inspires terror, so that it shocks even our souls, which nature has so molded that they love their own existence; for otherwise there would be no need to prepare ourselves, and to whet our courage, to face that towards which we should move with a sort of voluntary instinct, precisely as all men tend to preserve their existence.

Seneca, *Epistles* 36.8

> Death belongs among those things that are not evils in truth, but still have an appearance of evil; for a love of self is implanted in us, and a desire for existence and survival, and a dread of disintegration. Death seems to rob us of many good things and to remove us from all we have come to know. And there is another element that estranges us from death: we are already familiar with the present, but are ignorant of the future into which we will go, and we shrink from the unknown.... Even if death is something indifferent, then, it is nevertheless a thing that cannot be easily ignored.

Seneca, *Epistles* 82.15–16

As will become clear, death has a deep importance in Stoicism that is not shared by other conditions we fear. But at times the Stoics analyze death simply as an external – a thing that gains its meaning from the ways in which it is costumed by the mind. What we must overcome is not death but the way we think about it.

> Neither death nor pain is to be feared, but the fear of pain or death.... Confidence should therefore be our attitude toward death, and caution should be our attitude toward the fear of it. But now we have the opposite: toward death, avoidance;

Epictetus, *Discourses* 2.1.13–14

toward our opinions about it, carelessness, indifference, and neglect.

Epictetus, Discourses 2.1.17

What is death? A mask to frighten children. Turn it and examine it. See, it does not bite. The poor body must be separated from the spirit as it was before, either now or later. Why then are you troubled if it be now? For if not now, later.

Seneca, Natural Questions 6.32.8–9

The thing itself is trifling; that we fear it is serious. Better that it happen once than that it always be threatening.... Therefore exhort yourself as much as you can, Lucilius, against the *fear* of death. This is the thing that makes us abject; this is what disturbs and destroys the man whose life itself it has spared; this is what magnifies all those things like earthquakes and lightning.

2. *Fearlessness of death.* Freedom from the fear of death is regarded by the Stoic as one of the central goals of philosophical work, from which many other liberties and goods follow. One who regards death without fear steps more lightly through life, and is free from many other fears as well; for death is the master fear that lies behind them. From Seneca:

Seneca, Epistles 36.8

"What then should he study?" That which is helpful against all weapons, against every kind of foe – contempt for death.

Seneca, Epistles 26.10

He who has learned to die has unlearned slavery. He is above any power, and certainly beyond it. What terrors have prisons and bonds and bars for him?

Seneca, Epistles 4.5–6

Make life as a whole agreeable to yourself, then, by banishing all worry about it. No good thing makes its possessor happy unless his mind is prepared for its loss; and nothing is easier to let go of than that which, once gone, cannot be missed.

We must make ready for death before we make ready for life.

Seneca, *Epistles* 61.4

From others:

The whole life of a philosopher ... is preparation for death.

Cicero, *Tusculan Disputations* 1.30

A correct understanding that death is nothing to us makes the mortality of life enjoyable, not by adding to life a limitless time, but by taking away the yearning after immortality. For life has no terrors for him who has thoroughly understood that there are no terrors for him in ceasing to live.

Epicurus, *Letter to Menoeceus*

After Philip forced his way into the Peloponnesus, someone told Damindas that the Spartans would suffer greatly if they did not get back into Philip's good graces. "Coward," he replied; "what can people suffer who do not fear death?" Agis was similarly asked how people could live in freedom; to which he replied, "By holding death in contempt."

Montaigne, *A Custom of the Isle of Cea* (1580)

Montaigne took these bits from Plutarch's *Apophthegmata Laconica* (Sayings of the Spartans). The passage speaks of the advance toward Sparta by Philip II of Macedon in 346 BC (or thereabouts), and the Spartans' lack of interest in conciliating him. Philip elected not to seek the conquest of Sparta. Agis was one of the many kings of Sparta by that name.

3. *Correctives to fear*. The Stoic approach to the fear of death is the same as to other externals: use reason to see the thing clearly and peel away its frightening features.

a. *The unknown experience of death*.

Does it do any harm to a good man to be smeared by unjust gossip? Then we should not let the same sort of thing do damage to death, either, in our judgment; for death also has a bad reputation, but none of those who malign death have tried it.

Seneca, *Epistles* 91.20

See also:

Plato, *Apology* 29a

To fear death, gentlemen, is nothing else than to think one is wise when one is not; for it is thinking one knows what one does not know. For no one knows whether death be not even the greatest of all blessings to man, but they fear it as if they knew that it is the greatest of evils.

Montaigne, *Use Makes Perfect* (1580)

In dying, which is the greatest task we have to perform, practice is no help. We may use habit and experience to strengthen ourselves against pain, poverty, shame, and other misfortunes, but death we can try only once; we are all apprentices with respect to it. There were some in ancient days so meticulous in the use of their time that they even tried to taste and to savor the moment of their deaths; they bent their faculties of mind to discover what it was to cross over. But they never came back to tell their stories.

b. *The painlessness of death.* Dying might be painful. So far as we know, death itself is not.

Seneca, *Consolation to Marcia* 19.4

Reflect that there are no ills to be suffered after death, that the reports that make the underworld terrible to us are mere tales, that no darkness threatens the dead, no prison, no blazing streams of fire, no river of Lethe, no seats of judgment, no defendants, nor in that freedom so complete are there any tyrants to meet again. All those things are the sport of the poets, who have stirred us up with terrors that are empty.

Seneca, *Epistles* 4.3

Death is coming to you; it would be a thing to dread if it could stay. But necessarily it either doesn't come, or it comes and is gone.

Marcus Aurelius, *Meditations* 8.58

He who fears death fears either the loss of sensation or a different kind of sensation. But if you will have no sensation, you will feel nothing bad; and if you have a different kind of sensation, then you will be a different kind of living being and will not have ceased to live.

The similar view of Epicurus:

> Accustom yourself to thinking that death is nothing to us, since every good and evil lies in perception, while death is the deprivation of perception…. Something that causes no trouble when it is present causes pain to no purpose when it is merely expected. Death, the most horrible of evils, is therefore nothing to us – since so long as we exist, death is not present, and when death is present, we do not exist.

Epicurus, *Letter to Menœceus*

As for dying itself, it doesn't usually take very long.

> It is not against death that we prepare; that is too momentary a thing. A quarter of an hour's suffering, without aftereffects and without damage, does not require special instruction. In truth, we prepare ourselves against the preparations for death.

Montaigne, *Of Physiognomy* (1580)

c. *Death as transformation.* Stoics view the arrival of death as a transition not so different from others we know.

> Do not despise death, but be content with it, since this too is one of those things nature wills. For what it is to be young and grow old, and to increase and reach maturity, and to have teeth and beard and grey hair, and to father children, and to be pregnant and to give birth, and all the other natural operations the seasons of your life bring – so also is dissolution. This, then, is the way of one who is reflective: to be neither careless nor impatient nor arrogant with respect to death, but to wait for it as one of the operations of nature.

Marcus Aurelius, *Meditations* 9.3

Stoicism regards death more specifically as a natural transformation of matter into other forms.

Marcus Aurelius, *Meditations* 8.18

That which has died does not fall out of the universe. If it stays here, it also changes here, and is dissolved into its proper parts, which are elements of the universe and of your self. And these change, too, and they do not complain.

Epictetus, *Discourses* 3.24.94

So I won't exist anymore? No, you won't – but something else will, which the universe now needs. For you also came into existence not when you chose, but when the world had need of you.

Marcus Aurelius, *Meditations* 7.23

From the essence of the universe, as if it were wax, nature molds now a little horse; and when it has broken this up, it uses the material for a little tree, then for a little man, then for something else; and each of these things exists for a very short time. But it is no hardship for a box to be broken up, just as there was none in its being fastened together.

d. *Comparisons to the time before birth.* A classic Stoic response to death is to contemplate its similarity to our position before birth, which we have no reason to think was difficult.

Seneca, *Epistles* 54.4–5

"What?" I say to myself; "does death so often test me? Let it do so; I myself have for a long time tested death." "When?" you ask. Before I was born.... Unless I am mistaken, my dear Lucilius, we go astray in thinking that death follows, when it has both preceded and will follow. Whatever condition existed before our birth, was death. For what does it matter whether you do not begin at all, or whether you end, when the result in either case is non-existence?

Cicero, *Tusculan Disputations* 1.4

"Perhaps I do not yet express what I mean, for I look upon this very circumstance, not to exist after having existed, to be very miserable." What, more so than not to have existed at all? It follows that those who are not yet born are miserable because they are not; and we ourselves, if we are to be miserable after death, were miserable before we were born: but I do not remember that I was miserable before I was born; and I should be glad to know, if your memory is better, what if anything you recollect of your own situation.

Those who have died return to the same state in which they were before they were born. Just as there was nothing either good or bad for us before we were born, so neither will there be after the end. And just as things before us were nothing to us, so neither will things after us be anything to us.

Plutarch, *Consolation to Apollonius* 15 (109e–109f)

How ridiculous to worry about passing into freedom from all worry! Just as our birth brought us the birth of all things, so will our death be the death of them all. And so to be sorry we will not be alive a hundred years from now is as foolish as to be sorry we were not alive a hundred years ago.

Montaigne, *That to Study Philosophy is to Learn to Die* (1580)

e. *Comparisons to unreasoning creatures.* A recurring line of Stoic argument points to creatures with weak understanding – children, or the foolish, or animals – who avoid the fear of death and other fears that encumber the philosophical type. A kind of inspiration can be drawn from those fearless examples; a larger endowment of reason should not make the philosopher worse off than the person, or pig, who has less of it. Some of these examples involve matters other than death, but all are applicable to it.

Infants, and boys, and those who have gone mad, have no fear of death. It is most shameful if reason cannot give us the same peace of mind to which they are led by their simplicity.

Seneca, *Epistles* 36.12

Seneca, *Epistles* 4.4

"It is difficult," you say, "to bring the mind to a point where it can scorn life." But do you not see that people sometimes do scorn life, and for trifling reasons? One hangs himself in front of the door of his mistress; another hurls himself from a housetop so that he will no longer have to bear the taunts of a bad-tempered master; a third, to be saved from arrest after running away, drives a sword into his vitals. Do you not suppose that virtue will be as effective as overwhelming fear?

Marcus Aurelius, *Meditations* 5.18

The same ills befall another, and either because he does not see that they have happened or because he would make a display of pride, he is firm and remains unharmed. It is a shame, then, that ignorance and the desire to impress should be stronger than wisdom.

Montaigne, *That the Taste of Good and Evil Things Depends in Large Part on the Opinion We Have of Them* (1580)

Pyrrho the philosopher was once aboard a ship during a very great storm. To those near him who were most frightened, he pointed to a hog that was there and that was not in the least concerned, and sought to encourage them by its example. Do we dare to say that the gift of reason, of which we speak so highly and which we think makes us masters and kings of the rest of creation, was put into us as a source of torment? What good is knowledge if it causes us to lose the peace of mind and the calm we would enjoy without it, and leaves us in a condition worse than that of Pyrrho's hog?

Pyrrho was a Greek philosopher born in the 4th century BC. He is considered the founder of the school of thought known as skepticism.

f. *Relief; the value of mortality.* Marcus Aurelius's view of humanity gave him a reason not to fear death: the human race, seen accurately, is not the sort of company one should be too sorry to leave behind.

If you want a vulgar form of comfort that touches the heart, reconcile yourself to death by observing, above all, the things from which you will be removed, and the morals of those with whom your soul will no longer have to associate. Do not take offense at them – it is your duty, rather, to care for them and to gently put up with them – but nevertheless remember that you will be departing from others who do not have the same opinions you do. That is the one consideration, if any, that would pull the other way and attach us to life – if we could live with those who share our opinions. But when you see how much trouble arises from the discord of all of them living together, it is enough to make you say, "Come quickly, O Death, lest somehow I too forget myself."

Marcus Aurelius, Meditations 9.3.2

The following passage is in a similar vein; it is not directly linked to death, but urges the same sort of detachment from life, and for the same reasons.

Turn to the habits of those you live with. They are nearly unbearable, even the most accomplished of them; I hesitate to say it, but a man can scarcely bear even himself. In such darkness and filth, then – in such a constantly changing flow of substance and of time, of motion and things moving – what is worth prizing highly or seriously pursuing, I cannot conceive.

Marcus Aurelius, Meditations 5.10.1

Seneca reflected on the suffering that comes with life, and on our eventual decrepitude, and on the shameful things people do to make life a little longer when they can, and he ended with this conclusion: mortality is a gift.

Deny, now, if you can, that Nature is very generous in making death inevitable.

Seneca, Epistles 101.14

Montaigne elaborated in the guise of speaking for nature:

Montaigne, *That to Study Philosophy is to Learn to Die* (1580)

Just imagine how much less bearable and more painful an immortal life would be for mankind than the life I have given you. If you did not have death, you would curse me forever for depriving you of it. Indeed, I have deliberately mixed death with a little bitterness to prevent the advantages of it from causing you to embrace it too quickly or too rashly. To keep you in the moderate state that I wish, not fleeing either from life or from death, I have tempered each of those states with pleasure and with pain.

4. *The progressive character of death.* The Stoic seeks to befriend death by removing illusions about it. One is that death is an eventuality in the distance. The Stoics attack that impression in several ways. First, they view death as a continuous process rather than an event. We all are dying; each day that passes is an increment of mortality.

Seneca, *Epistles* 1.2

Who can you show me that places any value on their time, who knows the worth of each day, who understands that they are dying daily? For we are mistaken when we see death ahead of us; the greater part of it has happened already. Whatever of our life is behind us is in death's hands.

Seneca, *Epistles* 24.19

We do not suddenly fall on death, but advance toward it by slight degrees. We die every day. For every day a little of our life is taken from us; even when we are growing, our life is on the wane. We lose our childhood, then our boyhood, and then our youth. Right up to yesterday, all past time is lost time; the very day we are now spending is shared between ourselves and death. It is not the last drop that empties the water-clock, but all that has flowed out already.

Why fear your last day? It does no more to advance you toward death than any other day did. The last step does not cause your fatigue; it reveals your fatigue. Every day is a step toward death. The last one arrives there.

Montaigne, *That to Study Philosophy is to Learn to Die* (1580)

Compare:

Each day is a little life: every waking and rising a little birth, every fresh morning a little youth, every going to rest and sleep a little death.

Schopenhauer, *Our Relation to Ourselves* (1851)

5. *The availability of death.* The Stoic regards death as an option rather than a terror. The option becomes, in turn, a source of courage in life. The ability to end one's own life is therefore an important freedom. If life is intolerable, as Epictetus puts it, "the doorway out is open."

What is pain? A scary mask. Turn it around and examine it. The poor flesh is sometimes treated roughly, sometimes smoothly. If this does not profit you, the doorway out is open: if it does, bear it.

Epictetus, *Discourses* 2.1.19

Seneca:

The best thing eternal law ever ordained was one entrance into life but many exits. Must I await the cruelty either of disease or of man, when I can depart in the midst of torture and shake off my troubles? This is the one reason why we cannot complain of life; it keeps none of us against our will. Humanity is well situated, in that none are unhappy except by their own fault. Live, if it suits you; if not, you can go back where you came from.

Seneca, *Epistles* 70.14–15

However:

We need to be warned and strengthened in both directions – not to love or to hate life overmuch. Even when reason advises us to make an end of it, the impulse is not to be adopted without

Seneca, *Epistles* 24.22, 24–25

reflection or at headlong speed. The brave and wise man should not flee from life but withdraw from it.

Montaigne:

Montaigne, *A Custom of the Isle of Cea* (1580)

The most voluntary death is the finest. Our life depends on the will of others; our death depends on our own. In nothing should we defer to our own feelings as much as in this. What others think has nothing to do with this business; it is madness to even consider it. Living is slavery if the freedom to die is lacking.

Montaigne, *An Apology for Raymond Sebond* (1580)

Here are the words of the law on this subject: If chance delivers some great misfortune that you cannot remedy, a haven is always nearby. You can swim away from your body as you would from a leaking boat. Only fools are attached to their bodies by a fear of death rather than a love of life.

6. *Duration vs. quality.* The impression that death lies in the distance can create a desire to keep it there, or as far away as possible – to treat the length of a life as the most important thing about it. The Stoic, to the contrary, is more concerned with the quality of life than its duration. Virtue and honor are goods not measured in time; the person who has them has lived long enough.

Seneca, *Epistles* 22.17

Men do not care how nobly they live, but only how long, although it is within the reach of every man to live nobly, but within no man's power to live long.

Seneca, *Epistles* 101.15

What matters is not how long you live, but how well; and often living well means that you cannot live long.

Seneca, *Epistles* 77.4

A journey will be incomplete if you stop halfway, or anywhere on this side of your destination; but a life is not incomplete if it is honorable. Wherever you leave off, provided you leave off nobly, your life is a whole. Often, it is true, one must leave off bravely, and not necessarily for momentous reasons; for neither are the reasons momentous that hold us here.

One who roams through the universe will never weary of the truth; it is the false things that will bring on disgust. And on the other hand, if death comes near with its summons, even though it be untimely in its arrival, and even if it cuts you off in your prime, you will have had the enjoyment of all that the longest life can give. The universe in great measure will have been known to you. You will understand that honorable things do not depend on time for their growth, while every life must seem short to those who measure its length by pleasures that are empty and for that reason unbounded.

Seneca, *Epistles* 78.26–27

You ask what the finest life span would be? To live until you reach wisdom. The one who gets there has arrived, not at the farthest goal, but at the most important. That man, indeed, may boldly congratulate himself, and give thanks to the gods – and to himself along with them – and count in his reckoning with the universe the fact that he has lived. His account will be in credit: he has given it back a better life than he received.

Seneca, *Epistles* 93.8

While commendation is not high on the list of Stoic aims, this comment from Plutarch is in the same spirit as those just considered.

Not the longest life is the best, but the best-lived. For it is not the one who has played the lyre the most, or made the most speeches, or piloted the most ships, who is commended, but the one who has done these things well.

Plutarch, *Letter to Apollonius* 17 (111a–b)

To turn the point around: a life lived trivially is, in effect, short.

Seneca, *On the Shortness of Life* 7.10

There is no reason for you to think anyone has lived long just because he has grey hairs or wrinkles. He has not lived long; he has existed long. For suppose you should imagine that a man had a great voyage when in fact he was caught by a fierce storm as soon as he left harbor, was swept this way and that by strong winds from different directions, and was driven along the same path in circles. He did not make a great voyage. He was greatly tossed about.

Seneca, *Epistles* 93.11

"He didn't live as long as he might have." And some books contain few lines, but are admirable and useful in spite of their size. Then there are the *Annals* of Tanusius – you know how ponderous the book is, and what people say about it. The long life of a certain sort of person is like that – a kind of *Annals* of Tanusius!

Seneca appears to be referring to Tanusius Geminus, a historian from the 1st century BC who evidently was long-winded, but from whom, for better or worse, very little has survived. Catullus, a Roman poet from around the same era, famously made fun of a historian from that time by referring to his writings as *cacata carta* (politely translated as toilet paper). One scholarly school of thought holds that Catullus was referring in a veiled way to the *Annals* of Tanusius, and that this is what Seneca meant when he referred, with a delicate lack of specificity, to "what people say" about that book.

The party whose death is under discussion in that last passage is Metronax, a friend of Seneca's who will appear again in Chapter 7, Section 8.

7. *The manner of death.* Fearlessness of death is regarded by the Stoics as a great achievement. And the way one

confronts death when it arrives is considered a test of that achievement, and of character – perhaps the true test.

> This is what I mean: your debates and learned talks, your maxims gathered from the teachings of the wise, your cultured conversation – all these afford no proof of the real strength of your soul. Bold speech may issue even from the timid. What you have accomplished will only become evident when you draw your last breath. I accept the terms; I do not shrink from the judgment.

Seneca, *Epistles* 26.6

> It is with life as with a play: what matters is not how long it is, but how good. It makes no difference at what point you stop. Leave off where you choose; just be sure to give it a good ending.

Seneca, *Epistles* 77.20

> [I can show you] not only brave men who have made light of the moment when the soul breathes its last, but some who, if undistinguished in other respects, matched the spirit of the bravest when it came to this one thing. Consider Scipio, Pompey's father-in-law, when he was being driven back toward Africa by headwinds and saw his ship being seized by the enemy. He ran himself through with his sword. To the men who were asking "where is the Commander?" he answered, "All is well with the Commander!" That statement made him the equal of his ancestors, and it did not allow the glory of the African Scipios, ordained by destiny, to be interrupted. It was a great deed to conquer Carthage, but a greater deed to conquer death. "All is well with the Commander!"

Seneca, *Epistles* 24.9

The Scipio to whom Seneca refers – Metellus Scipio, as he is sometimes known – was a commander who, like Cato the Younger, sided against Cæsar in the Roman civil war, and who, like Cato, took his own life at the end of it. The ancestors of Metellus Scipio that Seneca has in mind most prominently include Scipio Africanus, the Roman general who had defeated Hannibal in the Second Punic War against Carthage about 150 years earlier. Metellus was not regarded as one of the more impressive of the Scipios – very much the contrary – but he was felt to have died well.

To return to our theme via Montaigne:

Montaigne, *That Men Are Not to Judge of Our Happiness Till After Death* (1580)

> Epaminondas, asked which of the three should be held in highest esteem, Chabrias, Iphicrates, or himself, replied, "You must first see us die before deciding."

The characters in the anecdote were Greek generals who fought for Athens or Thebes against Sparta in the 4th century BC.

8. *Death as a universal and equalizer.* The Stoic finds consolation for death in the reflection that it is a fate common to everyone.

Seneca, *Consolation to Polybius* 1.4

> We therefore will find the greatest comfort in the thought that what has befallen us was suffered by all who came before and will be suffered by all to come; and Nature has, it seems to me, made universal that which she made hardest to bear, so that the equality of our fate might console us for its cruelty.

Seneca, *Epistles* 77.13

> What multitudes doomed to death will follow you, what multitudes will accompany you! You would feel more brave, I suppose, if many thousands were to die with you; and yet there are many thousands, both humans and animals, who at this very moment, while you are irresolute about death, are breathing their last in their various ways.

Death equalizes all people, which might encourage magnanimity in life.

Marcus Aurelius, *Meditations* 6.24

> When Alexander of Macedon and his mule driver died, they came to the same thing: for either they

were absorbed back into the same principles that produced them, or they were scattered alike among the atoms.

Why are you angry with your slave, with your master, with your patron, with your client? Wait a little. Behold, death comes, which will make you equals.

Seneca, On Anger 3.43.1

Toward death, at different paces, moves the entire crowd that now squabbles in the forum, that looks on at the theaters, that prays in the temples; both those you love and revere and those you despise, one heap of ashes will make equal.

Seneca, Consolation to Marcia 11.2

We are born unequal; we die equal. I say the same thing about cities as about their inhabitants: Ardea was captured, so was Rome. The founder of human law has not distinguished us based on lineage or illustrious ancestry – except while we are alive.

Seneca, Epistles 91.16

Ardea is an ancient town south of Rome that was once sacked by the Samnites (a group of tribes from southern Italy). By Seneca's time it was lightly populated and best known for its malarial climate and the imperial elephants kept nearby.

9. *The proximity of death.* Once the fear of it is subdued, death is regarded by the Stoics as a resource – a remedy for pride and a teacher of wisdom. They therefore pursue a kind of closeness with death rather than distance from it. Stoics observe that the possibility of death is nearer than we usually imagine, a point offered not to cause anxiety but to dispel it; rather than a frightening thing that advances on us, death is next to us all the time. It is best accepted as a reason to live well in the time that remains.

The fatted bodies of bulls fall from a tiny wound, and creatures of great strength are felled by a

Seneca, On Providence 6.8–9

single stroke of the human hand.... No deep retreat conceals the soul; you need no knife at all to root it out, no deeply driven wound to find the vital parts. Death lies near at hand.

Seneca, *Epistles* 4.8–9

Reflect that a bandit or an enemy can put a knife to your throat; and though he is not your master, every slave has the power of life and death over you. Therefore I declare to you: whoever scorns his own life is master of yours.

Seneca, *Epistles* 49.11

You are mistaken if you think that only on an ocean voyage is there a very slight space between life and death. No, the distance between is just as narrow everywhere. It is not everywhere that death shows himself so near at hand; yet everywhere he is as near at hand.

Montaigne, *That to Study Philosophy is to Learn to Die* (1580)

In truth, dangers and risks do little or nothing to bring us closer to death. If we think of the millions of threats that hang over us, apart from whichever one now seems to threaten us most, we will realize that death is equally nearby whether we are healthy or feverish, at sea or at home, in battle or at rest.

Melville was a reader of Seneca and Montaigne.

Melville, *Moby-Dick* (1851)

All men live enveloped in whale-lines. All are born with halters round their necks; but it is only when caught in the swift, sudden turn of death, that mortals realize the silent, subtle, ever-present perils of life. And if you be a philosopher, though seated in the whale-boat, you would not at heart feel one whit more of terror, than though seated before your evening fire with a poker, and not a harpoon, by your side.

Seneca had a related idea to offer: causes for fear are everywhere; oddly enough, this can relieve us from fear about any one of them, or all of them. Anything might kill you anytime, so you might as well forge on without worrying about it.

> I say that there is no lasting peace for anything that can perish and cause to perish. But I place this fact in the category of solace, actually a very powerful solace, since fear without remedy is what foolish men have.... If you wish to fear nothing, consider that everything is to be feared.

Seneca, *Natural Questions* 6.2.1

10. *Intimacy with death.* The nearness of death as a physical matter is matched by the Stoic's efforts to keep it nearby in the mind. Stoics recommend thinking about death often, as they find that it helps toward virtue without a need for argument.

> Nothing will give you so much help toward moderation as the frequent thought that life is short and that the little we have is uncertain. Whatever you are doing, be mindful of death.

Seneca, *Epistles* 114.27

> Let death and exile and every other thing that appears dreadful be every day before your eyes, but most of all death; and you will never harbor any low thoughts, nor have an extravagant desire for anything.

Epictetus, *Enchiridion* 21

> No one can have a peaceful life who thinks too much about lengthening it, or who believes that living through many consulships is a great blessing. Rehearse this thought every day, so that you may be able to peacefully give up this life to which so many clutch and cling, just as those snatched away by a rushing stream clutch and cling to briars and sharp rocks.

Seneca, *Epistles* 4.4–5

Montaigne:

> Let us strip death of its strangeness; let us spend time with it, let us get used to it, let us have nothing on our minds more often. At every moment

Montaigne, *That to Study Philosophy is to Learn to Die* (1580) let us imagine death in all of its aspects. When a horse stumbles, when a tile falls, when a pin pricks us even slightly, let us immediately turn over this thought: "What if that had been death itself?"

Johnson:

Johnson, *The Rambler* no. 17 (1750)

The disturbers of our happiness, in this world, are our desires, our griefs, and our fears, and to all these, the frequent consideration of death is a certain and adequate remedy.

Epicurus was succinct on the subject.

Epicurus, in Seneca, *Epistles* 26.8

Think on death.

11. *Mortality as inspiration*. Reflection on death, as we have seen, is viewed by the Stoic as a way to reduce the fear of it, but also as a cause for urgency in living and a source of inspiration. Some further comments on the latter theme from Marcus Aurelius:

Marcus Aurelius, *Meditations* 7.69

The perfection of moral character consists in this: to spend each day as if it were the last, to be neither agitated nor numb, and not to pretend.

Marcus Aurelius, *Meditations* 7.56

Think of yourself as having died, and as having finished the life you have lived until now. The portion that is allowed to you beyond this, live out according to nature.

Marcus Aurelius, *Meditations* 4.37

You are going to die at any minute, and yet you still are not simple and straightforward, nor do you have peace of mind, nor are you free from suspicion that you will be hurt by external things, nor are you kind to everyone, nor do you see that being wise consists solely in being just.

From Seneca:

Seneca, *Epistles* 23.10

We must make it our aim to have already lived long enough.

Let us order our minds as if we had come to the end. Let us postpone nothing. Let us balance life's account every day.

Seneca, *Epistles* 101.7–8

Take as much as Fortune gives, remembering that it comes with no guarantee. Snatch the pleasures your children bring, let your children in turn find delight in you, and drain joy to the dregs without delay; nothing is promised for this night – nay, I have granted too long an extension! – not even for this hour. We must hurry, the enemy is right behind us!

Seneca, *Consolation to Marcia* 10.4

Chapter Five

DESIRE

We saw in Chapter 1 the foundational Stoic claim that we react not to things but to our judgments about them. It doesn't necessary follow, though, that those judgments are wrong. Indeed, one might react to the Stoic proposition by offering to concede it without effect: if we desire or dread something, and the desire or dread arises from our thoughts about it, maybe the thoughts are right. How are we to know?

Chapter 2 provided a general answer to that question: attachment to externals is a trap. And we have seen the start of specific answers in Chapters 3 and 4, which showed how the Stoics think we misjudge time, space, and death. But this chapter begins a series of closer inquiries into some more particular judgments we make about the world. The Stoics' notion that "everything is opinion" becomes, for them, a warrant to examine our usual thinking more closely, department by department, to see whether it squares with reason and with what we know of human nature. To simplify only a bit, Stoicism views most of our miseries as driven by the ways we relate to desires and fears about the future, and to pleasures and pains in the present. This chapter begins by considering desire – how it works and how we might handle it more rationally.

We have noted that the Stoic teachers each have certain specialties – for Epictetus, externals; for Marcus Aurelius, perspective. On the subject of psychology, which comes to the fore in this chapter, the great Stoic specialist is Seneca the Younger. Seneca, along with others we will see, gave early recognition to many tendencies of the mind that are relearned, often the hard way, by every generation and most individuals: that we most desire what we do not or cannot have; that the pursuit of a thing is more pleasing than the possession of it; that possession of a good and familiarity with it tend to produce indifference or disgust; that we mismeasure the value of what we have, or don't have, by comparing it to our expectations or to the holdings of others. In sum, we talk to ourselves about our desires in ways that are constantly misleading. The Stoics seek to give us more accurate things to say, as well as some advice about how to avoid or outwit our irrationalities.

1. *The insatiability of desires.* The Stoic's first observation about desire is that getting what we want tends not to produce the satisfaction that we imagined. It makes us want more. New desires appear when other ones are spent; our minds seem to have an appetite for desire itself, and for the illusion that fulfilling it will bring us to an endpoint. The end never arrives.

Who was ever satisfied, after attainment, with that which loomed up large as he prayed for it?

Seneca, *Epistles* 118.6

Why wait until there is nothing left for you to crave? That time will never come. We say that there is a succession of causes from which fate is put together. There is likewise a succession of desires: one is born from the end of another.

Seneca, *Epistles* 19.6

You will learn the truth by experience: the things that people value highly and try hardest to get do them no good once they have them. Those who don't have them imagine that, once they do, everything good will be theirs; then they do get them, and the heat of their desires is the same, their agitation is the same, their disgust with what they possess is the same, and their wish for what they don't have is the same.

Epictetus, *Discourses* 4.1.174

Disordered physical appetites are a frequent source of analogy to explain desires of other kinds.

Seneca, *Epistles* 15.11

At last, then, away with all these treacherous goods, better when hoped for than when attained! If there were anything of substance in them, they eventually would bring satisfaction. As it is, they are a drink that makes you more thirsty.

Epictetus, *Discourses* 4.9.4–5

Don't you know how thirst works in someone with a fever? It is nothing like the thirst of a man in good health. He drinks and is no longer thirsty. The sick man is happy only for a moment, then is nauseous; he converts the drink into bile, he vomits, his stomach hurts, and then he is thirstier still. It is just like this to crave riches and have riches, to crave power and have power, to crave a beautiful woman and sleep with her.

Plutarch, *On Virtue and Vice* 4 (101c)

Pile up gold, heap up silver, build covered walks, fill your house with slaves and the town with debtors, unless you lay to rest the passions of the soul, and put a curb on your insatiable desires, and rid yourself of fear and anxiety, you are but pouring out wine for a man in a fever, and giving honey to a man who is bilious, and laying out a sumptuous banquet for people who are suffering from dysentery, and can neither retain their food nor get any benefit from it, but are made even worse by it.

This general theme of the Stoics – the illusion that fulfillment of a desire will bring us to a certain longed-for state of mind (which never quite arrives) – has been taken up by many of their cousins and descendants.

Plutarch, *On Love of Wealth* 3 (524c–d)

He who has more than enough and yet hungers for still more will find no remedy in gold or silver or horses and sheep and cattle, but in casting out the source of mischief and being purged. For his ailment is not poverty, but insatiability and avarice, arising from the presence in him of a false and unreflecting judgment; and unless someone removes this, like a tapeworm, from his mind, he will never cease to need superfluities – that is, to want what he does not need.

Whatever falls into our possession and knowledge fails to bring satisfaction; we go panting after things unknown and things to come, because the things that are present are never enough. It is not, in my view, that they lack what it takes to satisfy us, but rather that we hold them in an unhealthy and immoderate grip.

Montaigne, *Of a Saying of Cæsar* (1580)

A new way to think about the pyramids:

I consider [a Pyramid] as a monument to the insufficiency of human enjoyments. A king, whose power is unlimited, and whose treasures surmount all real and imaginary wants, is compelled to solace, by the erection of a Pyramid, the satiety of dominion and tastelessness of pleasures, and to amuse the tediousness of declining life, by seeing thousands laboring without end, and one stone, for no purpose, laid upon another. Whoever thou art that, not content with a moderate condition, imaginest happiness in royal magnificence, and dreamest that command or riches can feed the appetite of novelty with perpetual gratifications, survey the Pyramids, and confess thy folly.

Johnson, *Rasselas* (1759)

Schopenhauer offered some interesting ways to explain the Stoic observation.

When a piece of good fortune befalls us, our claims mount higher and higher, as there is nothing to regulate them; it is in this feeling of expansion

Schopenhauer, *The Wisdom of Life* (1851)

that the delight of it lies. But it lasts no longer than the process itself, and when the expansion is complete, the delight ceases; we have become accustomed to the increase in our claims, and consequently indifferent to the amount of wealth which satisfies them.

Schopenhauer, *The Wisdom of Life* (1851)

There is no absolute or definite amount of wealth which will satisfy a man. The amount is always relative, that is to say, just so much as will maintain the proportion between what he wants and what he gets; for to measure a man's happiness only by what he gets, and not also by what he expects to get, is as futile as to try and express a fraction which shall have a numerator but no denominator. A man never feels the loss of things which it never occurs to him to ask for; he is just as happy without them; whilst another, who may have a hundred times as much, feels miserable because he has not got the one thing he wants.

2. *Natural vs. unnatural appetites.* The Stoics sometimes explain bottomless desires by reference to their unnatural character. We have two kinds of appetites. Some are implanted by nature, such as hunger. These are finite and can be fully satisfied. Of course they then recur; the satisfaction isn't permanent. But the measure of them is clear. We eat until we aren't hungry, and the same thing that was satisfying yesterday can be satisfying today. Other desires, such as the wish for status, are produced by social life, or are created by stimulating the appetite for things we don't need. Desires of this artificial kind are never quite satisfied; their fulfillment isn't as pleasing as we imagined, and newer and bigger objects of them must always be sought. And because they aren't linked to a particular need, they have no natural stopping place.

Seneca, *Consolation to Helvia* 11.4

Every want that springs, not from any need, but from vice, is of a like character; however much you pile up for it will serve not to end but to advance desire. He who keeps himself within natural limits will not feel poverty; he who exceeds them will be pursued by poverty even amid the greatest wealth.

The measure of what is necessary is what is useful. But what standard can limit the superfluous? It is for this reason that men sink themselves in pleasures, and then cannot do without them when once they have become accustomed to them; and it is for this reason they are most wretched – that they have reached such a pass that what was once superfluous to them has become indispensable.

Seneca, *Epistles* 39.5–6

Let the possessions of many wealthy men be piled up together for you! Assume fortune takes you far beyond a mere private income: it covers you in gold, dresses you in purple, brings you to that stage of luxury and riches at which you hide the ground under marble floors, so that you're able not only to have wealth but to walk on it. Add statues and paintings and whatever art has devised in the service of luxury. What you will learn from these things is to long for more. Natural desires are finite; those born of false opinion have no place to stop. There is no terminus to what is false. When you are travelling on a road, there must be an end; but wanderings have no limit.

Seneca, *Epistles* 16.8–9

Some good later reworkings:

The laws of Nature teach us what we legitimately need. The sages tell us that no one is poor according to Nature; everyone is poor according to opinion. They then distinguish skillfully between desires that come from Nature and desires arising from our disordered imaginations. The desires that have limits come from Nature. The ones that run away from us and never have an end are our

Montaigne, *Of Managing the Will* (1580)

own. Poverty in material things is easy to cure; poverty of the soul, impossible.

Johnson, *The Idler* no. 30 (1758)

The desires of man increase with his acquisitions; every step which he advances brings something within his view, which he did not see before, and which, as soon as he sees it, he begins to want. Where necessity ends, curiosity begins; and no sooner are we supplied with every thing that nature can demand, than we sit down to contrive artificial appetites.

This theme is pursued further in Chapter 6, Section 8.

3. *Chasing vs. having.* Another deception identified by the Stoics: when we work toward a goal, we imagine the happiness that its attainment will bring; but the pursuit itself turns out to be more enjoyable than the capture of the thing pursued.

Seneca, *Epistles* 9.7

The philosopher Attalus used to say: "It is more pleasant to make a friend than to have one, as it is more pleasant to the artist to paint than to have painted." When one is busy and absorbed in one's work, the very absorption affords great delight; but when one has withdrawn one's hand from the completed masterpiece, the pleasure is not so keen. Now it is the fruit of his art that he enjoys; it was the art itself that he enjoyed while he was painting.

Attalus was a Stoic philosopher and one of Seneca's early teachers. Seneca described himself as having "practically laid siege to his classroom, the first to arrive and the last to leave." (*Epistles* 108.3) Seneca's father described Attalus as the subtlest and most articulate philosopher of his times.

Shakespeare, *The Merchant of Venice*, 2, 6

GRATIANO.   All things that are
Are with more spirit chased than enjoyed.

The pleasure of expecting enjoyment is often greater than that of obtaining it, and the completion of almost every wish is found a disappointment.

Johnson, *The Rambler* no. 71 (1750)

4. *Disgust with possession.* A related but distinct Stoic law of desire: having a thing tends to bring about indifference or contempt towards it. Sometimes this is because finally possessing what one wanted allows its unimportance to be exposed.

You regard the objects you seek as lofty because you lie far away from them. To him who has reached them, they are small and mean. And I am very much mistaken if he does not desire to climb still higher; that which you regard as the top is merely a rung on the ladder. Now everyone suffers from ignorance of the truth; deceived by what they hear others say, they seek these ends as if they were good, and then, after having won their wish, and suffered much, they find them evil, or empty, or less important than they had expected.

Seneca, *Epistles* 118.6–7

Compare:

To obtain something we have desired is to find out that it is worthless; we are always living in expectation of better things, while, at the same time, we often repent and long for things that belong to the past.

Schopenhauer, *On the Vanity of Existence* (1851)

But the Stoics regard the difficulty as deeper still. Anything loses its power to satisfy once it is possessed, not just because we see it more realistically but because possession itself changes how we feel about it. No acquisition or stimulation makes the same impression on us with long exposure.

Do you not realize that all things lose their force because of familiarity?

Seneca, *Natural Questions* IV B, 13.11

Seneca, *Epistles* 81.28

We value nothing more highly than a benefit when we are seeking it, and nothing less highly once we obtain it.

Seneca, *Epistles* 115.17

Would that those who crave wealth could compare notes with those who have it! Would that those who seek political office could confer with the ambitious who have gained the highest honors! They would then surely change their desires, seeing that these grandees are always gaping after new gains and despising what they formerly sought. For there is no one in the world who is contented with his prosperity, even if it is continuous. People complain about their plans and about getting what they planned. They always prefer what they have failed to win.

An example of the pattern on a social rather than individual level, from a visit Seneca made to the villa of Scipio Africanus:

Seneca, *Epistles* 86.8

In Scipio's bathhouse there are tiny chinks – you cannot call them windows – cut out of the stone wall in such a way as to admit light without weakening the fortifications. Nowadays, however, people regard baths as fit for moths unless they have been so arranged that they receive the sun all day long through the widest openings. Unless you can bathe and get a tan at the same time. Unless there is a view from the tub over land and sea. So it goes; the establishments that had drawn crowds and admiration when they were first opened are avoided and accounted old-fashioned as soon as luxury has worked out some new way to outdo itself.

Montaigne was a close observer of the corrosive effect that familiarity and surfeit have on our affections.

Montaigne, *Of Presumption* (1580)

I am bothered by a defect in my soul that I dislike both for its injustice and, even more, for the trouble it causes. I try to correct it but cannot get it out by the roots. It is that I value too lightly the things that I have, just because I have them, and overvalue things that are foreign, things that are absent, and things that don't belong to me.... Possession breeds contempt for whatever we hold and control.

Nothing is as distasteful and clogging as abundance. What appetite would not be repelled by seeing three hundred women at its mercy, as the Grand Turk has in his seraglio? And what appetite for so-called hunting did one of his ancestors maintain for himself, who never went into the fields with fewer than seven thousand falconers?

Montaigne, *Of the Inequality Amongst Us* (1580)

Johnson also had remarks on this theme.

Corporal sensation is known to depend so much upon novelty, that custom takes away from many things their power of giving pleasure or pain. Thus a new dress becomes easy by wearing it, and the palate is reconciled by degrees to dishes which at first disgusted it.... Something similar, or analogous, may be observed in effects produced immediately upon the mind; nothing can strongly strike or affect us, but what is rare or sudden. The most important events, when they become familiar, are no longer considered with wonder or solicitude, and that which at first filled up our whole attention, and left no place for any other thought, is soon thrust aside into some remote repository of the mind, and lies among other lumber of the memory, overlooked and neglected.

Johnson, *The Rambler* no. 78 (1750)

Such is the emptiness of human enjoyment, that we are always impatient of the present. Attainment is followed by neglect, and possession by disgust; and the malicious remark of the Greek epigrammatist on marriage may be applied to

Johnson, *The Rambler* no. 207 (1752)

every other course of life, that its two days of happiness are the first and the last.

Johnson was probably putting a more graceful construction onto an ugly saying of Hipponax, a Greek poet from the 6th century BC: "There are two days when a woman is a pleasure: the day one marries her and the day one carries out her dead body."

Our topic in this section might be considered an aspect of what psychologists today sometimes call adaptation – the tendency to become used to things, and to stop noticing them, and all that follows from this. Stoics are keen students of adaptation and its workings, some of which help us and some of which make us worse off. Adaptation was relevant to Chapter 1, for example, because getting accustomed to a condition can cause us to regard it as natural and inevitable when it isn't. Adaptation will be relevant again when we take up the subject of adversity, because adaptation helps with its management. Adaptation also is at the root of many desires, because it corrodes our ability to find pleasure in whatever we already have and so drives us on to new wants. Smith nicely tied the phenomenon to a larger Stoic claim.

Smith, *The Theory of Moral Sentiments* (1759)

The never-failing certainty with which all men, sooner or later, accommodate themselves to whatever becomes their permanent situation, may, perhaps, induce us to think that the Stoics were, at least, thus far very nearly in the right; that, between one permanent situation and another, there was, with regard to real happiness, no essential difference: or that, if there were any difference, it was no more than just sufficient to render some of them the objects of simple choice or preference; but not of any earnest or anxious desire: and others, of simple rejection, as being fit to be set aside or avoided; but not of any earnest or anxious aversion.

5. *Envy.* Attainment of our desires fails to satisfy in part because we measure our satisfaction with what we have by comparing it to what others have. It is always possible to find some who seem to be ahead of us or to have more than us, and those tend to be the only comparisons we care about.

That man will never be happy whom the sight of a happier man will torment.

Seneca, *On Anger* 3.30.3

No man when he views the lot of others is content with his own. This is why we grow angry even at the gods, because some person is ahead of us, forgetting how many men there are behind us, and how huge a mass of envy follows at the back of him who envies but a few. Nevertheless such is the presumptuousness of men that, although they may have received much, they count it an injury that they might have received more.

Seneca, *On Anger* 3.31.1

Suppose you regard wealth as a good. Poverty will distress you and, worst of all, it will be an imaginary poverty. However much you may have, still, because someone has more, you will feel that you fall short to the extent he is ahead. You consider official position a good: this man being made a consul will vex you, or that one's being reappointed, and you will be envious whenever you see another's name appearing frequently on the list of officeholders. Such is the madness of ambition that you will feel you have come in last if anyone is ahead of you.

Seneca, *Epistles* 104.9

Why should one person envy another? Why be awed by the rich or the powerful, especially those who are strong and quick to anger? For what will they do to us? What they can do, we don't care about; what we care about, they cannot do.

Epictetus, *Discourses* 1.9.20

Everyone can be envious of somebody – if not of one who is achieving more, then of one who is achieving something else.

Plutarch, *On Tranquility of Mind* 13 (473b)

Not only are men jealous of fellow-craftsmen and those who share the same life as themselves, but also the wealthy envy the learned, the famous the rich, advocates the sophists, and, by Heaven, free men and patricians regard with wondering admiration and envy successful comedians in the theatre and dancers and servants in the courts of kings; and by so doing they afford themselves no small vexation and disturbance.

Envy doesn't just make us less satisfied; it makes us desire things that we otherwise wouldn't want at all.

Seneca, *Epistles* 123.6

And how much do we acquire simply because our neighbors have acquired such things, or because most men possess them!

Envy, like other topics in this chapter, has provoked much discussion by descendants of the Stoics. Johnson was a perceptive analyst of the problem. He spun out this last idea of Seneca's a bit.

Johnson, *The Adventurer* no. 111 (1753)

Many of our miseries are merely comparative: we are often made unhappy, not by the presence of any real evil, but by the absence of some fictitious good; of something which is not required by any real want of nature, which has not in itself any power of gratification, and which neither reason nor fancy would have prompted us to wish, did we not see it in the possession of others.

He also observed, in his characteristic style, the universal character of the general problem: our imaginings of others.

Johnson, *The Rambler* no. 63 (1750)

It has been remarked, perhaps, by every writer who has left behind him observations upon life, that no man is pleased with his present state; which proves equally unsatisfactory, says Horace, whether fallen upon by chance, or chosen with deliberation; we are always disgusted with some circumstance or other of our situation, and imagine the condition of others more abundant in blessings, or less exposed to calamities.

And Johnson noted, finally, that while it may or may not make us happier to have what someone else does, we are definitely made unhappy by envy of it.

> Such is the state of every age, every sex, and every condition: all have their cares, either from nature or from folly: and whoever therefore finds himself inclined to envy another, should remember that he knows not the real condition which he desires to obtain, but is certain that by indulging a vicious passion, he must lessen that happiness which he thinks already too sparingly bestowed.

Johnson, *The Rambler* no. 128 (1751)

Schopenhauer added that envy is the rare vice that makes us unhappy on the spot.

> [Envy] is at once a vice and a source of misery. We should treat it as the enemy of our happiness, and stifle it like an evil thought. This is the advice given by Seneca; as he well puts it, we shall be pleased with what we have, if we avoid the self-torture of comparing our own lot with some other and happier one.

Schopenhauer, *Our Relation to Ourselves* (1851)

Envy can be considered an instance of a larger problem: useless comparisons, on which Smith again had a good comment.

> The great source of both the misery and disorders of human life, seems to arise from over-rating the difference between one permanent situation and another. Avarice over-rates the difference between poverty and riches: ambition, that between a private

Smith, *The Theory of Moral Sentiments* (1759)

and a public station: vain-glory, that between obscurity and extensive reputation. The person under the influence of any of those extravagant passions, is not only miserable in his actual situation, but is often disposed to disturb the peace of society, in order to arrive at that which he so foolishly admires. The slightest observation, however, might satisfy him, that, in all the ordinary situations of human life, a well-disposed mind may be equally calm, equally cheerful, and equally contented.

6. *Desires and opinions.* We turn from the Stoic diagnosis of desire to the remedies. The most direct antidotes, here and in most cases, are those introduced in the first two chapters of this book. One can work to view the object of a desire accurately, and thus seek detachment from it; attachments to externals are, in general, breeding grounds for envy and other vices. Or one can perceive a desire as just another misjudgment and, if the talent for doing so has been developed, simply dismiss it. To restate the point: the principle of Chapter 1 treats the mind and its opinions as responsible for what we want; it follows that any desire can be satisfied – or addressed, anyway – in two ways. One can go after the object of the desire, or one can get to work on the other half of the problem: the opinion that produces it. Solving the equation in this way (from the right-hand side rather than the left, as we might think of it) is standard Stoic procedure.

Epictetus, *Discourses* 4.1.175

Freedom is attained not by satisfying desires but by removing them.

Seneca, *Epistles* 123.3

No one can have whatever he wants. What he can do is not want what he doesn't have, and cheerfully enjoy what comes his way.

Marcus Aurelius, *Meditations* 9.40

One man prays: "Help me go to bed with that woman." You pray: "Help me not to lust after going to bed with her." Another: "Help me be released

from that!" You: "Help me not need to be released."
Another: "How shall I not lose my little son?" You:
"How shall I not be afraid to lose him?" Turn your
prayers this way, and see what happens.

Wouldn't anyone admit how much better it is,
instead of working hard to get possession of
someone else's wife, to work hard to restrain your
desires; instead of being distressed about money,
to train yourself to want little; instead of working
to become famous, to work not to thirst for fame;
instead of finding a way to hurt someone you
envy, to find a way not to envy anyone; and instead
of acting as a slave to false friends, as sycophants
do, to suffer hardships in order to find true
friends?

Musonius Rufus, *That One Should Disdain Hardships*

Epicurus offered a statement of this point of which Seneca approved.

If you wish to make Pythocles rich, do not add to
his store of money, but subtract from his desires.

Epicurus, quoted in Seneca, *Epistles* 21.7

Seneca liked it well enough that he thought the logic
could be multiplied.

If you want to make Pythocles distinguished, don't
add to his distinctions, but diminish his desires. If
you want Pythocles to have endless enjoyment,
don't add to his enjoyments, but diminish his
desires. If you want to make Pythocles an old man,
living his life to the full, don't add to his years, but
diminish his desires.

Seneca, *Epistles* 21.8

7. *Useful comparisons to other people.* Dealing with desires
by dropping them, as just shown, is the first line of Stoic
response, and perhaps all that is needed on a purist's
view. But the late Stoics knew that such a direct approach
can be very difficult, so they offered other psychological
strategies for the management of desire as well. The Sto-

ics criticize comparisons that cause discontent, as we have seen. But they recommend comparisons that have the opposite effect. One might suppose that all comparisons to others ought to be held strictly irrelevant – that to reduce unhappiness by looking at others who are unhappier makes no more sense than reducing happiness by looking at others who are happier still. But this is another instance of pragmatism in the late Stoics, especially Seneca. They judge a perspective by its consequences. A comparison may be recommended just because it helps free us from tendencies of the mind that have already been diagnosed as unwanted.

Some of the healthy comparisons suggested by the Stoics are to people and circumstances from the past.

Seneca, *On Tranquility of Mind* 12.4

Whenever I look back at the examples of antiquity I am ashamed to seek any consolations for poverty – the extravagance of our day having reached the point that the travel expenses of exiles are more than the inheritances of princes in former times.

Comparisons to others who have been in the same boat can likewise be productive.

Plutarch, *On Tranquility of Mind* 6 (467e)

It will also help greatly toward tranquility of mind to observe that famous men have suffered nothing at all from evils the same as yours. Does childlessness, for example, vex you? Consider the kings of Rome, of whom not one was able to bequeath the kingdom to a son. Are you distressed by your present poverty? Well, what Bœotian rather than Epaminondas, what Roman rather than Fabricus, would you have preferred to be?

Epaminondas was a revered Greek statesman and general in the 4th century BC who was well known for his simple manner of living. Fabricus was a consul in early Rome. He, too, had a reputation for austerity.

Useful comparisons can also be drawn to those in the

present who are worse off than oneself. Our tendency is always to look in the other direction – up rather than down.

> No man in public life thinks of the many whom he has surpassed; he thinks rather of those by whom he is surpassed. And these men find it less pleasing to see many behind them than annoying to see anyone ahead of them. That is the trouble with every sort of ambition; it does not look back.

Seneca, *Epistles* 73.3

The Stoics recommend changing the direction in which we look for comparisons to decide how we are doing. Envy may, in effect, be reversed.

> Are there many who surpass you? Consider how many more are behind than ahead of you. Do you ask me what is your greatest fault? Your book-keeping is wrong. What you have paid out, you value highly; what you have received, low.

Seneca, *On Anger* 3.31.3

Plutarch made this point well, too: it is up to us to choose the people to whom we compare ourselves. This allows us to rig the contest. Whether or not this is good philosophy, it is helpful psychology.

> In the Olympic games you can't win by choosing your competitors. But in life, circumstances allow you to take pride in your superiority to many, and to be envied rather than envious of others – unless, of course, you make Briareus or Hercules your opponent.... When you are marveling at the greatness of Xerxes crossing the Hellespont, as a local once did, look also at those who are digging through Mount Athos beneath the lash, and those whose ears and noses are mutilated because the bridge was broken by the current. Consider that at the same time, they are thinking how happy your life and your fortunes are.

Plutarch, *On Tranquility of Mind* 10 (470e)

Xerxes I of Persia had sought to invade Greece in 480 BC. His path required his army to dig a canal near Mount Athos in Greece, and to build a 4,000-foot pontoon bridge over the Hellespont (now the Dardanelles) – the strait separating Asia from Europe. The first version of the bridge collapsed, after which Xerxes ordered terrible retributions against those he held responsible, along with a vengeful flogging of the nearby waters by his soldiers. Upon seeing Xerxes make his crossing at last, a local is said to have compared him to Zeus (as recounted in Herodotus, *Histories* 7.56). As for Briareus, he was a creature from Greek mythology with 50 heads and 100 arms. An example that needs less explanation:

Plutarch, *On Tranquility of Mind* 11 (471b)

When that renowned Pittacus, whose fame for bravery and for wisdom and justice was great, was entertaining some guests, his wife entered in a rage and upset the table; his guests were dismayed, but Pittacus said, "Every one of us has some trouble. He that has only mine is doing very well indeed."

Pittacus was one of the Seven Sages of Greece – the circle of statesmen and philosophers from the 6th century BC who were celebrated for their wisdom in classical times. Some more recent continuations of these ideas:

Montaigne, *On Vanity* (1580)

In all circumstances, we compare ourselves to what is above us and look to those who are better off. Let us measure ourselves instead by what is below. None are so miserable that they cannot find a thousand examples to provide consolation.

Boswell, *Life of Johnson* (1791)

I mentioned the advice given us by philosophers, to console ourselves, when distressed or embarrassed, by thinking of those who are in a worse situation than ourselves. This, I observed, could not apply to all, for there must be some who have nobody worse than they are. Johnson. "Why, to be sure, Sir, there are; but they don't know it. There is no being so poor and so contemptible, who does not think there is somebody still poorer, and still more contemptible."

It is a fact that if real calamity comes upon us, the most effective consolation – though it springs from the same source as envy – is just the thought of greater misfortunes than ours; and the next best is the society of those who are in the same luck as we – the partners of our sorrows.

Schopenhauer, *Our Relation to Ourselves* (1851)

A variant:

When any calamity has been suffered, the first thing to be remembered is how much has been escaped.

Johnson, Letter to Hester Thrale (1770)

Our current teaching might be further illustrated by imagining a marketplace for miseries and asking whether we would want to make trades there. If this notion does not seem directly related to the problem of desire, consider it another device for increasing contentment with what one has.

If we were all to bring our misfortunes into a common store, so that each person should receive an equal share in the distribution, the majority would be glad to take up their own and depart.

Plutarch, *Letter to Apollonius* 9 (106b)

Herodotus offered a similar idea:

This, however, I know full well – that if all men were to carry their own private troubles to market for barter with their neighbors, there would not be a single one who, when he had looked into the troubles of other men, would not be glad to carry home again what he had brought.

Herodotus, *Histories* 7.152

8. *Useful comparisons to loss.* Another valuable comparison considers how desirable the goods we have would seem if they were absent. We saw earlier the role that adaptation plays in creating desires that never end. Getting used to what we have causes us to lose appreciation

for it. The Stoics respond by trying to see old things freshly. Instead of changing their possessions, they try to change the way they view them.

Marcus Aurelius, *Meditations* 7.27

Don't imagine having things that you don't have. Rather, pick the best of the things that you do have and think of how much you would want them if you didn't have them.

Epicurus, Vatican Sayings 35

Don't spoil what's here by longing for what's not here, but realize that these too were things to be prayed for.

Schopenhauer, *Our Relation to Ourselves* (1851)

We should sometimes try to look upon our possessions in the light in which they would appear if we had lost them.

Compare:

Epictetus, *Discourses* 3.9.21

To you everything you have appears small; all my things appear great to me.

The same idea can be applied to conditions rather than to things. It is a way to build gratitude not just for what one has but for one's circumstances and situation.

Plutarch, *On Tranquility of Mind* 9 (469e–f)

We should not overlook even common and ordinary things, but take some account of them and be grateful that we are alive and well and look upon the sun ... These things when they are present will afford us greater tranquility of mind, if we but imagine them to be absent, and remind ourselves often how desirable is health to the sick, and peace to those at war, and, to an unknown stranger in so great a city, the acquisition of reputation and friends; and how painful it is to be deprived of these things when we have once had them. For it will not then be the case that we find each one of these important and valuable only when it has been lost, but worthless while securely held.

Chapter Six

WEALTH AND PLEASURE

Chapter 5 considered some general properties of desires – their never-ending character, and the ways they are fed by comparisons; how they deceive us, and how they might be tamed. This chapter considers more specific Stoic teachings on two temptations in particular: wealth and pleasure. Every such temptation is accompanied by its own origins, snares, and illusions, and also by questions about whether or how it can be enjoyed in a way that is consistent with peace of mind and other Stoic aspirations. A few ideas from the previous chapter will be revisited here and applied to more particular problems.

On a Stoic view, money and our fascination with it – greed – tends to make us ridiculous and to cause much misery to ourselves and to others. The Stoics hold that attachment to wealth has predictable consequences. Once we have money, we worry about keeping it, are anxious for more of it, and feel pain when it is lost. We feel a desire for more of whatever we have, and gradually value all sorts of things more highly than they are worth. These points can be applied to pleasure more generally: we overrate pleasures and underrate the cost of trying to gain them. Pleasure and pain are parts of a cycle; they go together, and have to be addressed together.

After considering those ideas, this chapter will turn from warnings about wealth and pleasure to ideas about the use and management of them. Stoicism suggests first that we rethink what we want, how much of it, and why. Stoics value moderation, and they don't view it as a compromise of pleasures. They regard moderation, rather, as enhancing pleasures – indeed, as making the true and healthy enjoyment of them possible. A second Stoic resource is detachment. One can learn to enjoy wealth and pleasures without grasping for them, holding them too tightly when one has them, or being crushed when they are gone. Third, to continue a theme from the previous chapter, the easiest way to real wealth is by learning to be happy with less – with enough. There is no difference, so far as contentment is concerned, between having something and not caring whether you have it. The second route often is easier.

The last sections of the chapter consider the pleasures that Stoics do embrace – the kind they regard as natural, and that we experience when we satisfy the appetites we are born with. Seneca considers recreation and games to be among these (and he recognizes a place for drinking as well). Above all, though, the Stoic is attracted to the pleasures of the mind. Stoics regard wisdom and understanding as producing a kind of joy that is immune from interruption by circumstance.

1. *Hazards of money.* The Stoics generally consider money to be a great corrupter of the individual and of social life. Money is hard to see and understand clearly; it causes us to misjudge the value of things, and it drives those who worship it into low behavior.

Seneca, *Epistles* 115.10

That very thing which occupies so many magistrates and so many judges, which *makes* both magistrates and judges – money! – since it began to be regarded with honor, has caused true honor to fall into ruin. Becoming alternately merchants and merchandise by turns, we ask not what a thing truly is, but what it costs.

Seneca, *On Anger* 3.33.1

Most of the outcry is about money. It is this that wearies the courts, pits father against son, brews poisons, and gives swords to the legions and to cut-throats alike.... Because of it, nights resound with the quarrels of husbands and wives, crowds swarm to the tribunals of the magistrates, kings rage and plunder and overthrow states that have been built by the long labor of centuries, in order that they may search for gold and silver in the very ashes of cities.

Seneca rejected the claim that riches are no more harmful in themselves than swords.

> Posidonius holds that riches are a cause of evil, not because they do evil themselves but because of the evil they goad men to do…. Riches puff up the spirit and beget pride. They bring on envy and unsettle the mind to such an extent that a reputation for having money delights us, even when that reputation will do us harm.

Seneca, *Epistles* 87.31

Posidonius was a Stoic philosopher of the "middle" period in the ancient life of the school (2nd century BC).

Dr. Johnson emphasized the worthlessness of money on its own.

> Wealth is nothing in itself, it is not useful but when it departs from us; its value is found only in that which it can purchase, which, if we suppose it put to its best use by those that possess it, seems not much to deserve the desire or envy of a wise man.

Johnson, *The Rambler* no. 58 (1750)

2. *The effect of wealth on its holder.* The previous chapter discussed ways in which acquisitions fail to satisfy the appetite for them. The same can be said for money, which Stoics view as having no particular tendency to make people happier.

> Consider how many more people are poor than rich; and yet you will observe that that the poor are no unhappier and no more anxious than the rich.

Seneca, *Consolation to Helvia* 12.1

> I will borrow from Epicurus: "The acquisition of riches has been, for many men, not an end of

Seneca, *Epistles* 17.11–12

troubles but a change of them." I do not wonder. For the fault is not in one's wealth but in the mind itself. That which had made poverty a burden to us has made riches a burden as well. It matters little whether you lay a sick man on a bed of wood or a bed of gold; wherever he be moved, he will carry his disease with him. So, too, it matters not whether a diseased mind is set down in wealth or in poverty. The malady follows the man.

Plutarch, *On Love of Wealth* 1 (523d)

When some persons praised a tall fellow with a long reach as having the makings of a fine boxer, the trainer Hippomachus remarked: "Yes, if the crown were hung up and to be got by reaching." So too we can say to those who are dazzled by fine estates, great houses, and large sums of money and regard them as the greatest of blessings: "Yes, if happiness were for sale and to be got by purchase."

Hippomachus was a trainer of boxers and wrestlers; he evidently had a talent for philosophy as well. He will appear again in Chapter 7, Section 3.

The Stoics' suspicion of money goes further than just shown. They hold not only that wealth fails to satisfy but that it tends to rule those who possess it and bring about its own forms of unhappiness.

Seneca, *Epistles* 14.18

He who has need of riches feels fear on their account. But no man enjoys a blessing that brings anxiety. He is always trying to add a little more. While he puzzles over increasing his wealth, he forgets how to use it.

Seneca, *Epistles* 115.16

What tears and toil does avarice exact! How wretched it is in desiring, how wretched in what it has acquired! Add to this the daily worries that torment us in proportion to our possessions. To have money brings more anxiety than the effort to acquire it. How we grieve over our losses, which

may be great and which seem even greater! And
then even if fortune takes nothing away from us,
we regard as a further loss whatever we cannot get.

Seneca regarded the eventual consequence of greed to be
a certain type of diseased judgment.

We might define the disease this way: to strive too   Seneca, *Epistles* 75.11
hard for things that are only worth wanting a little
or not at all, or to value things highly that ought
to be valued only somewhat or not at all.

3. *Hazards of pleasure*. The Stoic attitude toward wealth
can be generalized to pleasure. Stoics view pleasures as
costlier than they seem – as not lasting long, as always
exacting a price, and as invariably alternating with some
sort of loss or pain.

One person seeks joy in feasting and self-indul-   Seneca, *Epistles* 59.15
gence; another, in elections and crowds of sup-
porters; another, in his mistress; another, in the
idle display of culture and in literature that has no
power to heal. All of them are led astray by
delights that are deceptive and short-lived – like
drunkenness, for example, which pays for a single
hour of hilarious madness with a long-lasting
sickness; or like applause and enthusiastic popularity and approval that are gained, and atoned
for, at the cost of great mental disquietude.

The day a man becomes subject to pleasure, he   Seneca, *On the Happy Life* 4.4
will also be subject to pain. And you see what
wretched and hateful slavery a person is in when
pleasures and pains – those most capricious and
tyrannical masters – take captive of him in turn.

The sages teach us well to beware the treachery of   Montaigne, *Of Solitude* (1580)
our appetites, and to distinguish true and com-
plete pleasures from those that are mixed and
interwoven with even more pain. Most pleasures,

they say, caress and embrace us only to strangle us, like the thieves the Egyptians called Philistæ. If we felt the headache before getting drunk, we would be careful not to drink to excess. But pleasure, to deceive us, walks in front and hides its train.

Montaigne, *That We Taste Nothing Pure* (1580)

Ease crushes us. That is the sense of an ancient Greek verse, which says the gods sell us every good they give us; that is to say, they give us nothing pure and perfect, nothing that we do not buy at the cost of some evil.

The Greek verse Montaigne mentions is from Epicharmus, a Greek poet (c. 540–c. 450 BC). He was reputed in classical times to be a great master of drama and comedy, but very little has survived from him. The line at issue here was preserved in Xenophon's *Memorabilia of Socrates* 2.1.20.

Marcus Aurelius expressed the value of moderation, and his skepticism of pleasures, in a different way. He observed that we don't admire those who set a high value on pleasures; they are as likely to be bad people as good. And he held that we're never sorry after we have set a low value on pleasure ourselves.

Marcus Aurelius, *Meditations* 6.34

How many pleasures have been enjoyed by robbers, patricides, tyrants.

Marcus Aurelius, *Meditations* 8.10

No one who is good and honorable would regret having passed a pleasure by.

Compare:

Plutarch, *Advice About Keeping Well* 7 (125d)

Just as Simonides used to say that he had never been sorry for having kept silent, but many a time for having spoken, so we have never been sorry either for having put a dainty to one side, or for having drunk water instead of wine, but the opposite.

Simonides of Ceos was a Greek poet (c. 556–468 BC).

4. *Things unneeded*. We turn, after our familiar pattern, from the Stoic analysis of wealth and pleasure to Stoic ideas about how to manage them. Chapter 5 introduced the Stoic idea that desires generally can be managed either by fulfilling them or decreasing them, and that the latter method is both overlooked and more effective in producing satisfaction. Here we consider the more specific application of that idea to wealth. Stoics view wealth not as an absolute state but as a favorable relationship between what one has and what one wants. Most people devote themselves to enlarging the first when they would do better to reduce the second. This is the classic Stoic inversion.

> It is in the power of any man to despise all things, but of no man to possess all things. The shortest way to riches is to despise riches.

Seneca, *Epistles* 62.3

> What I will teach you is the ability to become rich as speedily as possible. How excited you are to hear the news! And rightly so; I will lead you by a shortcut to the greatest wealth.... My dear Lucilius, not wanting something is just as good as having it. The important thing either way is the same – freedom from worry.

Seneca, *Epistles* 119:1–2

The things one *doesn't* want or need can thus be counted as a form of wealth. Seneca comments further on them:

> Do you think that these don't count as riches, just because no man has ever been condemned to death on their account? Because no one's son or wife has ever poisoned him for their sake? Because in wartime they are not looted? Because they are idle in peace? Because it is not dangerous to possess them, or troublesome to dispose of them?

Seneca, *Epistles* 119:6

Johnson's articulation of the idea:

Johnson, *The Adventurer*
no. 119 (1753)

Every man may grow rich by contracting his wishes, and by quiet acquiescence in what has been given him, supply the absence of more.

And the converse is also true: desires are a form of poverty.

Seneca, *Epistles* 2.6

It is not one who has little, but one who craves more, who is poor. What does it matter how much you have laid up in your safe or in your warehouse, how large are your flocks or your investments, if you covet your neighbor's property, and if you count not what you have but what remains for you to have?

Johnson, *The Rambler* no. 163
(1751)

Every man is rich or poor, according to the proportion between his desires and enjoyments; any enlargement of wishes is therefore equally destructive to happiness with the diminution of possession; and he that teaches another to long for what he never shall obtain, is no less an enemy to his quiet, than if he had robbed him of part of his patrimony.

5. *Acceptance.* A related idea, but applied more broadly: the value of accepting one's lot, and what one has. Again, the Stoics often made the point with comparisons.

Epictetus, Fragment (Stobæus
3.4.91)

When we are invited to a banquet, we take what is put before us. If someone should order the host to serve him fish or pastries, he would seem eccentric. But out in the world, we ask the gods for things they do not give us – even though there are many things they *have* given us.

Epictetus, *Enchiridion* 17

Remember that you are an actor in a play of whatever kind the producer may choose. If a short one, short; if a long one, long. If he wants you to play a beggar, see that you act even this part naturally; or a cripple, or a ruler, or an ordinary citizen. Your task is to give a good performance of the part that you are assigned. To select the part belongs to someone else.

The idea applied to a lifespan:

> You're not upset because you weigh only so many pounds and not three hundred; but you are sorry that you have only so many years to live and not more? Just as you are satisfied with how much substance has been allotted to you, be content also with the time.

Marcus Aurelius, *Meditations* 6.49

More literal treatments:

> Knowing how fleeting these ancillary comforts are, I never neglect, even while enjoying them fully, to make it my highest prayer to God that he render me content with myself and the goods that come from within me.

Montaigne, *Of Solitude* (1580)

> Examine the records of history, recollect what has happened within the circle of your own experience, consider with attention what has been the conduct of almost all the greatly unfortunate, either in private or public life, whom you may have either read of, or heard of, or remember; and you will find that the misfortunes of by far the greater part of them have arisen from their not knowing when they were well, when it was proper for them to sit still and to be contented. The inscription upon the tomb-stone of the man who had endeavored to mend a tolerable constitution by taking physic; "I was well, I wished to be better; here I am;" may generally be applied with great justness to the distress of disappointed avarice and ambition.

Smith, *The Theory of Moral Sentiments* (1759)

One path to acceptance is to imagine the position in which we hope to be left once a desire is fulfilled, and to ask whether the wished-for state might be attained more directly. Smith had a choice anecdote on this point, too, which he adapted from Plutarch.

Smith, *The Theory of Moral Sentiments* (1759)

What the Favorite of the king of Epirus said to his master, may be applied to men in all the ordinary situations of human life. When the King had recounted to him, in their proper order, all the conquests which he proposed to make, and had come to the last of them; And what does your Majesty propose to do then? said the Favorite. – I propose then, said the King, to enjoy myself with my friends, and endeavor to be good company over a bottle. – And what hinders your Majesty from doing so now? replied the Favorite.

The king of Epirus (a Greek state) was Pyrrhus, who ruled it in the years around 300 BC. His "Favorite" was an advisor named Cineas, who had been a student of the famous orator Demosthenes. To Pyrrhus we owe the expression "pyrrhic victory" – a victory not worth winning because of its cost. Pyrrhus incurred appalling casualties in wars with the Romans that he fought after the time of the anecdote above.

By way of epilogue:

Seneca, *Epistles* 71.37

When do we reach the point at which we disdain fortune, whether good or bad, at which – all our emotions having been overcome and brought within our control – we utter the words, "I have conquered"? Conquered whom, you ask? Not the Persians, nor the distant Medes, nor any warlike people (if such there be) beyond the Dahæ, but avarice, ambition, and fear of death – a foe that has conquered the conquerors of the world.

The three groups that Seneca mentions – the Persians, Medes, and Dahæ – were all inhabitants of areas that we now know as Iran or Turkmenistan. The Dahæ (or the

Scythians, of which the Dahæ were one tribe) were a standard classical reference for peoples beyond the boundaries of civilization.

6. *Detachment.* The Stoics have more to say about wealth and pleasure than "learn not to want them," for they recognize that everyone would rather have those things than not. So the next half of this chapter is about when and how wealth and pleasure can be acquired and used in a healthy way.

First and most generally, Stoics regard wealth and other such externals as "indifferent," not as good or bad in themselves. But Stoicism allows that we might legitimately want some of those things – in other words, that some of them are so-called preferred indifferents. This notion has sometimes been considered troublesome because a "preferred indifferent" sounds like a contradiction in terms, and because it might seem to be a kind of fudge factor: the bad Stoic who cannot let go of greed for material goods will shrug them off as preferred indifferents. But the idea serves an important role in Stoicism. It is reasonable, though not easy, to seek detachment from the things one wants in the world. It is not realistic to eradicate all preferences about them. The Stoics understand this.

> Count yourself happy only when all your joys are born of reason, and when, having seen the things that everyone clutches at, or prays for, or watches over, you find – I do not say nothing you *prefer* – but nothing you require.

Seneca, *Epistles* 124.24

So there are externals that Stoics agree are better to have than to lack, and that one might reasonably work to get. And there are disadvantages that a Stoic might reasonably want to avoid as well: non-preferred indifferents, such as ill-health or poverty. Aids to physical wellness are in the "preferred" category.

Seneca, *On the Happy Life*
22.2–3

The wise man will not despise himself no matter how short he may be, but nevertheless he will wish to be tall.... If his health is bad he will endure it, but he will wish for it to be good. Certain things, even if they are trifles when compared with the whole, and can be withdrawn without destroying the essential good, nevertheless add something to the perpetual joy that comes from virtue.

Wealth is another example.

Seneca, *On the Happy Life* 21.4

Nor does the wise man regard himself as undeserving of any of the gifts of Fortune. He does not love riches, but would prefer them; he does not admit them to his heart, but to his house; he does not reject the riches he has, but keeps them to supply fuller material for the exercise of his virtue.

Seneca, *On the Happy Life*
22.3–4

As a favorable wind, sweeping him on, gladdens the sailor, as a bright day and a sunny spot in the midst of winter and cold give cheer, just so riches have their influence on the wise man and bring him joy. And besides, who among wise men – I mean those of our school, who count virtue the sole good – deny that even those things we call "indifferent" do have some inherent value, and that some are more desirable than others? To some of them we accord a little honor, to others much. So make no mistake – riches are among the ones more desirable.

What is the difference between a preferred indifferent and the desires that Stoics regard as hazardous? Detachment. This distinction was introduced at the start of the first chapter. An attachment to an external causes one's happiness, and equilibrium, to depend on it. The Stoic tries to avoid that position under all circumstances. But money, if held without attachment, is unobjectionable – for the money isn't the point. The point is the health of the mind.

The word "detachment" risks creating the wrong impression, since it can connote a lack of real interest in whatever is the subject of it. That isn't the idea. Detachment refers more to the way in which something is held and to whether the mind has been given over to it in an excessive way. The detachment of the Stoic thus can be viewed as a kind of moderation – that is, moderation in one's relationship to externals. A good way to test such a relationship, and to know whether you have an attachment to a thing or just a preference about it, is to consider how well you would handle its loss.

No one is worthy of the gods except he who has disdained riches. I do not forbid you to possess them, but I want to bring you to the point at which you possess them without fear. There is only one way to achieve this: by persuading yourself that you can live happily without them, and by regarding them as always about to depart.

Seneca, *Epistles* 18.13

"Why does a philosopher say that wealth is to be despised, and yet have it? ... And why does the philosopher declare that there is no difference between a longer and a shorter life, and then – if nothing stands in the way – prolong his years, and flourish peacefully in green old age?" He says those things are to be despised not in order that he not have them, but in order that he not worry about keeping them.

Seneca, *On the Happy Life* 21.1–2

Rehearsing the loss of a thing in the mind is one way that Stoics try to keep the right distance from it. This sort of detachment makes the subject of it both safer and easier to enjoy.

Wealth and reputation and power and public office delight most of all those who least fear their opposites. For the violent desire for each of these implants a most violent fear that they may not

Plutarch, *On Tranquility of Mind* 16 (474c–d)

remain, and so renders pleasure in them weak and unstable, like a fluttering flame.

Epictetus offered some similar imaginative steps for achieving detachment from pleasures.

Epictetus, *Enchiridion* 34

When you are tempted by some apparent pleasure, guard yourself – just as with other impressions – against being carried away by it. Let the thing wait for you, and give yourself some delay. Then think about two times to come: the time when you will enjoy the pleasure, and the time afterwards when, having enjoyed it, you will regret it and reproach yourself. Compare this with how pleased you will be, and how you will congratulate yourself, if you don't do it. Still, if it seems that the time is right to do the thing, just take care that the charm and pleasure and attraction of it do not overcome you; compare how much better it is to know you have won this victory against it.

7. *Moderation*. We just saw that the detachment of the Stoic can be viewed as a form of moderation. That makes moderation itself the most natural topic to consider next, for the Stoics value it generally. Moderation is regarded by the Stoic not only as an admired virtue but as a helpful technique. It doesn't mean "less pleasure"; it means the possibility of actual and lasting pleasure – a way to enjoy something without spoiling it, and without the costs and regrets that come with excess. Epictetus liked to show the value of moderation by using comparisons.

Epictetus, *Discourses* 3.9.21

To children who put their hand into a narrow necked earthen vessel and bring out figs and nuts, this happens: if they fill the hand, they cannot remove it, and then they cry. Drop a few of them and you will get it out.

Moderation, for the Stoic, isn't just a question of not taking too much or doing too much of something. It is an attitude of restraint.

Remember that in life you ought to behave as you would at a banquet. Suppose something is passed around and is across from you. Reach out your hand and take some politely. It passes by: do not hold it back. It has not yet come to you: do not stretch to reach it, but wait till it comes to you. Behave this way toward children, toward a wife, toward wealth, and you will eventually be a worthy fellow banqueter of the gods. But if you do not take the things set before you, and even despise them, then you will be not only a fellow banqueter with the gods, but also a fellow ruler.

Epictetus, Enchiridion 15

Self-control restrains our desires. Some it hates and gets rid of, others it manages and restores to a healthy level; nor does it ever seek to satisfy desires for their own sake. Self-control knows that the best measure of the appetites is not how much you want to take, but how much you ought to take.

Seneca, Epistles 88.29

Lack of moderation is the plague of pleasure. Moderation is not the scourge of pleasure, but the seasoning of it.

Montaigne, Of Experience (1580)

Seneca encouraged moderation more broadly in the Stoic way of living.

Just as it is a sign of extravagance to chase after delicacies, so it is madness to avoid what is customary and can be purchased at no great price. Philosophy calls for plain living but not for penance; and we may perfectly well be plain and neat at the same time. This is the mean of which I approve; our life should observe a happy medium between the ways of a sage and the ways of the

Seneca, Epistles 5.4–5

world at large. All men should admire it, but they should understand it also.

8. *Natural appetites (con't.)*. Resuming a theme from the previous chapter, we turn to Stoic ideas about which pleasures are suitable for enjoyment. The Stoics advocate, first, a life led according to nature. The meaning and sense of this instruction has been a matter of debate. The ancient Stoics regarded nature as purposeful and intelligent in ways that few would accept now, so living by the dictates of nature in that sense is no longer a helpful idea to most people. But "according to nature" had further meanings, too, some of which have held up better. It means a life of reason, as Stoics regard reason as nature's distinctive gift to mankind; and that approach to living will appeal to many regardless of the rationale for it.

More relevant to our immediate purposes, living according to nature also means taking satisfaction from fulfillment of the desires that nature creates in us, which the Stoic would say is not hard to achieve. We saw in Chapter 5, Section 2 the idea that appetites from nature are finite while unnatural appetites are infinite. The point has specific applications here. As a corrective to the excessive desire for money and what it can buy, Stoicism distinguishes between requirements of nature and luxuries beyond them.

Seneca, *Consolation to Helvia* 11.1–2

What it has made necessary for man, nature has not made difficult. But he desires clothing of purple steeped in rich dye, embroidered in gold, and decorated with a variety of colors and designs: it is not Nature's fault but his own that he is poor.

Seneca, *Epistles* 4.11

It is the superfluous things for which we sweat. Those are the things that wear our togas threadbare, that force us to grow old in army camps, that dash us on foreign shores. That which is enough is right at hand.

The Stoic holds that pleasures arising from natural sources are rightly enjoyed. It merely should be done with moderation. But most of our energies are instead spent chasing short-lived pleasures that we invent or inflate. Stoics try to align their sense of pleasure with the satisfaction of their actual needs.

Nature has mingled pleasure with necessary things – not to cause us to seek pleasure, but to make those things that are indispensable to existence look attractive to our eyes. If pleasure claims rights of its own, it is luxury.

Seneca, *Epistles* 116.3

I do not advise you to deny anything to nature – for nature is insistent, and cannot be overcome; it demands its due. But know that whatever goes beyond those demands is something extra, not a necessity.... I am thirsty: whether I drink water that comes from the nearest pool or water I chilled in the snow, nature does not care.

Seneca, *Epistles* 119.2–3

Won't you hurry to do what your nature requires? "But rest is also necessary." And so say I. Nature has allowed for due measure of that, too, as it has for eating and drinking. And still you go beyond those measures, beyond what is enough – except when it comes to getting things done, where you stop short of what is possible.

Marcus Aurelius, *Meditations* 5.1

Montaigne borrowed a taxonomy from Epicurus that is similar to the Stoic analysis and reaches the same conclusion.

Desires are either natural and necessary, such as eating and drinking, or natural and not necessary, such as mating with females – or neither natural nor necessary. Almost all of our desires are in this last category; they are all superfluous and artificial.... False judgments and ignorance of the good

Montaigne, *That Our Affections Carry Themselves Beyond Us* (1580)

have instilled so many extraneous desires in us that they have chased out most of the natural ones.

Montaigne, *Upon Some Verses of Virgil* (1580)

Philosophy does not contend against natural pleasures, so long as they are measured; it preaches moderation, not avoidance. Its powers of resistance are for use against those pleasures that are misbegotten and unnatural. Philosophy holds that the appetites of the body should not be increased by the mind, and ingeniously warns us not to stir up hunger by overfeeding; not to stuff the belly but to fill it; to avoid all enjoyments that put us in need, and all meats that bring hunger and drinks that bring thirst.

Montaigne, *Of Experience* (1580)

I consider it as wrong to reject natural pleasures as to be too much in love with them. Xerxes was a fool to offer a reward to whoever found new pleasures for him when he was surrounded already by every pleasure known to man; but it is hardly less foolish to cut yourself off from the pleasures that nature has found for you. We should neither chase them nor flee them; we should accept them.

9. *Uses of pleasure.* The Stoics talk a good deal about despising pleasures. By this they mean that pleasures should be viewed as minor or trivial things, and not as the point of living. They also think pleasures should be viewed with wariness because they often end up causing us trouble. But this isn't the same as saying that pleasures should be *hated.* Sometimes we need them, as Seneca understood.

Seneca, *On Tranquility of Mind* 17.7–8

Some great men, as I have said, used to give themselves a day of rest on certain days every month, while others divided each day between work and leisure.... Some at midday would move on to something requiring less effort, which they had put off to the afternoon hours.... We must be indulgent to the mind, and regularly grant it the leisure that serves as its food and strength.

Seneca endorsed a wider range of pleasures than is sometimes appreciated.

> The mind must not be kept invariably at the same tension, but must be diverted to amusements. Socrates did not blush to play with little children, Cato would relax his mind with wine when it was wearied by the cares of state, and Scipio would stir his triumphal and soldierly person to the sound of music.

Seneca, *On Tranquility of Mind* 17.4

Seneca regarded sports and play as natural pleasures as well, to be enjoyed in moderation like any others. He especially recommended them for people with certain types of temperaments, for whom those pleasures serve a valuable purpose. Stoics are supposed to be of good cheer. Some of them need to lighten up.

> Games will also be beneficial; for pleasure in moderation relaxes the mind and gives it balance. The more damp and the drier natures, and also the cold, are in no danger from anger, but they must beware the more sluggish faults – fear, moroseness, discouragement, and suspicion. And so such natures have need of encouragement and indulgence and the summons to cheerfulness. And since certain remedies are to be employed against anger, others against sullenness, and the two faults are to be cured, not merely by different, but even by contrary, methods, we shall always attack the fault that has become the stronger.

Seneca, *On Anger* 2.20.4

Seneca acknowledged the value of wine as well, and even of occasional intoxication – moderation in moderation, perhaps – for the freedom it gives the mind and for the access it can provide to insight. His reasoning:

Seneca, *On Tranquility of Mind*
17.10

Whether we agree with the Greek poet that "sometimes it's also fun to get a little wild," or with Plato that "the man in possession of himself knocks in vain at poetry's gates," or with Aristotle that "there has been no great genius without some touch of madness" – there can be no lofty utterance, above the commonplace, unless the mind is excited.

These views might not have been shared by all of Seneca's Stoic colleagues or be perfectly consistent with some of his own positions elsewhere (as in Section 3 of this chapter). But they suggest the range of opinions that might be held by Stoics in reasonably good standing.

10. *Pleasures of the mind.* The Stoics give their highest endorsement to the pleasures associated with understanding and wisdom, which might be enjoyed even immoderately without fear of recoil. Stoics regard the mind as the site and the source of true happiness.

Seneca, *Epistles* 124.2

Those who rate pleasure as the supreme ideal hold that the Good is found by the senses; but we Stoics maintain that it is found by the understanding, and we assign it to the mind.

Seneca, *Consolation to Helvia*
11.5

It is the mind that makes us rich. It goes with us into exile; and in the most untamed wilderness, when it has found all that the body needs to be sustained, it relishes the enjoyment of its many own goods.

Epictetus, *Enchiridion* 41

It shows a lack of natural talent to spend much time on bodily activities, as by being excessive in exercise, excessive in eating and drinking, excessive in emptying the bowels and in copulating. These things should be done incidentally, and our attention should be devoted to the mind.

The penultimate activity Epictetus mentions might seem a strange one to associate with a danger of excess. But Romans often did their eliminating in public latrines that were communal and unpartitioned, and socialized while they went about it. Perhaps there were those who got carried away and forgot about the time.

In any event, real happiness for the Stoic comes from seeing the world in an accurate way and with benevolence. The latter point has appeared before and will be developed further in Chapter 11, but is made in this context by Marcus Aurelius.

> As for me, I am happy if the ruling force in my mind is sound, if I do not turn away from anyone, nor any of those things that happen to men, but can look upon all things with kindly eyes, and value everything according to its true worth.

Marcus Aurelius, *Meditations* 8.41

If these statements seem to be wanting in specifics about the form and complexities that the pleasures of understanding might involve, consider a more recent elaboration from Schopenhauer.

> The world in which a man lives shapes itself chiefly by the way in which he looks at it, and so it proves different to different men; to one it is barren, dull, and superficial; to another rich, interesting, and full of meaning. On hearing of the interesting events which have happened in the course of a man's experience, many people will wish that similar things had happened in their lives too, completely forgetting that they should be envious rather of the mental aptitude which lent those events the significance they possess when he describes them.... Since everything which exists or happens for a man exists only in his consciousness and happens for it alone, the most essential thing for a man is the constitution

Schopenhauer, *The Wisdom of Life* (1851)

of this consciousness, which is in most cases far more important than the circumstances which go to form its contents. All the pride and pleasure of the world, mirrored in the dull consciousness of a fool, are poor indeed compared with the imagination of Cervantes writing his *Don Quixote* in a miserable prison.

It isn't really clear how much of *Don Quixote* was written in prison, but one should not quibble when the point is so good.

Chapter Seven

WHAT OTHERS THINK

This chapter considers the Stoic way of looking at approval and criticism – that is, what others think. The approval may be the immediate kind that we call praise or the collective type known as fame; the criticism may be insult or infamy. This chapter can also be considered a Stoic examination of vanity and pride, for these all are externals of a common family. They involve social life: the desire for status within it and for the good opinion of others. Most people seek those things as intently as they chase money or pleasure, and work just as hard to avoid the loss of them.

The first rule of this branch of Stoic teaching is contempt for conformity, for the opinion of the majority, for the habit of looking to others when thinking about what to prefer and how to act. The problem runs deep. A large share of what most people say, think, and do is a product of convention. Its force is hard to resist because getting in line with what others expect causes them to think well of us. Deviating from it tends to be punished swiftly by others who are more comfortable saying, doing, and enforcing what is expected. Much of Stoicism is the effort to see the truth and act on it, and to learn a noble contempt for the consequences that follow.

Turning to details, then, the Stoics regard the appetite for praise as one of the mainsprings of conformity in particular and human behavior in general. They set out to tame it. They start by asking why we care what others say and think about us, especially when the others are people we probably do not hold in notably high esteem. The Stoic develops a distrust for popular judgments, and a suspicion of people and things that have mass appeal.

Stoicism tries instead to substitute a greater respect for one's own opinions, and practice at valuing things for what they are rather than for what anyone else thinks about them.

The other side of our topic is criticism and insult. Of course the Stoic urges indifference to these things. They are externals we can't control. But the Stoics also offer specific ways to think about attacks and respond to them. One is to regard the contempt of others with contempt (or to regard the others themselves with contempt), or to welcome the contempt when it is earned by doing the right thing. Any of these responses is better than fearing the opinions of others; for once one goes down that road, there is no end to it.

Another family of responses involves humility and forgiveness. Stoics usually can accept insults in good humor by reflecting that any such criticism probably understates their true faults; they are comfortable enough with self-inflicted ridicule to be unconcerned when others add to it. A second recourse is to make an assessment of the criticism. If we are criticized justly, we should accept it and change (or accept it and be done). If we are criticized unjustly, the critics are mistaken and entitled to compassion. They meant well, or at least said what seemed right and best to their limited capacities. And at any rate we all will be gone soon enough.

1. *Conformity; common opinion.* The Stoic regards conformity to social expectations as the source of much of our behavior and much of our imbecility. We live by imitating others, and so act out ways of life that have nothing in reason to recommend them. Convention, to be clear, is not merely irrelevant from a Stoic standpoint. It is a repository of error and engine of misjudgment, and a source of pressure that one must learn to resist. From Seneca:

Seneca, *Epistles* 123.6

> Many of our troubles may be explained by the fact that we live according to a pattern, and,

instead of arranging our lives according to reason, are led astray by convention.

On most journeys some recognizable road, and inquiries made of the locals, prevent you from going astray; but on this one the paths most worn and used are also the most deceptive. So nothing needs to be emphasized more than that we should not, like sheep, follow the lead of the flock in front of us – heading not where we ought to go, but where it goes.

Seneca, *On the Happy Life* 1.2–3

Who is not aware that nothing thought to be good or bad looks the same to the sage as it does to everyone else? He pays no mind to what others consider shameful or wretched; he does not walk with the crowd; just as the planets make their way against the whirl of heaven, he proceeds contrary to the opinion of the world.

Seneca, *On the Constancy of the Wise Man* 14.3–4

Marcus Aurelius:

How much trouble he avoids by not looking to see what his neighbor does or thinks – by looking only to what he does himself, that it may be just and pure. The part of the good man is not to peer into the character of others, but to run straight down the line without glancing to one side or the other.

Marcus Aurelius, *Meditations* 4.18

Kindred observations on the dangers of living by the opinions of others:

I have never wished to satisfy the crowd; for what I know, they do not approve, and what they approve, I do not know.

Epicurus, quoted in Seneca, *Epistles* 29.10

Whatever it be, whether art or nature, that has inscribed in us this condition of living by reference to others, it does us much more harm than good. We defraud ourselves out of what is actually

Montaigne, *On Vanity* (1580)

useful to us in order to make appearances conform to common opinion. We care less about the
real truth of our inner selves than about how we
are known to the public.

Johnson, *The Adventurer*
no. 119 (1753)

We trifle, because we see others trifle; in the same
manner we catch from example the contagion of
desire; we see all about us busied in pursuit of
imaginary good, and begin to bustle in the same
chase, lest greater activity should triumph over us.

2. *The appetite for praise.* As pernicious as the problem of
conformity, and a driver of it, is the desire for praise from
others, immediately or in the long run. We practice
things that will win praise; we should practice the art of
not needing it.

Epictetus, *Discourses* 2.16.5

When the orator knows that he has written a good
speech, that he has it committed to memory, and
that he will deliver it well, why is he still nervous?
Because he is not satisfied with this. What else does
he want? He wants to be praised by the audience.
About oratory he has been instructed; about praise
and blame he has not been instructed. For when
did anyone tell him the meaning of those things,
what they truly involve, what praise is worth seeking and what blame is worth avoiding? And when
did he practice the use of these principles?

The point on a larger scale:

Marcus Aurelius, *Meditations*
6.16.2

What then is to be valued? The clapping of hands?
No. Nor should we value the clapping of tongues,
for that is the praise of the masses.

Montaigne:

Montaigne, *Of Solitude* (1580)

Who does not willingly exchange health, tranquility, and life itself for reputation and glory –
the most useless, worthless, and counterfeit coin
that circulates among us?

Johnson noted that the appetite for praise is not limited to those trying for fame. Everyone wants the good opinion of those they define as their circle, or audience.

> Praise is so pleasing to the mind of man, that it is the original motive of almost all our actions. The desire of commendation, as of every thing else, is varied indeed by innumerable differences of temper, capacity, knowledge; some have no higher wish than for the applause of a club; some expect the acclamations of a county; and some have hoped to fill the mouths of all ages and nations with their names. Every man pants for the highest eminence within his view; none, however mean, ever sinks below the hope of being distinguished by his fellow-beings, and very few have by magnanimity or piety been so raised above it, as to act wholly without regard to censure or opinion.

Johnson, *The Rambler* no. 193 (1752)

> In all we do, almost the first thing we think about is, what will people say; and nearly half the troubles and bothers of life may be traced to our anxiety on this score; it is the anxiety which is at the bottom of all that feeling of self-importance, which is so often mortified because it is so very morbidly sensitive.

Schopenhauer, *The Wisdom of Life* (1851)

3. *Contempt for the judgments of others.* Epictetus suggested, as we just saw, that the orator who is nervous has been taught how to give a speech but not how to manage the appetite for praise. Education on that subject begins with a sober view of those whose good opinions we want. This is a point emphasized by all of the Stoic teachers.

> How foolish one must be to leave a lecture hall gratified by the applause of the ignorant! Why do you take pleasure in praise from those you cannot praise yourself?

Seneca, *Epistles* 52.11

Epictetus, *Discourses* 1.21.4

Who are these people whose admiration you seek? Aren't they the ones you are used to describing as mad? Well, then, is that what you want – to be admired by lunatics?

Marcus Aurelius, *Meditations* 7.62

Keep constantly in mind who these people are whose admiration you seek, and what guiding principles they have. Then you will not blame them when they carelessly offend you; and you will have no further wish for their approval once you look into the sources of their motives and opinions.

Schopenhauer, *The Wisdom of Life* (1851)

What goes on in other people's consciousness is, as such, a matter of indifference to us; and in time we get really indifferent to it, when we come to see how superficial and futile are most people's thoughts, how narrow their ideas, how mean their sentiments, how perverse their opinions, and how much of error there is in most of them.

The same reasoning can be adapted to the desire for fame, or the wish to be remembered after death.

Epictetus, *Discourses* 1.24.6

Diogenes, who was sent off as a scout before you, gave us a different report. He says that death is no evil, because it is not shameful; he says that fame is the noise of madmen.

Diogenes of Sinope (also known as Diogenes the Cynic) was a Greek philosopher who lived in the 4th century BC. Epictetus speaks with reverence of Cynicism and of Diogenes, sometimes describing him as a kind of idealized Stoic. At other points, as above, he depicts Diogenes as a divine scout and messenger who examined human life and was able to make reports like the one just shown. We will meet Diogenes again in Chapter 8, Section 4.

Cicero had pungent views on our current theme, viewing fame as the accumulated opinions of people whose views are worth nothing.

I pass over celebrity and popular fame, built by the consensus of knaves and fools.

Cicero, *Tusculan Disputations* 5.16

What could be more absurd than to suppose the same ignorant and common people you despise, when taken one by one, are of any greater consequence when taken together?

Cicero, *Tusculan Disputations* 5.36

True and philosophic greatness of spirit regards that virtue to which Nature most aspires as consisting in deeds, not in fame, and prefers to be first in reality rather than in name. And in truth, he who depends upon the caprice of the ignorant rabble cannot be numbered among the great.

Cicero, *On Duties* 1.65

The Stoic therefore regards widespread approval of something as a bad sign.

Human affairs are not so happily ordered that the better things are pleasing to the many; a proof of the worst choice is the crowd.

Seneca, *On the Happy Life* 2.1

The judgments of common and ordinary people rarely hit the mark. And in my own time, I am much mistaken if the worst writings are not those that have won the greatest share of public approval.

Montaigne, *On Vanity* (1580)

The same goes for people. Mass popularity suggests a want of quality or integrity in whoever obtains it.

It takes trickery to cultivate popular approval. You have to make yourself like them…. If I see you much acclaimed by the populace, if your entrances are greeted by the sound of cheers and applause (as we see given to actors), if the whole state, even the women and children, sing your praises – how can I help pitying you? For I know what road one must take to gain such popularity.

Seneca, *Epistles* 29.11–12

We must hope the following story is true.

Aelian, *Various Histories* 2.6

They say that the trainer Hippomachus, when an athlete he was training competed in wrestling and everyone who was present applauded, struck the student with his staff. "You did it badly, and not as you should have," he said. "You should have done better. If you had done it artfully they would not have applauded you."

4. *Futility*. Stoicism also applies the acid bath of reason to fame itself, arguing that it is useless and cannot last long anyhow. Marcus Aurelius came back to this idea often. There is some irony in repeating such claims written 2,000 years ago, but the Stoic would presumably say it's still early. And notwithstanding the good taste shown by the reader of this book, very few people now are familiar with the writers featured in it.

Marcus Aurelius, *Meditations* 7.21

Soon you will have forgotten everything; soon everything will have forgotten you.

Marcus Aurelius, *Meditations* 4.19

He who gets excited about fame after death doesn't consider that anyone who remembers him will also die very soon, then again the one who succeeds that one, until all recollection has been extinguished by passing through a succession of people who foolishly admire and perish.

Marcus Aurelius, *Meditations* 4.3

Or is it this thing called reputation that worries you? Look at the speed with which everything is forgotten; the vast gulf of boundless time on either side of us; the emptiness of applause; the changeable, undiscriminating nature of those who seem to praise; the tiny space in which it all takes place.

Dr. Johnson also commented on the small scale of even that which appears to us to be fame.

No man can be venerable or formidable, but to a small part of his fellow-creatures.

Johnson, *The Rambler* no. 118 (1751)

It is long before we are convinced of the small proportion which every individual bears to the collective body of mankind; or learn how few can be interested in the fortune of any single man; how little vacancy is left in the world for any new object of attention; to how small extent the brightest blaze of merit can be spread amidst the mists of business and of folly; and how soon it is clouded by the intervention of other novelties.

Johnson, *The Rambler* no. 146 (1751)

In addition to considering the desire for lasting fame to be futile, Marcus Aurelius regarded it as pointless. Why should anyone care what is said about them after they are gone?

How strange it is, what people do! They are reluctant to praise men who live at the same time they do; yet they think it is important to be praised by future generations – by those they have never seen and never will. This comes close to being aggrieved because those living in former times did not speak well of you.

Marcus Aurelius, *Meditations* 6.18

Those who try to achieve fame that will outlive them fail to reflect that the people of the future will be just like the ones they cannot bear now, and mortal as well. And what is it to you, really, if those in the future say one thing or another, or hold this or that opinion about you?

Marcus Aurelius, *Meditations* 8.44

5. *Valuing one's own judgments.* The Stoic response to praise and fame has a negative side that we have seen: the dissection of those things to show how little they are worth. But the Stoics would do more than learn contempt for public opinion. They would replace it with greater respect for opinions of their own. Marcus

Aurelius offers the point as a question: why do we worry more about what others think than about what *we* think?

Marcus Aurelius, *Meditations* 12.4

I have often wondered how it is that, though every man loves himself most of all, he gives less weight to his own opinion of himself than to the opinion of others. If a god or wise teacher should appear and order a man not to have any thought or plan in his mind that he does not instantly and loudly announce, he would not be able to stand it for even a day. Evidently we have more respect for the opinions our neighbors hold about us than we do for our own.

What others are thinking is more than a bad source of guidance. It is a distraction from our own thoughts and from all else that we should be doing.

Marcus Aurelius, *Meditations* 3.4

Do not waste the time you have left thinking about others unless it serves some good and useful purpose, for it takes you away from other work. Thinking about what so-and-so is doing, and why, and what someone else is saying, and what another is thinking or planning, and all things of that sort, causes you to wander away from the observance of your own governing principles.

And taking one's own perceptions seriously isn't just a better habit than listening to others or worrying about what they might think. It is an essential part of Stoic practice, which consists in the first place, after all, of speaking the truth to ourselves instead of repeating what everyone else says.

Seneca, *Epistles* 31.2–3

Be deaf to those who love you most of all; they pray for bad things with good intentions. And if you want to be happy, pray to the gods that none of their fond desires for you may be brought to pass. Those things they wish to have heaped upon you are not really good; there is only one good,

the cause and the support of a happy life – trust
in oneself.

No longer be concerned with what the world says
about you, but with how you talk to yourself.

Montaigne, *Of Solitude* (1580)

Seneca reduced these ideas to some advice about how we
might talk to ourselves more intelligently, and without
dependence on the opinion of an audience. As applied
to a case of sickness, for example:

A brave man can appear even wrapped in bed-
clothes. You have a task at hand: to wrestle coura-
geously with disease. If it cannot force you to do
anything, or persuade you to do anything, you are
setting a distinguished example. What a wealth of
material there would be for achieving honor, if we
were observed in our illness! Be your own spectator; seek your own applause.

Seneca, *Epistles* 78.21

He also gave an example of such a dialogue with oneself,
and added a good note on the advantages of keeping
it private.

When you want to be praised sincerely, why be
indebted to someone else for it? Praise yourself.
Say: "I devoted myself to the liberal arts. Although
my poverty urged me to do otherwise and tempted
my talents towards a field where there is an immediate profit from study, I turned aside to unremu-
nerative poetry and dedicated myself to the
wholesome study of philosophy…." After this, ask
whether the things you said about yourself are
true or false. If they are true, you are praised in
front of a great witness, yourself. If they are false,
no one is a witness to your being made a fool of.

Seneca, *Natural Questions* IV
A, Pref. 14, 18

Montaigne:

No one but you knows whether you are cowardly
and cruel or loyal and devout. Others never see

Montaigne, *Of Repentance*
(1580)

you; they only guess about you by uncertain conjectures. They do not see your nature so much as they see your artifice. So do not cling to their judgments; cling to your own.

Schopenhauer:

Schopenhauer, *The Wisdom of Life* (1851)

Most men set the utmost value precisely on what other people think, and are more concerned about it than about what goes on in their own consciousness, which is the thing most immediately and directly present to them. They reverse the natural order – regarding the opinions of others as real existence and their own consciousness as something shadowy; making the derivative and secondary into the principal, and considering the picture they present to the world of more importance than their own selves. By thus trying to get a direct and immediate result out of what has no really direct or immediate existence, they fall into the kind of folly which is called *vanity* – the appropriate term for that which has no solid or intrinsic value.

6. *Valuing things for their own sake.* The other affirmative branch of the Stoic view seeks to value things in themselves – for their goodness rather than their popularity.

Marcus Aurelius, *Meditations* 4.20

Everything that is beautiful in any way is beautiful in itself, and its beauty is self-contained. Praise is not part of it; nothing is made better or worse by being praised.

Seneca, *Epistles* 7.11

He too spoke well – whoever it was, for his identity is uncertain – who said, when asked why he took so much trouble over a piece of craftsmanship that would never reach more than a very few people: "A few is enough for me; so is one; so is none."

From the descendants of the Stoics:

It would perhaps be excusable for a painter or craftsman, or even a rhetorician or a grammarian, to try to acquire a name for himself through his works; but virtuous deeds are too noble in themselves to seek any reward other than their own value, and especially to seek it in the vanity of human judgments.

Montaigne, *Of Glory* (1580)

Not fame, but that which deserves to be famous, is what a man should hold in esteem.... Light is not visible unless it meets with something to reflect it; and talent is sure of itself only when its fame is noised abroad. But fame is not a certain symptom of merit; because you can have the one without the other; or, as Lessing nicely puts it, *Some people obtain fame, and others deserve it.*

Schopenhauer, *The Wisdom of Life* (1851)

7. *Insult and opinion.* We have considered one problem associated with social life: the irrational desire for the good opinion of others. Another problem – really the other side of the same issue – involves the irrational dread of criticism and insult. Some lines of Stoic response are familiar; others are distinctive to this challenge. Among the familiar replies, we can begin with a return to principles from earlier in the book. An effective insult requires a kind of cooperation from the victim – a judgment, for example, that the insult matters. The judgment can be dropped or withheld.

The success of an insult depends on the sensitivity and the indignation of the victim.

Seneca, *On the Constancy of the Wise Man* 17.4

Remember that you are insulted not by the person who strikes or abuses you but by your opinion that these things are insulting. So whenever another provokes you, be assured that it is your own opinion that has provoked you.

Epictetus, *Enchiridion* 20

What is it to be insulted? Stand by a stone and insult it; what will you gain? And if you *listen* like a

Epictetus, *Discourses* 1.25.28

stone, what will be gained by one who insults you? But if he has a stepping-stone in the weakness of his victim, then he accomplishes something.

8. *Contempt for contempt.* As we have seen in prior chapters, the Stoics routinely offer the solution just shown in reply to any disturbance: dismiss the opinion within you that is responsible for it. But perhaps in recognition that the simple solution can be hard to execute, the Stoics usually follow up with other or more specific strategies as well – in this case, some additional ways to think about insults. The Stoic regards the contempt of others with indifference, or contempt, or a welcoming spirit. Anything but fear will do. To begin with indifference, which is close to the dismissals seen a moment ago:

Marcus Aurelius, *Meditations* 5.3

So long as any word or deed is true to nature, consider it worthy of you, and do not be distracted by the comments or criticisms of others. If it is the right thing to say or do, don't disparage yourself for saying or doing it.

Marcus Aurelius, *Meditations* 11.13

Someone will disdain me? That is his concern. My concern is that I not be found doing or saying anything worthy of disdain.

Epictetus, *Enchiridion* 50

Whatever someone might say about you, pay no attention; it is no concern of yours.

The more aggressive stance, in which contempt is welcome if properly chosen or earned:

Seneca, *Epistles* 105.5

Contempt remains to be discussed. You have the measure of it under your control if you make it your own – if you are despised because you choose to be, not because you deserve to be.

Seneca, *Epistles* 76.4

On the way to Metronax's house, as you know, you pass right by the Neapolitan theater. The place is packed, and there is a vigorous debate inside about who is a good flute-player. Even the Greek trumpeter and the announcer draw a crowd. But over in the lecture hall, where the question is who can be called a good person and how to become one, the audience is very small. The few who are present seem, to most people, to be doing nothing worthwhile. They are called empty-headed idlers. Let that mockery apply to me. The insults of the ignorant should be heard with equanimity. For one who is progressing toward virtue, contempt should itself be regarded with contempt.

Unfortunately we know nothing of Metronax other than what Seneca mentions of him in brief references of this kind.

9. *Contempt for the source of the contempt.* A related but distinct response: not to belittle the contempt, but to belittle or ignore the person from whom it issues.

It is the mark of a great mind to rise above insults; the most humiliating kind of revenge is to treat your adversary as not worth taking revenge upon. Many have taken slight injuries too deeply to heart in the course of punishing them. The great and noble are those who, like a lordly beast, listen unmoved to the barking of little dogs.

Seneca, *On Anger* 2.32.3

Whoever gets into a fight becomes the antagonist of the other, and can only win by being on the same level. "But if the wise man gets punched, what should he do?" What Cato did when he was struck in the face. He did not get angry, he did not avenge the wrong, he did not even forgive it; he said that no wrong had been done. He showed finer spirit in not acknowledging it than he would if he had pardoned it.

Seneca, *On the Constancy of the Wise Man* 14.3

As Epictetus saw it, getting upset about an insult is a surrender of the self to the antagonist.

Epictetus, *Enchiridion* 28

If someone was going to put your body into the hands of anyone who happened to come along, you would be vexed. But that you entrust your mind to whoever you happen to meet, so that if he insults you, your mind is disturbed and confounded – aren't you ashamed of that?

10. *Endlessness*. Here is a repeating form of Stoic argument: once you start to worry about what other people think or say, where does it stop? You have made yourself vulnerable to any and all.

Seneca, *On the Constancy of the Wise Man* 13.5

The sage is not moved by an insult from anyone. For men may differ from one another, but the sage regards them as all equal on account of their equal stupidity. If he were to lower himself enough to be moved by insult or injury even once, there would never be an end to his worries.

Seneca, *On the Constancy of the Wise Man* 19.2

Liberty is having a mind superior to injury, a mind that makes itself the only source from which its pleasures spring, that separates itself from all external things, avoiding the unquiet life of one who fears everybody's laughter, everybody's tongue. For if there is anyone who can offer an insult, who cannot?

And such worry comes at a further cost. The time spent on it might have been spent on things that matter – another version of a point made by Marcus Aurelius in Section 5 of this chapter.

Seneca, *On the Constancy of the Wise Man* 19.1–2

All provocations given by unthinking people – and it is only from the unthinking that they can come – should be ignored, and the insults and honors of the crowd should both be valued the same. We must not be pained by the one or rejoice over the other; otherwise – whether from fear of insults or disgust with them – we will neglect many necessary things.

As we have seen, the Stoics say fame is pointless to seek because it can't last. The same idea can be used as a source of immunity from the effects of insult.

> What others may speak of you, let them worry about it – for speak they will. And all that talk will be confined to those narrow regions that you see, nor did it ever last long about anyone, but it is buried with the deaths of men and extinguished in the forgetfulness of future ages.

Cicero, *On the Republic* 6.25

11. *Humility.* The Stoic response to insults and other wrongs can also include humility and acceptance. We will see in Chapter 8 that Stoicism calls for a frank view of one's own flaws. That habit makes criticism from others easier to take.

> If you hear that someone has spoken ill of you, do not make excuses about what was said, but answer: "Evidently he didn't know about my other faults, or he wouldn't have spoken only of the ones he did."

Epictetus, *Enchiridion* 33.9

> And this thing we call an insult – what is it? They make jokes about my bald head, my weak eyes, my thin legs, my height. How is it an insult to be told what is obvious?

Seneca, *On the Constancy of the Wise Man* 16.3

A sense of humor about oneself also tends to defeat ridicule from others.

> No one becomes a laughingstock who laughs at himself. It is well known that Vatinius, a man born to be a butt for ridicule and hate, was a graceful and witty jester. He made jokes at the expense of his own feet and shriveled jowls; in this way he escaped the raillery of his enemies – chief among them Cicero – who were even more numerous than his deformities.

Seneca, *On the Constancy of the Wise Man* 17.2–3

Publius Vatinius, a tribune and a follower of Cæsar's, was a good illustration for Seneca's time and place. Montaigne preferred a different one for his own.

Montaigne, *Of Presumption*
(1580)

The lowest walk is the safest. It is the seat of constancy. There you need only yourself, and there constancy is self-supporting and relies on itself alone. The following example of a gentleman known to many has an air of philosophy about it, does it not? He married when he was well advanced in years, having spent his youth in lively company as a great talker and jester. Remembering how often the subject of cuckoldry had given him material for stories and jokes about others, he protected himself by marrying a wife he found in a place where women are available to anyone for money. They made an alliance to address themselves in these terms: "Good morning, whore!" "Good morning, cuckold!" And there was nothing he talked about more often or more openly than this plan of his when entertaining guests in his home. It curbed the private chattering of those who would mock him, and blunted the force of the insult.

Stoic uses of humor to dissolve aggression are further considered in Chapter 9, Section 8.

12. *Mistakes*. But suppose an insult is unjust. In that case the Stoic regards whoever delivered it not as a bad person but as mistaken, and as appropriately viewed in the way we look at anyone who blunders – mostly as a pitiful character.

Seneca, *On the Constancy of the Wise Man* 16.3

You need not be a sage to take insults lightly, but merely someone of sense – one who might say: "Do I deserve these things that happen to me? If I deserve them, there is no insult; it is justice. If I don't deserve them, let the one who does the injustice blush."

Stoics compare those who commit wrongs or mistakes, or who otherwise have bad judgment, to people with diminished physical capacities. We tend to be forgiving of such impairments; why shouldn't we have the same attitude toward those who insult us, or otherwise do wrong, because their understandings are defective?

> Mistakes are nothing to get angry about. What, now, should we be angry with those whose footsteps falter in the dark? With the deaf, when they don't listen to orders? With children, because – neglecting a proper attention to their duties – they watch the games and silly jokes of their fellows? Do you want to be angry with those who are weary because they are sick and growing old?

Seneca, On Anger 2.10.1

> So this robber, this adulterer, shouldn't they have been destroyed? Not at all, but rather ask this: "This man who has been misled and deceived about the most important things, who has been blinded – not in his vision, the ability to distinguish white from black, but in his judgment, the ability to distinguish good from evil – shouldn't we destroy him?" If you put it this way, you will see how inhumane your question is. It is like saying, "This blind man, shouldn't he be destroyed? This deaf-mute?"

Epictetus, Discourses 1.18.5–7

> Why is it that we are not stirred up when we meet someone whose body is disfigured or disabled, yet cannot tolerate a deformed mind without being enraged? Such vicious severity reflects more on the critic than on the defect.

Montaigne, Of the Art of Conference

Or, indeed, the one who gives an insult or does some other form of wrong may be infirm in ways that are common to all of us.

> Among the other misfortunes of humanity there is this one too – a darkness of our minds, not so much a compulsion to go wrong as a desire to do

Seneca, On Anger 2.10.1–2

so. Lest you be angry with men individually, you must pardon mankind as a whole, you must grant indulgence to the human race.

Seneca, *On Anger* 2.10.4

On an individual soldier, a general's severity may be unleashed; but pardon is unavoidable when the whole army deserts. What takes away the wise man's anger? The multitude of wrongdoers. He knows how unjust and how dangerous it is to be angry with vice that is widespread.

A last perspective: if you receive an insult that is wrongful, you may consider it to have been directed at someone else – the person you were thought to be. It was a case of mistaken identity. This was Joseph Addison's interpretation of the Stoic stance in a paraphrase of Epictetus that he devised.

Addison, *The Spectator* no. 355 (1712)

Does a man reproach thee for being proud or ill-natured, envious or conceited, ignorant or detracting? Consider with thy self whether his reproaches are true; if they are not, consider that thou art not the person whom he reproaches, but that he reviles an imaginary being, and perhaps loves what thou really art, tho he hates what thou appearest to be. If his reproaches are true, if thou art the envious ill-natur'd man he takes thee for, give thy self another turn, become mild, affable and obliging, and his reproaches of thee naturally cease: his reproaches may indeed continue, but thou art no longer the person whom he reproaches.

Compare these anecdotes that Montaigne relates, which he borrows and condenses from the writings of Plutarch and Diogenes Lærtius:

Montaigne, *Upon Some Verses of Virgil* (1580)

When Archelaus, king of Macedonia, was walking along the street, someone dumped water on him. The king's attendants said that he should punish the man. "Ah, but he did not dump the water on me," the king replied, "but on the man he thought I was." When Socrates was told that people spoke ill of him, he said, "Not at all. There is nothing in me of what they say."

13. *Empathy and forgiveness.* Beyond viewing antagonists as disabled by bad judgment, the Stoic meets them with empathy. This starts with the idea that those who give offense are seeking to do right by their own lights. Nobody *wants* to be wrong.

> "Every soul is deprived of truth against its will" – and is likewise deprived against its will of justice, self-control, kindness, and everything of the kind. It is necessary to keep this in mind always, because it will make you milder toward everyone else.

Marcus Aurelius, *Meditations* 7.63

The philosopher he quotes is Plato in *The Sophist* (228c) – or perhaps Epictetus, who once quoted that passage from Plato. Epictetus himself:

> Whenever someone does you a wrong or speaks ill of you, remember that he is doing what he thinks is proper. He can't possibly be guided by what appears right to you, but only by what appears right to him. So if he sees things wrongly, he is the one who is hurt, because he is the one who has been deceived.... Starting from this reasoning, you will be mild toward whoever insults you. Say each time, "So it seemed to him."

Epictetus, *Enchiridion* 42

The Stoic tries more specifically to understand what thoughts caused another to offer an insult or attack, and to be generous in interpreting them and in responding. Maybe you and your adversary are not so different.

> When someone does you wrong in some way, consider at once the understanding of good or evil that caused him to wrong you. For once you

Marcus Aurelius, *Meditations* 7.26

see this, you will have pity on him, and you will be neither surprised nor angry. For you yourself probably have the same understanding of the good as he does, or another of the same sort. If so, you must pardon him. And if you no longer understand the same things to be good and evil, you will more easily be gracious to one whom you know to be mistaken.

There is, finally, this solace with respect to an antagonist: you both will be dead before long.

Marcus Aurelius, *Meditations* 7.22

It is a peculiarity of man to love even those who stumble. This happens when it occurs to you that they are kinsmen, that they do wrong through ignorance and without intent, that in a little while you will both have died, and above all, that he has done you no harm – for he has not made your ruling faculty any worse than it was before.

Seneca, *On Anger* 3.43.2–3

At the morning shows in the arena we sometimes see a fight between a bull and a bear tied together. After they have roughed each other up, there's someone waiting to finish them off. We do the same thing: we provoke someone tied to us, though a speedy end hangs over both the victor and the vanquished. Let us rather spend what little time remains in peace and calm! Let our corpse be hateful to no one! The cry of "Fire!" in the neighborhood has often broken up a fight; the arrival of a wild beast has separated a bandit from a traveler. There's no time to struggle with lesser evils once a greater threat appears. Why do we concern ourselves with conflict and plotting? That man you are angry with – can you wish for him anything worse than death? He is going to die without your doing a thing.

Chapter Eight

VALUATION

This chapter is about another set of misjudgments we commit at our own expense: undervaluing the present, undervaluing time generally, undervaluing other intangible goods, overvaluing ourselves, and misjudging others by seeing our flaws in them. The treatment of these problems next to one another isn't inevitable. The second half of this chapter has little enough to do with the first. But the topics all involve mistakes of the mind that, unlike most of the errors the Stoics talk about in this book, do not involve desire or fear or pleasure or pain. Each is a kind of misjudgment about value.

Some teachings of the Stoics are found in other traditions as well. This chapter shows some prominent examples. One of them is appreciation of the present. The Stoics mean to correct our preoccupation with the past and future; they regard the time we pour into memories, hopes, and fears to be mostly ill-spent (though not always, as we shall see). They also regard us as unconscious of the value of time generally. We give it away lightly, and waste it with less alarm than we waste money, though time is more valuable in the end.

The Stoics' analysis of time resembles their more general view of intangible costs and benefits, which this chapter will consider as well. We overrate money and undervalue time, just as we overrate material goods and the approval of others while undervaluing the gains we get by forgoing them. Stoics look at many things that way. When something bad seems to happen, it often has quiet compensations; exciting opportunities, to the contrary, tend to be costlier than they first seem once their consequences, visible and not, have all been noticed and weighed. Grasping all this helps the Stoic toward an even keel in both circumstances.

Our errors of valuation continue with respect to ourselves and others. We overlook faults in ourselves but find them easily in those around us. Recognizing this is an encouragement to forgiveness. What another has done that annoys you is probably no worse than what you have done on another day. But the point is also subtler: we condemn in others precisely what we detest but cannot see in ourselves; we project our faults onto them. So the Stoic works hard for self-knowledge and makes unhesitant confessions of weakness.

1. *The present.* The Stoics are sensitive to misjudgments about time. Later we will see various other ways that time may be wasted or misunderstood, but here we examine the first and simplest: neglect of the present.

There is a parallel between the Stoic analysis of our mistakes in judging time and our mistakes in judging material things. Chapter 5 discussed the difficulty of being satisfied with anything once it belongs to us. The present moment fails to satisfy in a similar way. We worry and plan in the same spirit that we crave the next acquisition; whatever we look forward to, whether it be the future or some new object, looks more appealing than it ever quite turns out to be once it arrives. The Stoic holds that satisfaction can better be found by making peace with what we have than by chasing what we don't, and by paying attention to the present rather than by dwelling on the past and the future.

Some Stoic comments on this theme are of a general character, observing that the present moment is both elusive and all that really exists.

Seneca, *On the Shortness of Life* 10.6

Present time is very short – so short, indeed, that for some it seems not to exist. It is always in motion, it flows and hurries on; it ceases to be before it arrives.

Keep this in mind, that each of us lives only this present and indivisible moment. Everything else has either already been lived or is uncertain.

Marcus Aurelius, *Meditations* 3.10

Stoic reflections on the present are usually more practical, though. They seek to address the bad habit of burdening the mind with worry about the future. Part of the argument is that imaginings of the past and future are harder to bear than the present moment tends to be. The present is always tolerable.

Do not disturb yourself by imagining your whole life at once. Don't always be thinking about what sufferings, and how many, might possibly befall you. Ask instead, in each present circumstance: "What is there about this that is unendurable and unbearable?" You will be embarrassed to answer.

Marcus Aurelius, *Meditations* 8.36

Memory recalls the torments of fear, and foresight anticipates them. It is only the present that makes no one wretched.

Seneca, *Epistles* 5.9

Nothing is more pathetic than worry about the outcome of future events. How much time remains, and what it will be like – on these counts the troubled mind is vexed with fear that cannot be explained. How shall we escape this wallowing? There is only one way: if our life does not project forward, if it stays contained in itself. Those who worry about the future are failing to profit from the present.

Seneca, *Epistles* 101.8–9

Apart from the refuge the present moment provides from imagined troubles, it is the only place where actual living occurs. By spending our thoughts on the future, we fail to attend to what is happening now and so fail to live.

Think about individuals; consider men in general; there is not one whose life is not focused on

Seneca, *Epistles* 45.12–13

tomorrow. What harm is there in that, you ask? Infinite harm. They are not really living. They are about to live.

Seneca, *Epistles* 5.7–8

Just as the same chain joins the prisoner and the guard, so do these two things, which are so dissimilar, keep pace with each other: fear follows hope. I do not find this surprising. Each is the mark of a mind in suspense, a mind troubled by awaiting the future. The principal cause of either hope or fear is that we do not adapt ourselves to the present, but send our thoughts far ahead. Thus foresight – the greatest blessing of the human condition – is turned into an evil.

Montaigne, *That Our Affections Carry Ourselves Beyond Us* (1580)

We are never home; we are always elsewhere. Fear, desire, and hope push us toward the future; they rob us of feeling and concern for what is by distracting us with what will be, even when we will be no more.

Schopenhauer's rendition of the Stoic point:

Schopenhauer, *Our Relation to Ourselves* (1851)

Those who strive and hope and live only in the future, always looking ahead and impatiently anticipating what is coming, as something which will make them happy when they get it, are, in spite of their very clever airs, exactly like those donkeys one sees in Italy, whose pace may be hurried by fixing a stick on their heads with a wisp of hay at the end of it; this is always just in front of them, and they keep on trying to get it. Such people are in a constant state of illusion as to their whole existence; they go on living *ad interim*, until at last they die.

Instead, therefore, of always thinking about our plans and anxiously looking to the future, or of giving ourselves up to regret for the past, we should never forget that the present is the only reality, the only certainty; that the future almost always turns out contrary to our expectations; that the past, too, was very different from what we suppose it to have been. But the past and the future are, on the whole, of less consequence than we think. Distance, which makes objects look small to the outward eye, makes them look big to the eye of thought. The present alone is true and actual; it is the only time which possesses full reality, and our existence lies in it exclusively.

2. *Using the past.* All this makes it sound as though the Stoic wants to live entirely in the present, but that is a bit too strong. Stoics do not think the future should be ignored or met without planning. They mean that we should pay attention to the present; and they mean that we should carefully make decisions about the future that belong to us, but then waste no energy wondering and worrying about what is to come. (See Chapter 2, Section 6.) As for the past, Seneca holds to the pragmatic strain of Stoicism – that is, deciding whether and how to do a thing (in this case, looking back) by considering how it helps toward a better state of mind. Compare these passages:

> Two things we must therefore root out: fear of distress in the future and the memory of distress in the past. The one concerns me no longer. The other concerns me not yet.

Seneca, *Epistles* 78.14

> The man who is only happy with present things sets narrow limits to his enjoyment. Both the future and the past can delight us – one in anticipation, the other in memory – but one is uncertain and may not happen, while the other cannot fail to have been. What madness it is, therefore, to lose our grip on that which is the surest thing of all!

Seneca, *Epistles* 99.5

In that last passage, from a letter on the subject of grief, Seneca is advising the bereaved to value their memories. So he does not say that recollection of the past should be avoided on principle. He discourages the recollection of the bad but encourages happy memories, for they help us. The Stoic goal is not just to see time accurately but to make good use of it – the past as well as the present. Plutarch had a similar recommendation about the benefits of memory.

Plutarch, *On Tranquility of Mind* 14 (473b–473c)

That each of us keeps within ourselves the storerooms of tranquility and despondency – and that the wine-jars of good and evil are not stored up "in the abode of Zeus" but in our own spirits – the difference in our feelings makes clear. For the foolish overlook and neglect even the good things at hand, because their thoughts are always intent on the future; while the wise, by memory, make vivid to themselves even those things that are no more.

For more on Stoic uses of memory, see Chapter 9, Section 13.

3. *Time*. On a Stoic view, we fail to see the significance not only of the present moment but of time in general. Seneca thought that most of us are barely conscious of its passage.

Seneca, *Epistles* 49.2–3

It was just a moment ago that I sat, as a lad, in the school of the philosopher Sotion, just a moment ago that I began to argue cases in the courts, just a moment ago that I lost the desire to argue them, just a moment ago that I lost the ability. The swiftness of time is infinite – something that appears more clearly to people looking backwards. It escapes the notice of those focused on the present, so gentle is the passage of its headlong flight. Do you ask the reason? All bygone time is in the same place; it looks the same, it lies together. Everything falls into the same abyss.

Sotion was a philosopher originally from Alexandria, and (along with Attalus) another of Seneca's early teachers. He was an instructor in the school of Sextius, which blended Stoic and Pythagorean thought.

> Even as conversation or reading or deep thought on some subject beguiles travelers, and they find that they have reached the end of their journey before realizing that they were approaching it, just so with this unceasing and most swift journey of life, which we make at the same pace whether waking or sleeping; those who are preoccupied become aware of it only at the end.

Seneca, *On the Shortness of Life* 9.5

Inattention to time leads to waste of it. To make the point, Seneca introduces a favorite theme: comparisons of time to material wealth.

> Life as we receive it is not short, but we make it so; nor do we have any lack of it, but we are wasteful of it. Just as great and princely wealth is scattered in a moment when it comes into the hands of a bad owner – while wealth, however limited, if it is entrusted to a good guardian, increases with use – so our life is amply long for him who orders it properly.

Seneca, *On the Shortness of Life* 1.4

Johnson's variation:

> An Italian philosopher expressed in his motto, that *time was his estate;* an estate, indeed, which will produce nothing without cultivation, but will always abundantly repay the labors of industry, and satisfy the most extensive desires, if no part of it be suffered to lie waste by negligence, to be over-run with noxious plants, or laid out for show rather than for use.

Johnson, *The Rambler* no. 108 (1751)

The Italian philosopher Johnson mentions was Girolamo Cardano (1501–1576), who had the phrase Johnson mentions (*Tempus ager meus*) inscribed over the door to his library.

Seneca viewed time as the most valuable thing we own – really the only thing. Yet we guard it with none of the care we apply to our property. To lose some cash is alarming to anyone; to lose some time is alarming to few.

Seneca, *On the Shortness of Life* 3.1

None will be found willing to distribute their money to others; but among how many others do each of us distribute our lives! Men are tight-fisted in guarding their fortunes, but extravagant when it comes to wasting time – the one thing about which it is right to be greedy.

Seneca, *Epistles* 42.7

Our stupidity can be seen by this, that we only think we have bought those things for which we pay cash, while we regard as free those things for which we expend our very selves. Things that we would never be willing to buy if we had to give our house in exchange, or some attractive and productive estate, we are fully prepared to attain at the cost of anxiety, danger, lost honor, lost freedom, and lost time – for we treat nothing as cheaper than ourselves.

Seneca, *Epistles* 1.3

All things, Lucilius, belong to others; only our time is our own. Nature has put us in possession of this one fleeting and uncertain property, from which anyone who wishes can eject us. And so great is the stupidity of mortals, that when they have obtained the cheapest and most unimportant things, easily replaced, they agree to be charged for them; yet no one considers himself indebted if he has taken up our *time* – though this is the one thing that even a grateful debtor cannot repay.

Seneca offered some mental exercises to help make the value of time more vivid. If we fail to grasp that time is more important than money, for example, we might compare the distress typically felt by those who are running out of each.

No one values time; everyone spends it extrava-
gantly, as if it were free. But see how these same
people clasp the knees of physicians if they fall ill
and the danger of death draws nearer; see how
ready they are, if threatened with capital punishment, to spend all that they have to live longer!

Seneca, *On the Shortness of Life*
8.2

If each of us could have the number of our future
years set before us, as we can with the years that
have passed, how alarmed we would be, and how
sparing of them, if we saw only a few remaining!
And while it is easy to manage something when
the amount you have is known, even if it is small,
you must guard what you have more carefully if
you don't know when it may give out.

Seneca, *On the Shortness of Life*
8.3

These views lead to particular alarm at the prospect of
one's time being lightly seized by another.

I am often amazed when I see some nagging others for their time, and those who are asked so
indulgent. Each of them is looking at the object
for which the time is sought, neither of them at
the time itself, as if nothing were being asked and
nothing given.

Seneca, *On the Shortness of Life*
8.1

4. *Invisible prices, intangible benefits.* Stoicism calls for
attention to the invisible and overlooked half of an equation: the wealth gained not by having money but by
being indifferent to it, the destitution created by giving
away our time with less concern than our property, and
other forms of intangible gain and loss. This is a recurrent theme in Epictetus.

Keep this thought close, whenever you lose some
external thing: what are you getting in exchange?
And if what you have received is more valuable,
never say "I have suffered a loss" – not if you get a
horse in place of an ass, or a cow in place of a

Epictetus, *Discourses* 4.3.1–3

sheep, or a good deed in place of a little money, or cultured leisure in place of pointless chatter, or self-respect in place of obscenity.

Epictetus, *Enchiridion* 12.2

Is a little oil spilled, is a little wine stolen? Say "this is the price of equanimity, this is the price of peace of mind" – for nothing comes free.

Epictetus, *Enchiridion* 25.4–5

You have not been invited to someone's dinner party? You did not give the host the price he charges for the dinner. He sells it for praise, he sells it for personal attention.... So don't you have anything in place of the dinner? Certainly you do: not to have praised the fellow you did not want to praise, and not to have put up with the people at his door.

The idea can be turned from oneself toward others. Before resenting or envying them, one should consider the prices that they paid for what they have.

Epictetus, *Discourses* 1.29.21

This is why I lost my lamp: because a thief was better than I am at staying awake. But he bought the lamp at a high price. In return he became a thief, he became untrustworthy, he became an animal. This seemed to him a good bargain!

This style of inquiry is not limited to the plain wrongdoing of the thief. It applies to all the choices people make. Holders of office are a frequent subject of this kind of Stoic analysis.

Seneca, *On the Shortness of Life* 20.1

When you see someone often wearing the robe of office, or someone whose name is famous in the Forum, do not be envious; those things are bought at the cost of one's life.

Epictetus, *Discourses* 4.9.1–2

Whenever you see another man holding office, set against this the fact that you have no need to hold office. If someone else is wealthy, see what you have instead. For if you have nothing instead, you are miserable; while if in place of wealth you have no need of wealth, know that you possess something more than he does, and much greater in value.

I have good manners, he has a governorship; he has the rank of general, I have self-respect.

Epictetus, *Discourses* 4.3.9

So whenever we hear someone say that our affairs are insignificant and woefully minor because we are not consuls or governors, we may reply, "Our affairs are splendid and our life is enviable: we do not beg, or carry burdens, or flatter."

Plutarch, *On Tranquility of Mind* 10 (470f–471a)

Again, Seneca had a knack for visual comparisons to bring a point to life – here, the cost of things that usually seem free.

So in all our plans and activities, let us do just what we are accustomed to do when we approach a sidewalk vendor who is selling some merchandise or other: let's see what it will cost to get this thing we have our hearts set on. The thing for which nothing is paid often comes at the highest price. I can show you many things whose pursuit and acquisition has cost us our freedom. We would belong to ourselves if these things did not belong to us.

Seneca, *Epistles* 42.8

Imagine the following scene: Fortune is holding games, and over this mob of humanity she is shaking out honors, riches, influence. Some of these trinkets have been torn in the hands of people trying to grab them, some shared by a treacherous partnership, some caught with great injury to those who get them. Some fell to people doing other things entirely; some were dropped because people were trying too hard to catch them, and knocked away from those snatching at them

Seneca, *Epistles* 74.7

greedily. But even among those to whom this booty has luckily fallen, there is no one whose joy in it has lasted until the next day. So it is that the wise run from the theater as soon as they see the trinkets being brought in. They know that these small things come at a high price.

A typical Stoic conclusion:

Seneca, *Epistles* 104.34

If you set a high value on liberty, you must set a low value on everything else.

A relevant anecdote of Diogenes the Cynic, narrated by Diogenes Lærtius (no relation):

Diogenes Lærtius, *Lives of Eminent Philosophers* 2.8.68

Once Diogenes, who was washing vegetables, jeered [Aristippus] as he passed by, and said, "If you had learned to eat these vegetables, you would not have been a slave in the palace of a tyrant." But Aristippus replied, "And you, if you had known how to behave among men, would not have been washing vegetables."

In retellings since, the sequence in that anecdote is often reversed and given a more Stoic flavor: Aristippus taunts Diogenes that he would not have to live on lentils if he would learn to flatter the king. Diogenes replies that Aristippus would not have to flatter the king if he had learned to live on lentils.

Guillaume du Vair offered a way to express our current point: before envying others, ask whether you would accept an offer to pay what they did to get what they have.

du Vair, *The Moral Philosophy of the Stoics* (1585)

I find that most of the time we envy others for their wealth, honor, and privilege; but if someone were to say to us, "You can have the same amount that they have for the same price," we would not want it. For in order to have these things that they do, we must flatter, we must endure insult and injury, we must give up our freedoms.

5. *Self-knowledge; humility.* We turn to another family of self-deceptions: those involving our own qualities. Stoicism, as we have seen at many points, is a humble philosophy. It starts with candid assessment of one's own flaws and foolishness. As the Stoic sees it, a confession of weakness is not weakness; it is the way to wisdom.

> The beginning of philosophy – at least for those who take hold of it in the right way, and through the front door – is an awareness of one's own weakness and incapacity when it comes to the most important things.

Epictetus, *Discourses* 2.11.1

Epicurus expressed the idea as a maxim:

> The knowledge of error is the beginning of deliverance.

Epicurus, in Seneca, *Epistles* 28.9

Seneca turned the point into a method: prosecution of the self by the self.

> He who does not know he is at fault does not wish to be corrected: you must catch yourself in the wrong before you can do better. Some people boast of their faults; when they count their vices as if they were virtues, do you think they intend any remedy? Therefore establish your own guilt as far as you can. Investigate yourself; play the part of the prosecutor, then of the judge, only then of the advocate. Offend yourself sometimes.

Seneca, *Epistles* 28.9–10

Johnson's version of self-prosecution:

> The learned, the judicious, the pious Boerhaave relates, that he never saw a criminal dragged to execution without asking himself, "Who knows whether this man is not less culpable than me?" On the days when the prisons of this city are emptied into the grave, let every spectator of the dreadful procession put the same question to his own

Johnson, *The Rambler* no. 114 (1751)

heart.... For, who can congratulate himself upon a life passed without some act more mischievous to the peace or prosperity of others, than the theft of a piece of money?

Herman Boerhaave (1668–1738) was a Dutch scientist and philosopher, and is often considered a founder of modern medicine.

6. *Love of self.* Against the efforts at self-examination just endorsed, Stoics identify a countervailing force: love of oneself. We humans habitually overrate ourselves and overlook or excuse our own shortcomings.

Seneca, *On Anger* 2.28.8

The faults of others we keep before our eyes, our own behind our back.

Montaigne, *Of Drunkenness* (1580)

Every man overrates the offense of his companions, but extenuates his own.

Johnson, *The Rambler* no. 155 (1751)

No weakness of the human mind has more frequently incurred animadversion than the negligence with which men overlook their own faults, however flagrant, and the easiness with which they pardon them, however frequently repeated.

These tendencies can be reduced to more particular mistakes they cause us to commit, such as making self-serving excuses and assignments of blame.

Seneca, *Epistles* 50.3–4

None of us recognizes that we ourselves are greedy or covetous. But while the blind at least ask for a guide, we wander around without one, saying "I'm not ambitious, but there's no other way to live in Rome. I'm not extravagant, but the city itself requires a significant outlay. It's not my fault that I'm irritable, that I haven't yet decided on a settled way of life – that's just my youth." Why do we fool ourselves? Our evil is not on the outside, it is within us, it is seated in our vitals – and it is that much harder to attain health when we do not know we are sick.

Or using double standards.

"Why, then, are we upset by the wrongs done to us by our enemies?" Because we did not expect them, or at least not wrongs so serious. This is the result of undue love of self; we think we should remain untouched even by our enemies. Each of us has within himself the royal mindset: license for what he does, but not for what is done to him.

Seneca, *On Anger* 2.31.3

Let us put ourselves in the place of the person with whom we are angry; from that point of view, we see that our anger comes from an unwarranted opinion of ourselves. We are unwilling to bear what we ourselves would have been willing to inflict.

Seneca, *On Anger* 3.12.3

Or being susceptible to flattery.

Our principal hindrance is that we are so easily satisfied with ourselves. If we come across someone who says that we are good men, that we are wise, that we are upright, we acknowledge the accuracy of the description. We are not content with moderate praise: whatever shameless flattery heaps upon us, we accept as our due. We agree with those who maintain that we are the best and wisest of all, though we know they are greatly given to lying.

Seneca, *Epistles* 59.11

If you stroke a cat, it will purr; and, as inevitably, if you praise a man, a sweet expression of delight will appear on his face; and even though the praise is a palpable lie, it will be welcome, if the matter is one on which he prides himself.

Schopenhauer, *The Wisdom of Life* (1851)

On the stubbornness of the tendency:

Why does no one confess his faults? Because he is still in their power. You tell your dreams when

Seneca, *Epistles* 53.8

you are awake; to confess your faults is the mark of a sound mind.

Montaigne made a similar point about why it is so hard to catch our own misjudgments. Our limited capacities prevent us from perceiving our limited capacities.

Montaigne, *Of Presumption* (1580)

It is commonly said that good sense is the gift Nature has distributed most fairly among us, for there is no one who is unsatisfied with the share he has been allotted – and isn't that reasonable enough? For whoever saw beyond this would see beyond his sight. I think my opinions are good and sound, but who does not think the same of his own?

The descendants of the Stoics have offered some additional theories to account for the trouble we have seeing our own flaws clearly. Another of Montaigne's was that we look at ourselves in the idealized way that people see anyone with whom they are in love.

Montaigne, *Of Presumption* (1580)

There is another variety of glory, which is the exaggerated opinion that we have of our own worth. We flatter ourselves with careless affection, and it shows us to ourselves other than as we are. It is like the passionate love that lends beauty and grace to whatever subject it embraces, and makes those who are caught up in it, by their disturbed and disordered judgments, regard what they love as other and more perfect than it is.

Johnson suggested a different mechanism – that we imagine others don't see what we know to be true about ourselves.

Johnson, *The Rambler* no. 155 (1751)

Self-love is often rather arrogant than blind; it does not hide our faults from ourselves, but persuades us that they escape the notice of others, and disposes us to resent censures lest we should confess them to be just. We are secretly conscious of defects and vices, which we hope to conceal from the public eye, and please ourselves with innumerable impostures, by which, in reality, nobody is deceived.

Smith had a different view still: self-knowledge is unbearably painful, so we look the other way.

> It is so disagreeable to think ill of ourselves, that we often purposely turn away our view from those circumstances which might render that judgment unfavorable. He is a bold surgeon, they say, whose hand does not tremble when he performs an operation upon his own person; and he is often equally bold who does not hesitate to pull off the mysterious veil of self-delusion, which covers from his view the deformities of his own conduct.... This self-deceit, this fatal weakness of mankind, is the source of half the disorders of human life. If we saw ourselves in the light in which others see us, or in which they would see us if they knew all, a reformation would generally be unavoidable. We could not otherwise endure the sight.

Smith, *The Theory of Moral Sentiments* 3.4.6 (1759)

7. *Projection.* An exaggerated love of self often comes with sensitivity to offense given by others and flaws found in them. The Stoics have a particular interest in one feature of this last tendency: the inclination to fault others for what is at least as objectionable in ourselves. Sometimes the point is just that we criticize people without reflecting on what similar faults we have within us. If we don't do the same things they do, we should admit that we have the capacity for it, or that we do other things as bad or worse.

> Whenever you take offense at someone else's fault, turn immediately to find the fault most similar in yourself – such as attachment to money, or

Marcus Aurelius, *Meditations* 10.30

pleasure, or reputation, or whatever it might be. In seeing this, you will quickly forget your anger; it will occur to you that he was forced to act that way. For what else could he do?

Seneca, *On Anger* 2.28.6

If anyone will recall how often he himself has fallen under undeserved suspicion, how many of his good services chance has clothed with the appearance of wrongdoing, how many people he once hated and learned to love, he will be able to avoid all hasty anger, particularly if as each offence occurs he will first say to himself in silence: "I myself have also been guilty of this." But where will you find such a fair-minded judge?

Seneca, *On Anger* 3.26.5

"That man has already injured me, but I have not yet injured him." But perhaps you have already harmed, perhaps you will someday harm, someone else. Do not count only this hour or this day; consider the whole character of your mind. Even if you have done no evil, you are capable of it.

But sometimes the problem is more insidious. It is not just that we criticize others without reflecting on our own culpabilities. It is that we see in others precisely those things that we find most uncomfortable in ourselves. In a word, we engage in projection.

Seneca, *On Anger* 2.28.7

The strictest enforcer of loyalty is the traitor, the punisher of falsehood is also a perjurer, and the unscrupulous lawyer deeply resents an indictment brought against himself.

Seneca, *On Anger* 3.26.4

We are all inconsiderate and unthinking, all untrustworthy, complaining, ambitious – why hide the universal sore in softer words? – we are all wicked. Each of us will find inside ourselves whatever fault we rebuke in another.... And so let us be more kindly toward one another; being wicked, we live among the wicked. Only one thing can bring us peace – a compact of mutual good nature.

Plutarch:

> Poverty of thought, emptiness of phrase, an offensive bearing, fluttering excitement combined with a vulgar delight at commendation, and the like, are more apparent to us in others when we are listening than in ourselves when we are speakers. So we ought to transfer our scrutiny from the speaker to ourselves, and examine whether we unconsciously commit such mistakes.... Everyone ought to be ready ever to repeat to himself, as he observes the faults of others, the utterance of Plato, "Am I not possibly like them?"

Plutarch, *On Listening to Lectures* 6 (40c–40d)

Montaigne describes this sort of projection as "the most universal and common error of mankind." He continues:

> We mock ourselves a hundred times a day when we mock our neighbors; we detest in others the defects that are more evident in us, and wonder at them with a marvelous absence of awareness and shame.

Montaigne, *Of the Art of Conference* (1580)

> We every day and every hour say things about others that we might more properly say about ourselves, if only we knew how to turn our observation on ourselves as skillfully as we extend it toward them.

Montaigne, *Of Drunkenness* (1580)

Johnson again had an idea about the source of this habit. Sometimes we are suspicious of others precisely because we deserve suspicion ourselves, and assume that others are the same.

> We can form our opinions of that which we know not, only by placing it in comparison with something that we know; whoever, therefore, is

Johnson, *The Rambler* no. 79 (1750)

over-run with suspicion, and detects artifice and stratagem in every proposal, must either have learned by experience or observation the wickedness of mankind, and been taught to avoid fraud by having often suffered or seen treachery, or he must derive his judgment from the consciousness of his own disposition, and impute to others the same inclinations, which he feels predominant in himself.

Schopenhauer thought that we have trouble seeing our vices because we live in the midst of them. Our criticisms of others therefore have a side benefit. They provide an unintentional glimpse at what is ugliest within us.

Schopenhauer, *Our Relation to Ourselves* (1851)

A man bears the weight of his own body without knowing it, but he soon feels the weight of any other, if he tries to move it; in the same way, a man can see other people's shortcomings and vices, but he is blind to his own. This arrangement has one advantage: it turns other people into a kind of mirror, in which a man can see clearly everything that is vicious, faulty, ill-bred and loathsome in his own nature; only it is generally the old story of the dog barking at its own image; it is himself that he sees and not another dog, as he fancies.

Chapter Nine

EMOTION

Stoicism connotes, to many people today, "unfeeling." Yet sometimes the Stoics not only welcome feeling but seek it. To borrow two passages we will meet in Chapter 11:

> This is the first promise that philosophy holds out to us: fellow-feeling, humanity, sociability.

Seneca, *Epistles* 5.4

> I should not be unfeeling like a statue; I should care for my relationships both natural and acquired – as a pious man, a son, a brother, a father, a citizen.

Epictetus, *Discourses* 3.2.4

Or recall Seneca's instruction at the end of Chapter 4 to "Snatch the pleasures your children bring, let your children in turn find delight in you, and drain joy to the dregs without delay." These are not the words of one who is hostile to feeling. Yet the Stoics do seek to avoid some varieties of it, especially those that take a form, or rise to a level, that we might call emotion. So which sorts of feeling are welcomed by the Stoics, and how much is too much?

In keeping with the approach of this book, some basic answers can be sketched without recounting the full theoretical apparatus that the Romans and especially the Greeks developed. First, it helps to view the Stoics not as against feeling or emotion (we will return to the distinction in a moment) but as in favor of seeing the world accurately, living by reason, and staying detached from externals. Feelings and emotions – any inner states – are unwanted to the extent that they interfere with those aims. Sometimes they do. Someone who is furiously angry is probably not making clear judgments, and an ill-advised attachment is probably the basis of the fury. The fellow-feeling Seneca endorses above is different because it does not unseat reason and does not involve an illusion or an attachment to any external. Those are the best measures of whether a feeling is more than a Stoic would welcome: has the happiness of whoever has the feeling come to depend on the subject of it? Does the feeling blur the vision, causing the holder of it to make misjudgments? If these questions can be answered in the negative, there is no need to disparage a state of feeling, or any similar state, on Stoic grounds.

It is useful to have simple words to refer to the distinction just explained – between a state of inner upheaval that involves attachment to externals or that threatens the priority of reason, and a state that doesn't have those properties. We do not have ready-made English terms for that difference. For the sake of convenience, I will sometimes refer to the first state as an emotion and the second as a (mere) feeling. There are modern definitions of "emotion" and "feeling" to which this usage does not conform; I don't mean to controvert those other definitions or create confusion about them. The words are only used here as rough placeholders for the practical difference sketched above, which is important to the Stoics.

Next, the Stoics, at least the late ones (this chapter belongs mostly to Seneca), are more realistic than their reputation sometimes suggests. Seneca does not begrudge surges of feeling – tears, trembling, lusts – so long as reason is able to get them under control. They are considered physical impulses. And he accepts that grief is inevitable after a loss; he dismisses doubts on that point as quickly as any non-Stoic would. The Stoic's aim, as he sees it, is to avoid making natural grief worse by talking to ourselves unhelpfully about it and taking our cues from convention. These are humane counsels. If they would cause some to say that Seneca was an insufficiently pure Stoic, let us be content with the philosophy in its impure form.

An essay in Chapter 13 provides some further discussion of these themes. It suggests that the Stoic tries to respond to events in a manner similar to what would be expected of anyone after long experience with them – the kind of response you might have after encountering the occasion for it a thousand times. The result is not an uncaring or unfeeling attitude, though it will probably not involve much emotion. It is the posture of the veteran.

This chapter starts with some Stoic analysis of emotions in general, then turns to three of them in particular: fear, anger, and grief. Stoicism offers ways of coping with all three, and those methods can be carried over easily enough to emotions of other kinds.

1. *Inevitabilities.* The Stoic is sometimes caricatured as denying a place for emotion in human experience. We therefore might start by showing what place Seneca *does* concede for them. First, some involuntary reactions can't be helped.

> There are certain things, Lucilius, that no courage can avoid; nature reminds courage of its own mortality. And so the courageous man will frown at sad things; he will be startled by a sudden occurrence; he will feel dizzy if, standing at the brink, he looks down from the precipice. This is not fear, but a natural feeling not to be overcome by reason.

Seneca, *Epistles* 57.4

> Whatever is implanted and inborn can be reduced with practice but not overcome. Some of those who appear in public most often will break into a sweat, just as if they were tired and overheated; some tremble in the knees when they are about to give a speech; in some cases teeth chatter, tongues falter, lips quiver. Neither training nor experience will ever get rid of these things. Rather, Nature is

Seneca, *Epistles* 11.1–2

exerting its strength to admonish even the strongest among us – each through his particular flaw.

Montaigne, *Of Constancy* (1580)

Nor do the Stoics believe that the soul of their sage can resist visions and imaginings when they first surprise him. Rather, they concede that it is in his nature to react to a loud noise from the sky or from a collapsing building (for example) by turning pale and tense; and likewise for all other emotions, provided his judgment remains sound and intact, that the seat of his reason does not suffer any damage or change, and that he does not give consent to his fear and pain.

Seneca also acknowledges that larger forms of feeling sometimes will not be denied no matter what we may think about them. Grief is like this, and we will return to it in more detail later in the chapter. But the basic goal of the Stoic is to make such reactions no worse by the way we think about them, or by the way that others encourage us to think.

Seneca, *Epistles* 13.6

Whenever you are surrounded by people trying to convince you that you are unhappy, consider not what you hear them say but what you yourself feel.

Seneca, *Epistles* 99.15–16

Now, am I urging you to be hard-hearted, do I ask that you betray no emotion at the funeral, do I refuse to let your spirit even be touched? Not at all. It would be barbarous, not courageous, to watch the burial rites of one's own – with the same eyes that watched them while living – and not be moved as one's family is first torn apart. Suppose I did forbid it: some things have rights of their own. Tears fall even from those trying to hold them back; being shed, they lift the spirit. What, then, shall we do? Let us allow them to fall, but not order them to do so; let there be as much weeping as emotion may produce, not as much as imitation may demand. Let us add nothing to grief, nor enlarge it to match the example of someone else.

Stoicism offers taxonomies to describe an emotion's development, and they can be hard to keep straight. The most important practical point to understand, however, is just the larger Stoic goal: to make reason the basis for one's choices, actions, and sense of equilibrium, and to maintain a detachment from externals.

> An emotion, then, does not consist in being moved by the appearances of things, but in surrendering to them and following up this casual impulse. For if anyone supposes that turning pale, bursting into tears, sexual arousal, deep sighs, flashing eyes, and anything of that sort are a sign of emotion and mental state, he is mistaken and does not understand that these are merely bodily impulses.... A man thinks himself injured, wants to be revenged, and then – being dissuaded for some reason – he quickly calms down again. I don't call this anger, but a mental impulse yielding to reason. Anger is that which overleaps reason and carries it away.

Seneca, *On Anger* 2.3.1–2, 4

2. *Fear.* We turn to specific emotions, and will treat fear as one of them. It qualifies under the definition of this chapter, as it is a state of feeling that sometimes interferes with reason and judgment. The Stoic technique is now familiar: identify the foolishness in a certain state of mind or way of reacting to the world, then suggest rational ways to reform it. The trouble with fear, first, is that it multiplies our problems. If something will be bad when it arrives later, we increase its effects when we pull them into the present by fearing them. Why suffer twice?

> If foolishness fears some evil, it is burdened by the anticipation of it, just as if the evil had already

Seneca, *Epistles* 74.32–34

come. What it fears lest it suffer, it suffers already through fear.... What then is more insane than to be tortured by things yet to be – not to save your strength for actual suffering, but to summon and accelerate your wretchedness? You should put it off if you cannot be rid of it.

And fear does more than bring misfortunes forward. It tends to overdraw them.

Seneca, *Epistles* 13.4–5

There are more things, Lucilius, that frighten us than affect us; we suffer more often in conjecture than in reality.... We magnify our sorrow, or we imagine it, or we get ahead of it.

In addition to causing us to endure twice, or many times, what might have been endured once, fear spoils the enjoyment of the present. The pain of whatever is coming is not here yet, so we can't feel it unless we impose it on ourselves by thinking about it. As discussed in the previous chapter, meanwhile, what *is* here is probably bearable.

Seneca, *Epistles* 98.6

It is ruinous when a mind is worried about the future, wretched before its wretchedness begins, anxious that it may forever hold on to the things that bring it pleasure. For such a mind will never be at rest, and in awaiting the future it loses sight of what it might have enjoyed in the present. The fear of losing a thing is as bad as regret at having lost it.

Seneca, *Epistles* 74.34

Bygone things and things yet to be are both absent; we feel neither of them. And there is no pain except from what you feel.

Fear also makes us worse off by causing us to think and do foolish and cowardly things.

Epictetus, *Discourses* 2.1.8

Well, then, we act like deer. When they are frightened and flee the feathers that the hunters are waving at them, where do they turn, toward what place of safety do they retreat? Into the nets. They are destroyed by confusing what should be regarded with fear with what might be regarded with confidence.

Montaigne recounted a long series of similar disasters involving people whose fears drove them into error and disgrace. His conclusion:

What I fear the most is fear.   Montaigne, *Of Fear* (1580)

Finally, fear and other emotions tend to accumulate once they get going. That is why Seneca is a skeptic about the possibility of indulging emotions moderately.

If reason prevails, the emotions will not even get   Seneca, *Epistles* 85.9
started; while if they begin in defiance of reason,
they will continue in defiance of reason. It is easier to stop their beginnings than to control them
once they gather force. This "moderation" is therefore deceptive and useless: we should regard it in
the same light as if someone should recommend
being "moderately insane" or "moderately sick."

Stoicism thus regards fear as akin to a sickness or form of enslavement. The conquest of it is a great priority for the philosopher.

Even when there is nothing wrong, nor anything   Seneca, *Epistles* 13.13
sure to go wrong in the future, most mortals exist
in a fever of anxiety.

No one who is afraid or distressed or troubled is   Epictetus, *Discourses* 2.1.24
free; and whoever is released from distress and
fear and trouble, is in the same way released from
slavery.

3. *Antidotes to fear; rational scrutiny.* From a Stoic per-spective, fears are opinions about what is to come. Those opinions can be reduced to a series of things that the

fearful person must believe, even if they aren't conscious or articulate – a belief that a certain thing is going to happen, that it is going to be terrible, that it is worth getting upset about now. The Stoics regard most such propositions as mistaken, and would defeat fear by dismantling them. First, fearful things should be examined directly, and their realism severely tested.

Seneca, *Epistles* 13.8

> We do not disprove and overthrow by argument the things that cause our fear; we do not examine into them; we tremble and retreat just like soldiers who have abandoned their camp because of a dust-cloud raised by stampeding cattle, or who are thrown into a panic by the spreading of some rumor of unknown veracity. And somehow or other it is the false report that disturbs us most. For truth has its own definite boundaries, but that which arises from uncertainty is delivered over to guesswork and the license of a mind in terror.

And if rational scrutiny doesn't dissolve fears, we can adjust our standard of proof until it does; Seneca invites us to fix the game in our favor. We might as well, because the adversary doesn't fight fair, either. It's another case of questionable philosophy but good psychology.

Seneca, *Epistles* 13.13

> Weigh your hopes against your fears. When everything is uncertain, favor your own side: believe what you prefer. If fear obtains more votes, bend more the other way nevertheless and stop troubling yourself.

4. *Don't borrow trouble.* A next line of response to a fear: the feared thing might not happen. We often fail to discount enough for this possibility. Since whatever is feared may not come, we are foolish to agonize about it. Rather than causing us to suffer twice when we might have suffered once, the fear can cause us to suffer once when we need not have suffered at all.

The things that terrify you, as if they were about to happen, may never come; certainly they have not come yet. Some things torment us more than they should, some before they should, some when they should not torment us at all.

Seneca, *Epistles* 13.4–5

It is likely that some bad thing will happen in the future, but it is not happening now. How often has the unexpected happened! How often has the expected never come to pass! ... Many things may intervene that will cause an impending or present danger to stop, or come to an end, or pass over to threaten someone else. A fire has opened up a means of escape; a disaster has let some men down gently; the sword has sometimes been withdrawn from the very throat; men have survived their executioners. Even ill fate has its quirks. Perhaps it will be, perhaps it will not be; meanwhile it is not.

Seneca, *Epistles* 13.10, 11

When Seneca urged this line of thought, he said that he wasn't speaking as a Stoic. The upshot nevertheless fits comfortably among his other ideas. Still, it is one of the points in this book that the purist may regard as a teaching of a Stoic rather than as a Stoic teaching.

Only those evils which are sure to come at a definite date have any right to disturb us; and how few there are which fulfill this description. For evils are of two kinds; either they are possible only, at most probable; or they are inevitable. Even in the case of evils which are sure to happen, the time at which they will happen is uncertain. A man who is always preparing for either class of evil will not have a moment of peace left him. So, if we are not to lose all comfort in life through the fear of evils, some of which are uncertain in themselves, and others, in the time at which they will occur, we should look upon the one kind as never

Schopenhauer, *Our Relation to Ourselves* (1851)

likely to happen, and the other as not likely to happen very soon.

5. *And what if it does?* Suppose, finally, that your fears do end up being realized. Maybe they are not so bad after all if looked at realistically; or their ultimate consequences may be harder to judge than they seem. In any event, you will deal with them by use of the same resources that allow you to cope here and now.

Seneca, *Epistles* 24.2

I will conduct you to peace of mind by another route: if you would put off all worry, assume that what you fear may happen will certainly happen. Whatever the evil may be, measure it in your own mind, and estimate the amount of your fear. You will soon understand that what you fear is either not great or not of long duration.

Seneca, *Epistles* 13.14

Let someone else say, "Perhaps the worst will not happen." You say, "And what if it does? Let us see who wins. Perhaps it is happening for my benefit, and such a death will dignify my life." The hemlock made Socrates great. Pry from his hand Cato's sword – the vindicator of his freedom – and you take away the greater part of his glory.

This theme – ways in which things that we fear sometimes turn out to be for the best – is taken up in more detail in Chapter 10, Section 8.

Marcus Aurelius, *Meditations* 7.8

Do not let things still in the future disturb you. For you will come to them, if need be, carrying the same reason you now employ when dealing with things in the present.

6. *Anger.* This is the passion that Seneca discusses most extensively. On the dangers and costs of anger:

Seneca, *On Anger* 1.2.1

If you will look at the effects of anger, and at the harm it has done, no plague has been more costly

to mankind. You will see slaughters and poison-
ings, the mutual vileness of litigants, the downfall
of cities and the destruction of entire nations;
princes sold into slavery at auction, houses put to
the torch, fires not confined within city walls but
vast stretches of countryside aglow with enemy
flame.

Reason considers nothing but the question at issue;   Seneca, *On Anger* 1.18.2
anger is moved by trifling things that lie outside
the case. An overconfident demeanor, a voice too
loud, unrestrained speech, overrefined attire, over-
solicitous advocacy, popularity with the public –
anger is inflamed by all of them. Many times it will
condemn the accused because it hates his lawyer;
even if the truth is piled up before its very eyes, it
loves error and upholds it; it refuses to be convinced, and counts persistence in what is wrongly
begun to be more honorable than penitence.

Great anger ends in madness, and therefore anger   Seneca, *Epistles* 18.15
is to be avoided – for the sake not of moderation
but of sanity.

Anger may have been of special interest to Seneca
because its destructive potential was on such lavish display during his times. He writes, for example, of the
wrath of Vedius Pollio. When angry with his slaves,
Vedius fed them to his lampreys – a species of toothed,
eel-like, bloodsucking fish that was a popular delicacy in
Rome (we met them in passing in Chapter 5). The
emperor Augustus was a guest when one of Vedius's
slaves was ordered to be killed in this way for breaking a
crystal cup. According to Seneca, Augustus ordered that
the slave's life be spared and that Vedius's other cups be
broken in front of him. Seneca, if he were here to do so,
might cite the decline in the incidence of this sort of
problem as some further evidence that the extent and
expression of our anger are up to us.

7. *Anger as opinion.* Anger provides, indeed, a good example of the necessary role of opinion, or judgment, in forming an emotion. Though anger may take on a life of its own, it begins and is supported by beliefs we hold about the subject of it. One can see this by thinking of any real case of anger and observing how the emotion tends to change or vanish if it is found to have been based on mistaken beliefs. You think that your goods have been carelessly damaged; they turn out to have been someone else's. You thought something bad was done to you on purpose; you discover that it was an honest mistake. The feelings follow the facts, or rather your thoughts about the facts. The Stoic views all cases of anger as open to this kind of analysis. Even if the factual details that support the anger aren't wrong in the ways just described, the anger still has to depend on other beliefs, too, that are certainly mistaken from a Stoic standpoint – such as a belief that the subject is worth getting angry about.

Seneca, *On Anger* 2.1.3

There can be no doubt that anger is aroused by the impression that we have been wronged. The question, however, is whether anger follows immediately from that impression and springs up without assistance from the mind, or whether it is aroused only with the mind's cooperation. Our opinion is that it ventures nothing by itself, but acts only with the approval of the mind. For to form the impression of having received an injury and to want to avenge it, and then to couple together the two propositions that one ought not to have been wronged and that one ought to be avenged – this is not a mere impulse of the mind acting without our volition.

So a first Stoic remedy for anger, as for other such problems, is a return to Chapter 1: recognize it as an opinion and let it go.

Still you are indignant and complain, and you don't understand that in all the evils to which you refer, there is really only one – that you are indignant and complain.

Seneca, *Epistles* 96.1

Nothing is heavy if we take it lightly; nothing need provoke anger if one does not add one's anger to it.

Seneca, *Epistles* 123.1

It is not what men do that disturbs us (for those acts are matters of their own control and reasoning), but our opinions of what they do. Take away those opinions – dismiss your judgment that this is something terrible – and your anger goes away as well.

Marcus Aurelius, *Meditations* 11.18

8. *Uses of humor.* But as we have seen at various earlier points in the book, the Stoics understand that inner disturbances aren't always possible to get rid of in that way. So we have here the same pattern seen in Chapter 7, Section 8 (on the handling of insults, a topic closely related to our current one): beyond treating anger as an opinion to be dropped, the Stoics offer other remedies as well – ways to redirect the mind and substitute better ideas for unproductive ones. One such response to anger is to make light of its cause. A Stoic needs a good sense of humor.

We should bring ourselves to see all the vices of the crowd not as hateful but as ridiculous; and we should imitate Democritus rather than Heraclitus. For the latter, every time he went out into public, used to weep; the former used to laugh. One saw everything we do as wretchedness, the other as absurdity. Things should be made light of, and taken more easily: it is more civilized to laugh at life than to bewail it.

Seneca, *On Tranquility of Mind* 15.2

Democritus and Heraclitus were pre-Socratic Greek philosophers. Heraclitus died early in the 5th century BC, and Democritus was born soon afterwards. Democritus became known as the laughing philosopher for finding the comic side of all things, Heraclitus as the weeping philosopher for his darker view. The pairing of the two in this way evidently was an invention of Sotion, one of Seneca's teachers from childhood.

It should be noted that Stoicism doesn't commend laughter at the expense of others.

Seneca, *On Tranquility of Mind* 15.5

> It is better to accept common behavior and human vices calmly, without bursting into either laughter or tears; for to be hurt by the sufferings of others is to be forever miserable, while to enjoy the sufferings of others is an inhuman pleasure.

It is good humor at the expense of oneself, and about the affronts one receives, that is fully endorsed by the Stoic. Self-effacing humor disarms an opponent and makes the user of it a less appealing target of attack. (See Chapter 7, Section 11.) Humor has other uses that the Stoics recognize as well; one who manages to be amused by an attack rises above it and diminishes the attacker. Above all, however – and most to our point – humor can cause anger to dissolve.

Seneca, *On the Constancy of the Wise Man* 18.6

> Let us look at the examples of those whose forbearance we praise – such as Socrates, who took in good humor the public jests made at his expense, seen on stage in the comedies, no less than when his wife Xanthippe had doused him with the chamber pot. Antisthenes was taunted with the fact that his mother was a barbarian, being a Thracian; he answered that even the mother of the gods came from Mount Ida [in Crete].

Seneca, *On Anger* 3.11.2

> There are various ways in which anger can be checked. Many things can be turned into a game and a joke. They say that when Socrates once received a blow on the head, he merely said that it

was too bad that a man could not tell when he ought to go out wearing a helmet. What matters is not how offense is given but how it is received.

> As Cato was arguing a case, Lentulus – that violent partisan, remembered by our fathers – gathered as much thick saliva as he could and spat right in the middle of Cato's forehead. Cato wiped off his face and said, "I'll assure everyone, Lentulus, that they're wrong when they say that you're not worth spit."

Seneca, *On Anger* 3.38.2

This last passage involves a pun that does not translate well literally. Cato really told Lentulus that they were wrong to say he had no mouth; it was a play on words in Latin. I've sought to suggest something equivalent in English.

> Some are offended if a hairdresser jostles them; they see an insult in the surliness of a doorkeeper, the arrogance of an attendant, the haughtiness of a valet. What laughter such things should draw! With what satisfaction should your mind be filled when you contrast your own peace of mind with the unrest into which others blunder!

Seneca, *On the Constancy of the Wise Man* 14.1

> Believe me, these things that incense us not a little are little things, like the trifles that drive children to quarrels and blows. Not one of them, though we take them so tragically, is a serious matter; not one is important. *That* is where your anger and madness come from, I tell you – the fact that you attach such value to trifles.

Seneca, *On Anger* 3.34.1–2

9. *Uses of delay.* Some simple Stoic advice: wait before acting when angry. The first essay in Chapter 13 will suggest that Stoicism is a shortcut to the frame of mind created naturally by the passage of time. Here the point is the reverse: those who can't maintain an even temper by

philosophical effort can get there by letting some time go by.

Seneca, *On Anger* 2.29.1

The best corrective of anger lies in delay. Ask this concession from anger at the outset, not in order that it may pardon, but in order that it may judge. Its first assaults are heavy; it will leave off if it waits. And do not try to destroy it all at once; attacked piecemeal, it will be conquered completely.

Plutarch, *On Controlling Anger* 11 (459f–460a)

Who among us is so harsh as to whip and chastise a slave because five or ten days ago he burned the food, or knocked over the table, or was slow to come when called? And yet these are the very things that – when they have just happened and are fresh in our minds – upset us and make us harsh and implacable. For just like bodies seen through a fog, so things seen through a mist of rage appear greater than they are.

10. *Avoiding causes for anger.* Here is more Stoic pragmatism. A good way to avoid anger is to avoid situations where it is likely to be aroused, or at least to avoid seeking them out in ways that we might find tempting. Seneca observes that people sometimes want to know whatever has been said about them that might be cause for resentment. But these provocations are so hard to see clearly and fairly that we're usually better off ignorant of them.

Seneca, *On Anger* 3.11.1

You don't want to be irritable? Don't be inquisitive. People who try to find out what has been said about them, who dig up malicious gossip even if it happened in private, are only upsetting themselves. Our interpretations can make things appear to be insults when some should be put aside, others laughed at, others forgiven.

Seneca praised the self-control of this kind showed by rulers who declined to expose themselves to causes for anger.

The great Julius Cæsar displayed this same quality, on showing himself so merciful in victory in the civil war. When he discovered packets of letters written to Pompey by people who probably belonged to the opposing or neutral party, he burned them. However moderate his tendency to anger might have been, he preferred to avoid any occasion for it. The most graceful form of forgiveness, he thought, was not to know the offense that might have been given by each of them.

Seneca, On Anger 2.23.4

In view of the Stoics' usual insistence on the unvarnished truth, one might wish they had discussed more fully when is it better not to know than to know. But it may be enough for the everyday Stoic to recognize it as a question that should be answered more deliberately than is common.

The same restraint can also be applied internally – that is, to how we interpret things once we do hear them. Seneca saw that we sometimes have an appetite for indignation, or at any rate are too quick to find grounds for it. We should tilt the other way, being slow to construe what others say as offensive or hostile and learning to distrust suspicious instincts.

Suspicion and surmise – those deceptive provocations – ought to be banished from the mind. "This man did not give me a civil greeting; that one did not embrace me as I kissed him; that one broke off the conversation abruptly; that one did not invite me to dinner; that one tried to avoid seeing me." Grounds for suspicion will never be lacking. But we need to be straightforward and to see things in their best light. We should believe only what is thrust under our eyes and becomes unmistakable. And every time our suspicion proves to be groundless we should blame our own credulity; this rebuke will develop the habit of being slow to believe.

Seneca, On Anger 2.24.1–2

The Stoics do not usually pause to acknowledge that a reaction may be easier for some to tame than for others just because we are born with different temperaments. But Seneca does sometimes talk about this. We saw examples in Section 1 of this chapter and in Chapter 6, Section 9 (on pleasures and games), where he distinguished between the challenges faced by fiery dispositions and those that might be described as either dry or watery. When it comes to anger, too, some need to take different precautions than others.

Seneca, *On Anger* 2.20.2

As for nature, it is difficult to alter it, and we may not change the elements that were combined once for all at our birth; but though this be so, it is profitable to know that fiery temperaments should be kept away from wine, which Plato thinks ought to be forbidden to children, protesting against adding fire to fire.

Plutarch, *On Controlling Anger* 13 (461f–462a)

Anyone who is quick to anger should abstain from rare and curiously wrought things, like drinking-cups and seal-rings and precious stones; for their loss drives their owner out of his senses more than do objects which are common and easily procured. This is the reason why, when Nero had an octagonal tent built, an enormous thing and a sight to be seen for its beauty and costliness, Seneca remarked, "You have proved yourself a poor man, for if you ever lose this you will not have the means to procure another like it." And indeed it did so happen that the ship which conveyed it was sunk and the tent lost. But Nero remembered Seneca's saying and bore his loss with greater moderation.

Nero was a prolific executioner – of his rivals, of his first wife, of his mother, and of various others (finally including Seneca); so one may wonder if Plutarch wrote that

passage with some irony. But what the "greater moderation" of Nero looked like in this case is not recorded.

11. *The endlessness of anger.* Seneca holds that if anger is
ever warranted by externals, it is warranted constantly;
life overflows with good grounds for annoyance.

> What is more unworthy of the wise man than that
> his emotions should depend on the wickedness of
> others? Shall great Socrates lose the power to carry
> back home the same look he had when he left? If
> the wise man is to be angered by low deeds, if he
> is to be upset and unsettled by crimes, surely
> nothing is more woeful than the wise man's lot;
> his whole life will be passed in anger and in grief.
> For what moment will there be when he will not
> see something to disapprove of?

Seneca, *On Anger* 2.7.1

That passage alludes to what Xanthippe, the wife of Socrates, is recorded as having said about him: "that when
the State was oppressed with a thousand miseries, Socrates still always went out and came home with the same
look. For he bore a mind smooth and cheerful on all
occasions, far remote from grief and above all from fear."
(Aelian, *Various Histories* 9.7)

The pattern of argument used by Seneca in the last
excerpt – the "no end to it" argument – is common in
Stoicism: if you are ever going to get upset about X, you
should realize that chances for X are everywhere, so you
might as well be upset all the time – or be sensible and
stop ever (or so often) getting upset about X at all. We
have seen this idea applied to sensitivity to insults, to
worry about what others think, and now to anger about
wrongdoing. Elsewhere Seneca applies it to sadness:

> Come, look about you, survey all mortals – every-
> where there is ample and constant reason for weep-
> ing.... Tears will fail us sooner than the causes for
> grief.... Such is the way we spend our lives, and so

Seneca, *Consolation to Polybius*
4.2–3

we ought to do in moderation this thing we must do so often.

12. *Justice without anger.* To conclude our discussion of anger, we might reflect briefly on whether it is needed to support values such as justice; the opposition of the Stoics to anger will sometimes raise questions about whether they are pacifists, and too detached to care about righting wrongs. Not in the least. The Stoic disposition affects the spirit in which justice is administered and in which the good is pursued, but it does not imply mild views about the *substance* of those things or timidity in securing them.

Seneca, *On Anger* 1.19.2

> If need be, reason silently, quietly wipes out whole families root and branch, and households that are a plague on the state it destroys along with wives and children; it tears down their very houses, levelling them to the ground, and exterminates the names of the enemies of liberty. All this it will do, but with no gnashing of the teeth, no violent shaking of the head, nothing that would be unseemly for a judge, whose countenance should at no time be more calm and unmoved than when delivering a weighty sentence.

The Stoic judge, in something like the spirit of the dispassionate physician, is concerned with deterrence and rehabilitation – with the good of the community and the good of the offender, very broadly understood – rather than with retribution. Some further thoughts on how such a judge might think:

Seneca, *On Anger* 1.19.7
(quoting Plato, *Laws* 11.934)

> He will look to the future, not to the past. For as Plato says: "A sensible person does not punish a man because he has done wrong, but in order to keep him from doing wrong; for while the past cannot be recalled, the future may be forestalled." And he will openly kill those whom he wishes to

have serve as examples of the wickedness that is
slow to yield, not so much that they themselves
may be destroyed as that their destruction may
deter others. These are the things a man must
weigh and consider, and you see how free he ought
to be from all emotion when he proceeds to deal
with a matter that requires the utmost caution –
the use of power over life and death.

The Stoic sees honor in fighting to the death for a good
cause, and takes a perspective broad enough to identify
virtue on both sides of a conflict.

> Great is Scipio, who lays siege to Numantia, and
> constrains and compels the hands of an enemy,
> whom he could not conquer, to resort to their own
> destruction. Great also are the souls of the defend-
> ers – men who know that, as long as the path to
> death lies open, the blockade is not complete, men
> who breathe their last in the arms of liberty.

Seneca, *Epistles* 66.13

Numantia, also mentioned in Chapter 4, was a city in
Spain that was besieged by the Romans in 134 BC. The
siege lasted for 13 months, at the end of which the inhabitants killed themselves rather than surrender. For readers wishing to keep their Scipios straight, the one
referenced here is Scipio Aemilianus, adoptive grandson
of Scipio Africanus (the Roman general who had
defeated Hannibal about 60 years earlier). Neither is to
be confused with Metellus Scipio (encountered in Chapter 4, Section 7).

As these passages show, Stoic detachment does not
imply a shortage of engagement with the world or reluc-
tance to act in it. The detachment of the Stoic is a technique for preserving one's equilibrium and seeing the
world accurately. The requirements of justice are a separate matter, and one very important to the Stoics. Choices
about how to spend one's time and energy are likewise a

separate issue – one on which the Stoic advice is exactly the opposite of withdrawal. (See Chapter 11 for more on those points.)

These excerpts, and the longer discussions from which they come, can still raise additional questions. How exactly do Stoics, with all their detachment, find the will or motivation to fight hard and successfully for things – to give them their all, so to speak – without caring *too* much about them, or (perhaps to say it better) without caring about them the wrong way? One possibility is that they cheat on their Stoicism a bit, and sometimes become more invested in externals than they say they should. We see glimpses of this from time to time in Seneca. But more satisfying answers are available as well. The good Stoic, while regarding any particular case with detachment, may have a strong commitment to ideals that allow the case to nevertheless be treated as urgent. The best doctors care intensely about their patients and will fight hard to help any one of them. They do give it their all. But those same doctors tend not to get emotional about it, and are able to move on from any individual failure quickly enough. (They have to.) This approximate mindset, with its combination of commitment and detachment, is one way to think about the balance to which Stoics aspire more generally. We will come back to this line of thought in Chapter 13.

13. *Grief.* The greatest challenge to the Stoic approach to emotion has probably been the unavoidability of grief over a loss. A fairly uncompromising view of the subject is suggested in the accounts of the early Stoics given by later authors. Seneca's view of grief is more measured. He acknowledges that no one can avoid grieving on some occasions, and he does not describe this as a mistake. He claims, rather, that natural grief creates a risk of excess when we feed it and urge it on with our thoughts.

a. *Grief and opinion.*

"But surely to grieve for one's relatives is natural." Who denies it – so long as it is in proper measure? Merely the parting, let alone the loss of those dearest to us, brings an unavoidable sting and a tightness even to the stoutest heart. But expectation adds something more to our grief than nature has commanded.

Seneca, *Consolation to Marcia* 7.1

When the news of a bitter death first hits us – when we are holding the body that is about to pass from our embrace into the flames – a natural compulsion wrings out our tears; the breath of life, struck by the blow of grief, shakes the whole body and likewise the eyes, from which it presses out and discharges the adjoining moisture. Such tears, being forced out, fall against our will. Tears of a different kind escape when we recall the memory of those we have lost: these we allow, but the former overcome us.

Seneca, *Epistles* 99.18–19

What we teach is honorable: that when emotion has wrung some tears from us and has, so to speak, stopped frothing, the mind is not to be given over to grief.

Seneca, *Epistles* 99.27

Seneca was careful to distinguish his position from others that he considered less reasonable. He was probably talking here about other Stoics:

I well know that there are those whose wisdom is harsh rather than brave, who deny that the wise man will ever grieve. But these people, it seems to me, can never have run into this sort of misfortune; if they had, Fortune would have knocked their proud philosophy out of them and forced them to admit the truth even against their will. Reason will have accomplished enough if it

Seneca, *Consolation to Polybius* 18.5–6

removes from grief only what is both excessive and superfluous; that reason should not allow grief to exist at all is neither to be hoped nor desired. Rather let reason establish a measure that will copy neither indifference nor madness, and will keep us in the state that is the mark of an affectionate, and not an unbalanced, mind. Let your tears flow, but let them also cease; let deepest sighs be drawn from your breast, but let those, too, come to an end; so rule your mind that you can win approval both from wise men and from brothers.

Seneca's writing on these themes was informed by experience. When he was in his forties, he had a son who died early. The passage just shown appears to have been written a few years later.

b. *Grief and mastery.* Seneca offered views on the process of overcoming grief. He thought it was appropriate to have the feeling for a while, to reckon with it, and then to reason it to the ground. This is preferable to dealing with grief by distracting ourselves or just waiting until it wears off.

Seneca, *Consolation to Helvia* 16.1

When you have lost one of those dearest to you, to suffer endless grief is foolish indulgence; to suffer none, inhuman hardness. The best middle course between devotion and reason is to feel a sense of loss and to subdue it.

Seneca, *Consolation to Helvia* 17.1–2

No emotion is governable, least of all that which is born of grief; it is wild and stubbornly resists every remedy. Sometimes we want to conceal it and to choke back our sobs, yet tears pour down the face despite its assumed composure. Sometimes we occupy the mind with games or gladiators; but amid the very sights meant to divert it, some slight reminder of grief makes the mind

break down. Therefore it is better to conquer sorrow than to trick it; for sorrow that has been
deceived, and diverted by pleasures and engage-
ments, rises again and from this very respite gath-
ers strength for its raging. But the grief that has
yielded to reason is settled forever.

I know that what I am about to add is very trite, but   Seneca, *Epistles* 63.12
I am not going to omit it just because everyone
says it. If grief is not brought to an end by the use
of your judgment, it is brought to an end by the
passage of time. Yet the basest remedy for grief, for
a person of sense, is to become tired of it. I would
rather you abandon your grief than have your grief
abandon you. You should stop doing soon that
which, even if you wish, you cannot do for long.

c. *Grief and futility.* The Stoics speak of conquering
grief with reason. Some of the reasoning they offer for
the purpose is found in Chapter 4 of this book (on death),
but they also offer ideas specifically about grief and its
reduction. One of them is that grief does no good for its
subject, nor perhaps for anyone else.

Does Panthea or Pergamus now sit by the tomb of   Marcus Aurelius, *Meditations*
Verus? Does Chaurias or Diotimus sit by the tomb   8.37
of Hadrian? Ridiculous. Well, suppose they did sit
there, would the dead be aware of it? And if the
dead were aware of it, would they be pleased?

Passages like this make their point whether or not one
knows who the author is talking about, but nevertheless:
Verus was the adoptive brother of Marcus Aurelius, and
they were co-emperors until Verus died in 169. Panthea
was Verus's mistress. Hadrian was an earlier emperor –
one of those known as the "Five Good Emperors," along
with Marcus Aurelius himself. The others he mentions
are unknown.

Seneca, *Consolation to Polybius*
2.1

And it will help you, too, not a little if you reflect that your grief can accomplish nothing either for the one whose loss you mourn or for yourself; for you will not want to prolong what is useless.

Seneca, *Consolation to Polybius*
5.1–2

No one is less pleased by your grief than the person to whom it seems to be offered. Either he does not want you to suffer, or he does not know that you do. So your supposed duty has no point. If he for whom it is performed is unaware of it, it is useless; if he is aware of it, he does not like it. I may say boldly that there is no one in the whole wide world who takes the slightest pleasure in your tears.

Cicero, *Tusculan Disputations*
3.27

Is there anything more effective in overcoming sorrow than realizing that it does no good and is pointless to take up?

d. *Grief and memory.* The Stoic also finds solace for grief in memories, which Seneca regards as things with an ongoing existence. Memories live securely in the world of all that has been, which need not be so different as existing in the present. They can have much value to us.

Seneca, *Epistles* 99.4–5

Believe me, a great part of those we have loved remains with us, even if some accident has taken them away. Bygone time belongs to us; nor is anything stored more securely than what has been. We are ungrateful for what we have already received because of our hope for what is yet to be – as if whatever is to be, if it comes to us at all, will not quickly pass over to what has already been.

Seneca, *Epistles* 63.6–7

If we believe our friend Attalus, "Thinking of friends who are alive and well is like enjoying honey and cake; the remembrance of friends who have died delights us, but with a certain bitterness. Yet who will deny that sour things, with a touch of sharpness, can also whet the appetite?" I don't agree: thinking of my deceased friends is sweet and pleasant to me. I had them as if I was going to lose them; I have lost them as if I have them still.

For more on the Stoic treatment of memory, see Chapter 8, Section 2.

14. *Limitations.* This chapter has sought to present the late Stoic teachings on emotion in a practical way. But I want to end by briefly noting some complexities that this discussion has avoided and that some readers may wish to pursue separately.

The early (Greek) Stoics took a hardline view of emotion along the lines discussed in section 8 of this chapter. They held that every emotion amounts to a judgment. A person experiencing an emotion is agreeing to a proposition (such as "this is something to be enraged about"), and the agreement is a mistake, because it involves attachment to an external: namely, whatever the object of the emotion might be. Seneca relaxed that approach a bit, as we have seen, but the basic idea is still present in all forms of Stoicism. It is a theory, especially in its strict form, that has been criticized on many grounds. Infants and animals seem to be capable of anger and fear, for example, but the Greek Stoic view makes it hard to understand how such creatures could have any emotions at all; for they lack the mental capacity to form propositions or assent to them. There have then been efforts to save the Stoic theory from this problem by revising it a bit. The late Stoics, at least, knew that the judgments we hold can be ingrained and nonverbal, as noted in Chapter 1. Maybe animals and infants, too, can be viewed as making nonverbal evaluations of events that produce their emotions.

The analysis of these and related questions by modern philosophers has been extensive and complex. And the thinking of the Greek Stoics about emotion is itself quite involved. It includes an elaborate taxonomy of the emotions and claims about where they each come from. None of that can be done justice in this space. But those who wish to pursue these avenues of Stoic theory can start by consulting the recent scholarly work of Martha Nussbaum and Margaret Graver, which discusses it all in detail.

Chapter Ten

ADVERSITY

Stoics avoid adversity in the ways that anyone of sense would. But sometimes it comes regardless, and then the Stoic goal is to see adversity rightly and not let one's peace of mind be destroyed by its arrival. Indeed, the aim of the Stoic is something more: to accept reversal without shock and to make it grist for the creation of greater things. Nobody wants hardship in any particular case, but it is a necessary element in the formation of worthy people and worthy achievements that, in the long run, we do want. Stoics seek the value in whatever happens.

Adversity resembles death in this respect: it is both an external that we misjudge and a resource that might be put to use. On a Stoic view, we don't like adversity – that's mostly what it means for something to *be* adversity – for the same reason that we misjudge many other externals: we view them with psychological parochialism, defining size and value and better and worse in terms of our immediate wishes and convenience. Stepping away from the wishes and convenience allows adversity to be seen as it is – as often less monstrous than it looks when it first comes, as sometimes producing important benefits, and in any event as inevitable.

Stoicism offers a series of strategies for turning adversity to good. We cannot choose what happens to us, but we can choose how to react to it. So when a setback comes, Stoics interpret it as constructively as possible – as a chance to prove oneself, or to learn, or to build anew; and the value of any of these responses may be greater than the cost of the adversity. Stoics also have a modest opinion of their ability to predict future events, so they are slow to assume that an apparently unwelcome development will be for the worse in the long run. Finally, the Stoics have techniques for reducing the force of adversity by thinking in certain ways about it: looking at their own adversity from another's point of view, anticipating it in advance, and understanding how acceptance of it, and adaptation to it, can help with its management.

1. *Preferences.* Since their philosophy has sometimes been misinterpreted on this point, we might begin by noting that the Stoics, while unafraid of adversity and ready to turn it to good use, prefer to avoid it.

Seneca, *Epistles* 85.26

"On your view," he says, "a brave man will expose himself to dangers." Not at all: he will not fear them, but he will avoid them. Caution suits him, not fear.

Seneca, *Epistles* 67.4

Why wouldn't I prefer that war not break out? But if it should come, my hope is to nobly bear the wounds, the starvation, and all else that it must bring with it. I am not so mad as to want to be ill; but if I must be ill, my hope is that I do nothing immoderate or weak. It is not hardships that are desirable, but the courage by which to endure them.

Montaigne, *Of Constancy* (1580)

All honorable means of protecting ourselves from harm are not only permitted but commendable. The chief function of constancy is to patiently endure those hardships that cannot be avoided.

The same goes for difficult people, encounters with whom may be considered a type of adversity. We can avoid them with dignity and without hatred or fear.

Marcus Aurelius, *Meditations* 6.20

Suppose someone in the ring has scratched you with his fingernails and butt you with his head, thus causing you some hurt. We don't mark him down as bad, we don't take offense, we don't suspect him later of plotting against us. We are merely on our guard – not treating him as an enemy or with suspicion, but with friendly avoidance. Something like this should be the rule in other parts of life. Let us disregard many things in those who are, as it were, our sparring-partners. For as I have said, it is possible to avoid them – without being suspicious, and without being hateful.

The friendly avoidance recommended by Marcus Aurelius is not high on the list of theoretical innovations made by the Stoics, but it rates well if one measures a teaching by how often it is of use.

2. *Inevitability*. The Stoic regards adversity as inseparable from existence, and so as best met with an accepting spirit.

> The condition of life is that of a bathhouse, a crowd, a journey: some things are thrown at you, others just happen by accident. Life is not a dainty affair. You have started on a long road; inevitably you will stumble, you will knock into things, you will fall, you will grow weary, you will cry out "O, for Death!" – in other words, you will tell lies. You will forsake a companion in one place; you will bury one in another; elsewhere you will be afraid of one. It is through troubles of that sort that this rugged journey must be made.

Seneca, *Epistles* 107.2

Marcus Aurelius used a different analogy – a comparison between the mind that receives adversity and other parts of the body that accept and process what comes to them.

> A healthy eye should see all there is to see, not say "I want to see green things" – for that is a sign that the eyes are diseased. And healthy hearing and a healthy sense of smell should be ready for all that there is to be heard and smelled.... So, too, a healthy mind should be ready for whatever may

Marcus Aurelius, *Meditations* 10.35

come to pass. The mind that says, "Let my children be safe," and "Let everyone praise whatever I may do," is an eye that seeks green things, or teeth that seek out only what is tender.

Montaigne offered yet another comparison: the variety of things that we experience, welcome and not, may be likened to the elements of music.

Montaigne, *Of Experience*
(1580)

We must learn to put up with what we cannot avoid. Our life, like the harmony of the world, is composed of contrary things – of diverse tones, sweet and harsh, sharp and flat, sprightly and solemn. The musician who only loved some of them – what would he be able to do? He has to know how to make use of them all, and be able to mix them together. We must do the same with the good and the bad, which are of the same substance as our lives.

These views of adversity – as an unavoidable part of life, and inseparable from the good – have some other implications for how we think and talk. For one, Stoics don't see the point of complaining about things that are inherent to human existence. Here we find the closest that philosophical Stoicism comes to the modern meaning of that word.

Marcus Aurelius, *Meditations*
8.50

"This cucumber is bitter." Throw it away. "There are brambles in the road." Turn aside. That's enough. Don't go on to say, "Why are there such things in the world?" You would be ridiculed by any student of nature, just as you would be laughed at by the carpenter and the shoemaker if you criticized them because you saw shavings and trimmings from the things that they make in their workshops.

Seneca, *On the Happy Life*
15.6–7

What madness to be dragged when one could follow! As much, I swear, as it is folly and ignorance of one's lot to grieve because you lack something, or because something affects you adversely, or to be surprised and indignant at those things that happen to the good and the bad alike – I mean deaths, funerals, infirmities, and all the other accidents besetting human life. Whatever the ways of the universe may require us to suffer, let us take it up with high-mindedness. This is the oath by which we are bound: to bear with the human condition, and not to be disturbed by what we do not have the power to avoid.

Nor are Stoics much interested in blame.

> It is the act of an ill-instructed man to blame others for his own bad condition; it is the act of one who has begun to be instructed, to lay the blame on himself; and of one whose instruction is complete to blame neither another nor himself.

Epictetus, *Enchiridion* 5

Stoics think the ills that come with life should be accepted by considering their potential in advance – before they happen to anyone in particular. They are, after all, potential hazards faced by everyone. We do not encounter the same misfortunes, but we often are equal in the risks to which we are subject as mortals.

> Let us not wonder at any of those misfortunes to which we are born, and which no one should complain of, because they are the same for all. The same, I say: for even what a man has escaped, he *might* have suffered. An equal law, indeed, is not one that all experience, but one that is established for all. Let your mind treat this sense of equity as a rule, and let us pay without complaint the taxes that come with mortality.

Seneca, *Epistles* 107.6

> It is unjust to complain that what may happen to anyone has happened to someone.

Montaigne, *Of Experience* (1580)

But the response of the Stoics to adversity involves more than a lack of blame and complaint. They seek to meet whatever they can't avoid with a welcoming spirit.

Seneca, *Epistles* 107.9–10

Whatever happens, let your mind suppose it was bound to happen, and do not rail at nature.

Epictetus, *Enchiridion* 8

Don't insist that what happens should happen as you wish; wish that things happen as they actually happen. Then your life will go well.

Friedrich Nietzsche was not a Stoic, but his notion of *amor fati* ("love of one's fate") has often been associated with the idea just shown from Epictetus.

Nietzsche, *Ecce Homo* (1888)

My formula for greatness in man is *amor fati*: the fact that a man wishes nothing to be different, either in front of him or behind him, or for all eternity. Not only must the necessary be borne, and on no account concealed – all idealism is falsehood in the face of necessity – but it must also be loved.

3. *Hermes' magic wand.* Stoics view adversity, or developments contrary to one's wishes, as misjudged in various ways we can now consider. Adversity is a raw material needed for building strong things. To adjust the comparison: an unwanted card has been dealt, or the dice have come up a certain way; the Stoic goal is to avoid even the feeling of "oh, no" wherever possible on these occasions, and to replace it with sentiments closer to "now what?" or "let's see what can be done with this." The work of life is to turn whatever happens to constructive ends. That is the most important Stoic idea about adversity, and a theme to which all of its authors contribute, often with metaphors. Epictetus adapted for Stoic use the caduceus, or wand, that Hermes was said to use to perform feats of magic. But the alchemy the Stoic has in mind turns adversity into advantage.

This is Hermes' magic wand: touch it to anything you like, they say, and the wand will turn it to gold. Not so; bring anything you like, rather, and I'll make it something good. Bring disease, bring death, bring poverty, bring insults, bring punishment for high crimes – all these things will be made beneficial by Hermes' magic wand.

Epictetus, *Discourses* 3.20.12

The obstacle in the path:

The mind turns around every hindrance to its activity and converts it to further its purpose. The impediment to action becomes part of the action; the obstacle in our way becomes the way forward.

Marcus Aurelius, *Meditations* 5.20

The fire that consumes setbacks and burns more strongly:

The power within that rules us, when it is aligned with nature, is so made as to adapt itself easily to whatever happens and to whatever is possible. It needs no particular material; it advances its purpose as circumstance allows. Whatever is placed in its way it makes into material for itself, as when fire overcomes the things that are thrown onto it, by which a little flame would have been put out; the strong fire quickly appropriates and consumes anything heaped on top, and from this the flames rise still higher.

Marcus Aurelius, *Meditations* 4.1

The sculptor who works with whatever materials are at hand:

Do you think that the wise man is burdened by evils? He makes use of them. It was not only from ivory that Phidias knew how to make statues; he made them also from bronze. If you had given him marble, or some still lesser material, he would have carved the best statue that could be made of it. So the wise man will display virtue amid riches if possible, but if not, in poverty; at home if he

Seneca, *Epistles* 85.40

can, but if not, in exile; as a general if he can, but if not, as a soldier; in sound health if he can, but if not, then in weakness. Whatever fortune he is dealt, he will make of it something remarkable.

The animal tamer:

Seneca, *Epistles* 85.41

There are some animal tamers who compel even the wildest beasts, and the most terrifying, to submit to man. Not satisfied with eliminating their ferocity, they pacify them to the point that they might be roommates. The lion-master puts his hand in the animal's mouth; the keeper kisses his tiger; the tiny Ethiopian commands the elephant to kneel down and walk the tightrope. In the same way, the sage is a skillful master of misfortune. Pain, want, disgrace, prison, exile are frightful anywhere – but when they come to the wise man, they are tamed.

Bees:

Plutarch, *On Tranquility of Mind* 5 (467b–467c)

Those who are without skill and sense as to how they should live, like sick people whose bodies can endure neither heat nor cold, are elated by good fortune and depressed by adversity; and they are greatly disturbed by both, or rather by themselves in both, and not less in those circumstances called good.... But men of sense, just as bees extract honey from thyme, the most pungent and the driest of plants, often in like manner draw from the most unfavorable circumstances something which suits them and is useful.

More literal expressions of the point are of course possible as well.

Plutarch, *On Virtue and Vice* 4 (101d–e)

By the aid of philosophy you will live not unpleasantly, for you will learn to extract pleasure from all places and things. Wealth will make you happy, because it will enable you to benefit many; and poverty, as you will then have few things to worry about; and glory, as it will make you honored; and obscurity, for you will then be safe from envy.

Seneca also notes the value of humor, a recurrent and underappreciated Stoic theme. Sometimes the force of unwanted events can be turned to good by viewing them with a sense of comedy.

> In any sort of life you will find amusements, recreations and pleasures, if you are willing to make light of evils rather than treat them as hateful.

Seneca, *On Tranquility of Mind* 10.1

4. *Equipment.* The Stoics consider us equipped to manage whatever adversity life may devise for us.

> Nothing happens to anyone that he is not formed by nature to bear.

Marcus Aurelius, *Meditations* 5.18

> Nature did not want us to be harassed. Whatever it requires of us, it has equipped us for.

Seneca, *Epistles* 90.16

> Whatever happens to you, remember to turn to yourself and ask what power you have for dealing with it. If you see a good-looking boy or woman, you'll find that the power for such things is self-control; if hard labor is at hand, you will find endurance; if abusive language, you will find patience. And if you make this a habit, the appearances of things will not carry you away with them.

Epictetus, *Enchiridion* 10

5. *Adversity as proving ground.* Turning to more specific ways in which adversity may be converted to good: it may be a chance to prove oneself. Setbacks show what we are really capable of doing.

> Fire tests gold, misfortune brave men.

Seneca, *On Providence* 5.10

Seneca's way of expressing this idea – *ignis aurum probat, miseria fortes viros* – became well known, but the substance of it was a proverb of long standing. It appears also in Ecclus. 2:5, part of the Biblical Apocrypha.

Seneca, *Epistles* 67.14

In this connection our friend Demetrius comes to mind. An untroubled life, in which fortune makes no inroads, he calls "a dead sea." To have nothing to stir you and rouse you to action, no attack by which to try the strength of your spirit, merely to lie in unshaken idleness – this is not to be tranquil; it is to be stranded in a windless calm.

In *De Bello Gallico*, Cæsar had once turned the phrase "malacia ac tranquillitas" (describing the sea); it meant "dead calm and stillness." Seneca played on this by saying, at the end of this last passage, "this is not *tranquillitas*, this is *malacia*." "Malacia" also had the meaning in Greek of moral softness. As for Demetrius, he was a Cynic philosopher and a friend of Seneca's. There was no windless calm for him; he was banished from Rome with other philosophers in 71 AD.

Another analogy: we should welcome adversity in the same way we welcome an adversary in a game.

Seneca, *On Providence* 2.4

Without an adversary, virtue shrivels. We see how great and how powerful it really is, only when it shows by endurance what it is capable of. Be assured that good men should act likewise; they should not shrink from hardships and difficulties, nor complain against fate; we should make the best of whatever happens and turn it to good.

Seneca, *On Providence* 4.2–3

You are a great man; but how do I know it if fortune gives you no opportunity to show your worth? You have entered the Olympic games, but you are the only contestant; you gain the crown, not the victory. I congratulate you not as a brave man, but as I would someone who had obtained a consulship or prætorship: "You're getting quite famous!" Likewise I might say to a good man, if no harder circumstance has given him the chance to show his strength of mind, "I judge you unfortunate because you have never been unfortunate: You have passed through life without an antagonist; no one will know what you can do, not even you yourself."

To strive with difficulties, and to conquer them, is the highest human felicity; the next is, to strive, and deserve to conquer: but he whose life has passed without a contest, and who can boast neither success nor merit, can survey himself only as a useless filler of existence; and if he is content with his own character, must owe his satisfaction to insensibility.

Johnson, *The Adventurer* no. III (1753)

6. *Adversity as training.* Adversity may be viewed as training, or as a chance to learn. No one is likely to accomplish anything great who doesn't know how to work with setbacks. So the Stoic thinks we need to gain a certain ease about them – an ability to adapt. A misfortune can be viewed as part of that learning process.

It is the crisis that reveals the man. So when it arrives, remember that God, like a wrestling coach, has put you up against a rough young antagonist. Why, you ask? So that you can be an Olympic champion; for this cannot be achieved without sweat.

Epictetus, *Discourses* 1.24.1–2

We should offer ourselves to Fortune so that, by our struggles with it, we may be hardened against it. Fortune will gradually make us an even match for itself. Constant contending with danger will instill a contempt for danger. In the same way the bodies of sailors are hardened by the beating of the sea, the hands of farmers are calloused, the arms of soldiers have the strength to throw their weapons, and the legs of a runner are nimble: we are strongest in what we have exercised. It is by

Seneca, *On Providence* 4.12–13

suffering ills that the mind learns defiance of suffering.

Schopenhauer, *Worldly Fortune* (1851)

We may regard the petty vexations of life that are constantly happening as designed to keep us in practice for bearing great misfortunes, so that we may not become completely enervated by a career of prosperity.

7. *Adversity as privilege.* Or adversity may be viewed as a kind of honor or good fortune because only some would be asked or able to rise to the occasion.

Seneca, *On Providence* 5.4

Toil summons the best men. The senate is often kept in session the whole day long, though all the while every worthless fellow is either enjoying his leisure at the recreation-ground, or lurking in a tavern, or wasting his time in some gathering. The same thing happens in the world at large. Good men work, spend and are spent, and they do so willingly. Fortune does not drag them; they follow it, and keep step.

Marcus Aurelius, *Meditations* 4.49

"How unfortunate I am, that this has happened to me!" Not at all – rather, "How fortunate I am, that although this has happened to me I am still unhurt, neither broken by the present nor dreading what is to come." For something of this sort might have happened to anyone, but not everyone would remain unhurt in spite of it.... Remember then, on each occasion that might lead you to grief, to make use of this idea: "This is no misfortune; to bear it nobly, rather, is good fortune."

8. *Humility in judgment.* The Stoic does not easily conclude that any apparent reversal must be for the worse. Even apart from the methods just described for turning adversity into good, it is hard to tell where an apparently bad thing will lead. Events that seem terrible when they happen sometimes result in greater things later. This

may be because the process of recovery produces a result that surpasses whatever was destroyed. Or it may be because the later events lead, even fortuitously, to a new and better result in some way that was hard to foresee. The general point: we usually take a short-term view of developments we don't like, and are poor judges of what their ultimate consequences will be. Events that look bad should therefore be judged with humility and calm.

A man may be wise, he may do everything with precise judgment, he may attempt nothing beyond his powers ... none of these desirable and precious things is of any use, unless you prepare yourself against the accidents of fate and their consequences, unless frequently and uncomplainingly and at every injury you will say, "the gods decreed otherwise!" Nay, by heaven! – let's try for a braver, truer note, and one by which you may better sustain your spirit – say this, every time something happens otherwise than as you expected: "the gods decreed better!"

Seneca, Epistles 98:3–5

Destruction has often made room for greater prosperity. Many things have fallen in order that they might rise higher. Timagenes, no friend to the city's happiness, used to say that fires at Rome troubled him for one reason only: he knew that better buildings would rise in place of those that had burned.

Seneca, Epistles 91.13

Timagenes was a Greek teacher of rhetoric who was captured and made a slave by the Romans, then later set free. He evidently found himself in conflict with Augustus, which caused him to flee Rome.

If you decide to try above all to have what is best for you, don't be annoyed at difficult circumstances, but consider how many things have already happened to you in life, not as you wanted, but as was best for you.

Musonius Rufus, Fragment 27

Plutarch had a funny way of expressing this.

Plutarch, *On Tranquility of Mind* 6 (467c)

This then we should practice and work on first of all – like the man who threw a stone at his dog but missed and hit his stepmother. "Not so bad!" he said. For it is possible to change what we get out of things that do not go as we wish. Diogenes was driven into exile: "Not so bad!" – for it was after his banishment that he took up philosophy.

9. *Point of view.* As we have seen elsewhere, much of Stoicism amounts to the art of perspective – that is, of finding the most useful point of view from which to look at anything that happens. The Stoic learns to see things from angles more helpful than the self-centered one that we are prone to use without reflection. As another example, Stoics respond to their own adversities by asking what they think when the same things happen to others.

Epictetus, *Enchiridion* 26

If your neighbor's slave has broken his wine cup, it is common to say right away that "These things happen." When your own cup is broken, your reaction should obviously be the same as when the neighbor's cup was broken. Apply the same idea to more important things. Someone else's child has died, or his wife: there is no one who wouldn't say, "This is our human lot." Yet when someone's own child dies, right away it's "Woe to me, how wretched I am!" We have to remember how we feel when we hear the same thing about others.

du Vair, *The Moral Philosophy of the Stoics* (1585)

Remember how you judged similar mishaps when they happened to others, and consider how you were hardly moved, and even blamed them and brushed aside their complaints.... The opinions we have of another man's cause are always more just than those that we have of our own.

Smith's interpretation of the Stoic view:

We should view ourselves, not in the light in which our own selfish passions are apt to place us, but in the light in which any other citizen of the world would view us. What befalls ourselves we should regard as what befalls our neighbor, or, what comes to the same thing, as our neighbor regards what befalls us.

Smith, *The Theory of Moral Sentiments* (1759)

10. *Anticipation.* The Stoics recommend that we think ahead about adversity. Anticipating it can take away its terrors and reduce its force when it arrives.

The wise man gets used to future evils: what other men make bearable by long endurance, he makes bearable by long reflection. We sometimes hear the inexperienced say, "I didn't know this was in store for me." The wise man knows that everything is in store for him. Whatever happens, he says, "I knew."

Seneca, *Epistles* 76.34

Other translations render the last phrase as "I knew it." In the original, it's just one word – *sciebam* (I knew) – and leaving it as shown seems to me better. But the reader might enjoy making the choice.

"What can happen to one can happen to any." If a man will let this sink into his inmost heart, and if he will look on all the evils besetting other people, of which there is daily an immense supply, in this light – as if there is nothing to stop them from finding him, too – he will arm himself long before he is attacked. It is too late to equip the mind for the endurance of dangers after the dangers have come.

Seneca, *On Tranquility of Mind* 11:8–9

Military analogies:

In days of peace the soldier performs maneuvers, throws up earthworks with no enemy in sight, and is wearied by unnecessary toil, in order that

Seneca, *Epistles* 18.6

he may be equal to that which is necessary. If you would not have a man flinch when the crisis comes, train him before it comes. Such is the course those men have followed who, in their imitation of poverty, have every month left themselves almost destitute, that they might never recoil from what they had often rehearsed.

Montaigne, *Of Solitude* (1580)

It is enough for me, when favored by fortune, to prepare myself for its disfavor; and while I am at ease, and so far as my imagination can stretch, to picture future evils to come – just as we use jousting and tournaments to accustom ourselves to war and imitate it in times of peace.

A famous anecdote of Anaxagoras was told by both Plutarch and Cicero.

Plutarch, *On Tranquility of Mind* 16 (474d–474f)

It is possible not only to admire the disposition of Anaxagoras, which made him say at the death of his son, "I knew that he was mortal when I got him," but also to imitate it and to apply it to all that fortune may bring: "I know that my wealth is ephemeral and insecure," "I know that those who gave me power can take it away," "I know my wife is excellent, but a woman, and that my friend is but a man, and by nature a changeable being, as Plato said." Those who are prepared and have dispositions of this sort, when something unwanted but not unexpected happens, refuse to accept the "I would never have supposed," the "I had hoped for other things," and the "I never expected this." They do away with the beatings and poundings of their hearts, as it were, and quiet down the madness and disturbance of their minds.

Anaxagoras was a pre-Socratic Greek philosopher, said to be the first to bring philosophy to Athens. Cicero, after telling the same story, comments:

There is no doubt but that all those things which are considered evils are the heavier from not being foreseen.... The excellence and divine nature of wisdom consists in taking a near view of, and gaining a thorough acquaintance with, all human affairs, in not being surprised when anything happens, and in thinking that there is no event that has not happened that may not happen.

Cicero, *Tusculan Disputations* 3.14

Schopenhauer offered a theory to explain why foresight helps to blunt misfortune.

The main reason why misfortune falls less heavily upon us, if we have looked upon its occurrence as not impossible, and, as the saying is, prepared ourselves for it, may be this: if, before this misfortune comes, we have quietly thought over it as something which may or may not happen, the whole of its extent and range is known to us.... But if no preparation has been made to meet it, and it comes unexpectedly, the mind is in a state of terror for the moment and unable to measure the full extent of the calamity; it seems so far-reaching in its effects that the victim might well think there was no limit to them; in any case, its range is exaggerated. In the same way, darkness and uncertainty always increase the sense of danger.

Schopenhauer, *Worldly Fortune* (1851)

The Stoic advice to anticipate misfortune may seem in conflict with the Stoic advice to avoid worrying about the future (see Chapter 9, Section 4). The advice is best reconciled by holding that the rehearsals recommended above do not entail *worry*. Just as Seneca recommends savoring good memories and not rehashing bad ones, the Stoics encourage the rehearsal of future evils but not anxiety about them.

Schopenhauer also had a supplementary recommendation: not just to imagine what might be coming, but to imagine that it already came.

Schopenhauer, *Our Relation to Ourselves* (1851)

There is some use in occasionally looking upon terrible misfortunes – such as might happen to us – as though they had actually happened, for then the trivial reverses which subsequently come in reality, are much easier to bear. It is a source of consolation to look back upon those great misfortunes which never happened.

11. *Pain and opinion.* The Stoics know that some kinds of distress can't be entirely dissolved by how we think about them, but they say that our reactions are still strongly affected by our judgments – by the ways we talk to ourselves or are conditioned to respond. Pain is the most obvious example. You can't reason your way out of the sensation of it. But the Stoics think that our minds still have much to do with how the sensation is experienced and how it affects us.

Seneca, *Epistles* 78.12–13

Don't make your ills worse for yourself and burden yourself with complaints. Pain is slight if opinion adds nothing to it. If, on the contrary, you start to encourage yourself and say, "It's nothing, or certainly very little; let's hold out, it will soon leave off" – then in thinking it slight you will make it so.

Marcus Aurelius, *Meditations* 7.64

For most pains, let this remark of Epicurus also come to your rescue – that pain is neither unbearable nor eternal if you consider its limits, and don't add to it in your imagination.

Montaigne, *That the Taste of Good and Evil Things Depends in Large Part on the Opinion We Have of Them* (1580)

I willingly grant that pain is the worst hardship of our existence; I am the man on earth who most hates pain and avoids it, probably because I am so unaccustomed to it, thank God. Still, it is up to us, if not to eliminate pain, then at least to lessen it with patience – and, even if the body is disturbed by it, to maintain our reason and our souls in sound condition.

Montaigne adds a little later: "It is with pain as with gemstones that look brighter or duller depending on the foil in which they are set; pain takes up only as much space as we allow to it." The reader interested in more on this theme can refer back to Chapter 1, Section 3.

12. *Adaptation.* The Stoic understands, finally, that acceptance of adversity is helped by time – another case of what we might now call adaptation, or the good and bad effects of familiarity, which the Stoics understand well. Adaptation isn't always beneficial. It can cause one to get used to bad things that ought to be fixed, or to good things that go unappreciated. (See Chapter 13, Section 1 for some more discussion.) But adaptation is unquestionably a great aid in making peace with adversities that cannot be helped. Most things that bother us when they arrive become more bearable once we are accustomed to them. The Stoic is mindful of this.

> To those with no experience of it, a large part of any evil is its novelty. You can see this in the fact that, after getting used to them, they bear more bravely the things they once had regarded as harsh.

Seneca, *Epistles* 76.34

> There is nothing for which nature deserves greater praise than this: knowing the hardships to which we were born, it invented habit as a salve to disasters; we quickly accustom ourselves to even the severest misfortunes. No one could withstand adversity if its persistence were felt with all the same force as its first blow.

Seneca, *On Tranquility of Mind* 10.2

Chapter Eleven

VIRTUE

Much of Stoicism involves stripping externals of illusion and gaining detachment from them. But of course Stoicism has an affirmative side as well, which many would regard as its most central and important idea: the pursuit of virtue. This topic could have come at the start of the book. It appears here instead because the Stoic meaning of virtue follows in part from lessons that by now we have considered. Virtue is the natural result of an accurate use of reason; reason is the distinct gift that sets humanity apart from animals, so the purpose of human life must be found there. Earlier chapters have shown us much of what reason means to the Stoics. For one thing – and most relevant here – it should cause us to accurately see our individual insignificance (a theme of Chapter 3); and from this we might infer our corresponding place in the world, which is to function faithfully as parts of a whole.

Stoics regard virtue as sufficient to produce happiness on all occasions, and also as necessary for it. The happiness centrally valued by the Stoic is *eudaimonia*, or well-being – the good life rather than the good mood. But the Stoic believes that virtue gives rise to joy and to peace of mind as well. Virtue produces these good consequences as side effects. The primary mission of the Stoics, in other words, is to be helpful to others and serve the greater good, and they don't do this to make themselves happy. They do it because it is the right and natural way to live. But doing it in that spirit, as it turns out, makes them happy.

The Stoics, as we have seen, have various ways of advancing their views and making them persuasive. They attempt to base their ideas about virtue mostly on logic; the Greeks in particular sought to establish their ethical conclusions by a coherent system of deductions. They held that nature commands us to live in obedience to reason and designed us to gravitate toward virtue. These often are viewed as among the less enduring arguments the Stoics made. That is partly because their view of nature as rational and providential is now shared by few. Critics have also complained of circularity in some of what the Stoics said. I don't propose to chase down those issues here, but will venture that the efforts of the Stoics to *prove* that we should pursue virtue, as they define it, are not likely to be compelling to anyone who is not already sympathetic to their claims.

And yet the Stoics' view of virtue is attractive in ways that can be separated from those doctrinal problems. Their belief about the relationship between virtue and happiness contains a good deal of psychological insight. Some states of mind are difficult to acquire directly; they come about only as byproducts of effort applied in other directions. Many have found that happiness is this way. Efforts to acquire it by direct pursuit don't work well; happiness has to be found while looking for something else. (This is a point often rediscovered in modern times with much fanfare.) The something else proposed by the Stoic consists primarily of a dedication to reason and a commitment to others – to service, to justice, to helping in the ways one can. These are appealing values to live by whether or not they are accompanied by a logical guarantee of their correctness. They also may be found a dependable path to happiness, or a more reliable one than any other. But recall that putting happiness aside just in order to find it later is cheating; happiness is not supposed to be the Stoic goal, not even covertly. The Stoic view, rather, is that one should embrace virtue for its own sake, and that doing so is necessary to get the good side effects of it. The interested reader can reflect and experiment.

This chapter, consistent with the rest of the book (and much as in Chapter 9, on emotion), does not attempt to set forth the theoretical framework and taxonomy of virtue that the early Stoics developed. It shows in outline form, rather, the applied teachings of the late Stoics on the meaning of virtue, the benefits of pursuing it, and the value and cultivation of a few virtues in particular: honesty, consistency, and kindness. We also will see the importance that the Stoics assign to involvement in public affairs and to being of service to others.

1. *Definitions.* The Stoics view virtue, first, as the use of sound reasoning and judgment.

Seneca, *Epistles* 66.32

Virtue is nothing else than right reason.

Seneca, *Epistles* 71.32

This may be taught quickly and in a few words. Virtue is the only good, or at least there is no good without virtue; virtue itself is situated in our nobler part, that is, the rational part. And what will this virtue be? True and steadfast judgment. From this will spring the impulses of the mind; by this, every external appearance that stirs such an impulse will be reduced to transparency.

Sound reasoning and judgment will in turn produce some specific qualities, or virtues, that the Stoic seeks, many of which have been discussed in earlier chapters.

Marcus Aurelius, *Meditations* 5.5

They're not going to admire you for your quick-wittedness. So be it! Still, there are many other qualities about which you don't have to say, "I just wasn't born with it." So show them those qualities that are entirely up to you: sincerity, dignity, endurance of hardship; not pleasure-seeking, not complaining of your lot, needing little; kindness and generosity; being modest, not chattering idly, but high-minded. Don't you see how many you could display immediately – having no excuse on

account of lack of natural capacity or aptitude –
yet you still willingly fall short?

Examples of the virtues that Marcus Aurelius valued can
also be found in thanks he gives to others, such as his
grateful entry about Claudius Maximus – a Roman consul, judge, and Stoic philosopher who had been one of
his teachers.

> From Maximus I learned self-government, and
> not to be led aside by anything; and cheerfulness
> in all circumstances, as well as in illness; and a just
> mixture in the moral character of sweetness and
> dignity, and to do what was set before me without
> complaining.... He had also the art of being
> humorous in an agreeable way.

Marcus Aurelius, *Meditations* 1.15

Seneca saw the value of studying the liberal arts, among
which he counted literature, music, and mathematics
(there is a note about this in Chapter 7, Section 5). But
he said they were all less important than philosophy
because none of them taught its students the meaning of
virtue. His exposition of the point provides an inventory
of many virtues valued by the Stoics.

> Bravery is a scorner of things which inspire fear; it
> looks down upon, challenges, and crushes the
> powers of terror and all that would drive our free-
> dom under the yoke.... Loyalty is the holiest good
> in the human heart; it is forced into betrayal by
> no constraint, and it is bribed by no rewards....
> Kindliness forbids you to be overbearing towards
> your associates, and it forbids you to be grasping.
> In words and in deeds and in feelings it shows
> itself gentle and courteous to all men.... Do "lib-
> eral studies" teach a man such character as this?
> No; no more than they teach simplicity, modera-
> tion, and self-restraint....

Seneca, *Epistles* 88.29–30

2. *Benefits of virtue.* Stoics regard virtue as the only source of true *eudaimonia*, a word that sometimes is translated as "happiness" but (as noted at the start of the chapter) means something closer to well-being or the good life. Virtue gives rise to it as a side effect, and brings about pleasure and joy as well.

Epictetus, *Discourses* 1.4.3

If virtue promises good fortune, peace of mind, and happiness, certainly also the progress toward virtue is progress toward each of these things.

Seneca, in turn, elaborated on the tranquility, or peace of mind, associated with virtue:

Seneca, *On Tranquility of Mind* 2.4

What we want to discover, then, is how the mind may always maintain an even and favorable course, may be well-disposed toward itself, may be happy in contemplating its own condition, and may have this happiness without interruption—how it can stay calmly in that position, never carrying itself off and never cast down. This will be peace of mind.

Seneca, *Epistles* 59.16

Here is the result of wisdom: a constant and unvarying kind of joy. The mind of the wise man is like the heavens beyond the moon: the sky up there is always clear.... This joy is produced only by a consciousness of the virtues.

Marcus Aurelius:

Marcus Aurelius, *Meditations* 8.1

You know from experience how far you have wandered without finding the good life anywhere: not in logic, not in wealth, not in fame, not in pleasure – nowhere. Where is it found, then? In doing what human nature wishes. How is that done? By having principles that govern your impulses and actions. What principles? Those concerned with what is good and evil – that there is nothing good for man except what makes him just, moderate, brave, and free, and nothing evil except that which produces the opposite.

The Stoics emphasize, though, that in their view virtue is not pursued for the sake of the good consequences it brings. Those consequences are welcome and prized, but nevertheless are incidental.

> "But you too cultivate virtue," he replies, "only because you hope to gain some pleasure from it." First of all, even though virtue will assure pleasure, it is not on account of pleasure that virtue is pursued. It is not pleasure that it assures, but pleasure as well; nor does virtue exert itself for pleasure, but its effort – though it aims at something else – achieves this too.... Thus pleasure is not the reward or cause of virtue, but the byproduct of it.

Seneca, *On the Happy Life* 9.1–2

Compare the general conclusion of John Stuart Mill, which he thought was an accurate account of how most people work.

> Those only are happy (I thought) who have their minds fixed on some object other than their own happiness; on the happiness of others, on the improvement of mankind, even on some art or pursuit, followed not as a means, but as itself an ideal end. Aiming thus at something else, they find happiness by the way.

Mill, *Autobiography* (1873)

Mill elsewhere described the writings of Marcus Aurelius as "the highest ethical product of the ancient mind."

3. *Honesty.* Various Stoic virtues, such as moderation, have been examined in other parts of the book. We now consider some that have not, beginning with honesty – not just speaking the truth, but living without hiding anything. On openness of action:

> When you have determined that something should be done and are doing it, do not hide it from others even if most of them will not approve. If it isn't the right thing to do, then don't do it; but if it is, why be afraid of those who will criticize you wrongly?

Epictetus, *Enchiridion* 35

Seneca, *Epistles* 43.3–4

Count yourself really happy when you are able to live in public, when your walls protect rather than hide you – though for the most part we regard our walls as around us not so that we may live more safely but so that we may sin more privately. I'll tell you a fact by which you can judge our conduct: you will scarcely find anyone who could live with his door open.

See also:

Epicurus, Vatican Sayings 70

Let nothing be done in your life that will cause you fear if it is discovered by your neighbor.

Montaigne, *Of Repentance* (1580)

It is a rare life that maintains its good order even in private. Everyone can play his role and act the honest man on the stage; but to be well-managed within, in his own breast, where everything is allowed and where everything is hidden – that is the point. The next closest thing is to be this way in your house, in your ordinary behavior, for which you are accountable to no one, and where there is nothing studied or artificial.

On openness of mind, or keeping to thoughts that one wouldn't be embarrassed to admit:

Marcus Aurelius, *Meditations* 3.4.2

A person should accustom himself to think only those things about which – if someone should suddenly ask, "What are you thinking about?" – he might answer this and that, frankly and without hesitation.

Seneca, *Epistles* 10.5

The madness of men these days! They whisper the most shameful prayers to the gods; if anyone is listening, they fall silent. What they don't want anyone to know, they tell to God! See if this wouldn't make a wholesome rule: Live among others as if God were watching; speak with God as if others were listening.

I have enjoined myself to dare to say all that I dare
to do; I am displeased even to have thoughts that
I would not publish. The worst of my actions and
qualities do not seem to me as vile as the vile cowardice of not daring to own them.

Montaigne, *Upon Some Verses
of Virgil* (1580)

4. *Consistency*. The Stoics had a test for virtue, and perhaps a shortcut to it: consistency. Consistency sounds
like a quality that has nothing to do with substance; it
might seem as easy to be consistently bad (or wrong) as
consistently virtuous. But consider the relationship
between consistency and the openness of thought and
action described in the previous section. True consistency would mean always thinking the same thing is
right and never deviating from it. It also would mean
acting and thinking the same way in all settings – in public, at home, and alone, never phony; for phoniness may
accurately enough be described not only as dishonesty
but as a form of inconsistency. Someone who managed
to be consistent in the senses just described would, the
Stoic suggests, inevitably be virtuous.

To abandon the old definitions of wisdom and
use one that covers the whole range of human life,
I can be content with this: What is wisdom? To
always want the same things and reject the same
things. No need to add that little qualification, "so
long as what you want is right" – since one could
not always be pleased with the same thing if it
were not right.

Seneca, *Epistles* 20.5

This is how a foolish mind is most clearly shown:
it appears now as one thing, now as another, and –
worst of all, in my opinion – it does not appear as
itself. Believe me, it is a great thing to act as just
one person.

Seneca, *Epistles* 120.19, 22

It is a hard matter, from all antiquity, to pick out a
dozen men who have formed their lives to one

Montaigne, *Of the Inconstancy
of Our Actions* (1580)

certain and constant course, which is the principal design of wisdom.

5. *Love, kindness, compassion.* These are underestimated themes in Stoicism and so are worth illustrating at some length. What follows will be instructive in its own right and also as something to show to those who think of Stoicism as a cold or sour thing. Marcus Aurelius:

Marcus Aurelius, *Meditations* 6.39

Adapt yourself to the circumstances you have drawn; and the men among whom your lot has fallen, love them, and truly.

Marcus Aurelius, *Meditations* 11.1.2

Further characteristics of the reasoning soul are love of its neighbors, truth, compassion, and valuing nothing above itself, which is also the property of law. Thus there is no difference between correct reasoning and just reasoning.

Marcus Aurelius, *Meditations* 11.18

Kindness is invincible, if it is genuine and not insincere or put on as an act.

Epictetus:

Epictetus, *Discourses* 3.2.4

I should not be unfeeling like a statue; I should care for my relationships both natural and acquired – as a pious man, a son, a brother, a father, a citizen.

Seneca:

Seneca, *On Anger* 1.5.3

Our common life is founded on kindness and harmony; it is bound in a compact of mutual assistance, not by fear, but by love of one another.

Seneca, *Epistles* 5.4

This is the first promise that philosophy holds out to us: fellow-feeling, humanity, sociability.

Seneca, *Epistles* 47.11

Treat your inferiors as you would be treated by your betters.

The translation of the passage just shown is attractive but liberal. The original shows more clearly that Seneca was thinking about how people live with their slaves.

Keep an eye on one man to avoid being hurt; on another, to avoid hurting him. Rejoice in the happiness of all, and sympathize with them in their misfortunes; remember what you should take upon yourself, and what you should guard against.

Seneca, *Epistles* 103.3

So long as we draw breath, so long as we live among humans, let us cherish humanity. Let us not cause fear to anyone, nor danger; let us rise above losses, outrages, conflicts, and taunts; let us bear our short-lived ills with magnanimity.

Seneca, *On Anger* 3.43.5

If we were able to examine the mind of a good man, what a beautiful sight we should see: how pure, how astonishing in its noble calm – bright with justice and strength, with moderation and wisdom. In addition to these, thrift and moderation and endurance, kindness and affability, even *humanity* – a quality, hard as this is to believe, rarely encountered in humans – would add their own brilliance.

Seneca, *Epistles* 115.3

Seneca, *On Mercy* 2.5.2–3

People object that the Stoic school does not allow the wise man to be compassionate or forgiving. These propositions are detestable on their face. They would seem to leave no hope for human failings, but to make all transgressions lead to retribution. And if that were so, what kind of theory is it that commands us to unlearn our humanity and blocks the mutual assistance that is our surest refuge from ill fortune? But in fact there is no school more kind and gentle, none more affectionate toward humanity, none more concerned with the common good, to the point that its avowed purpose is to be of service and assistance, to have regard not only for oneself but for each and for all.

We have seen Seneca and Marcus Aurelius refer to the value of compassion. That is a nuanced topic for the Stoics. Their philosophy calls for a felt sense that all of humanity are their relations. It also calls for help to those who need it. But the Stoic does not favor compassion in the different sense of feeling sorry for other people and making their sadness one's own – that is, becoming despondent because others are despondent. Seneca's position was that good Stoics will *do* all that would be done by anyone who feels pity for others, but that they will not feel the pity themselves; pity is considered a form of distress that serves no purpose and impairs good judgment.

Seneca, *On Mercy* 2.6.1–2

Sorrow is not suited to seeing things accurately, to understanding how to get things done, to avoiding dangers, or to knowing what is just. So the wise man will not indulge in pity, because there cannot be pity without mental suffering. All else that those who feel pity are inclined do, he will do gladly and with an elevated spirit; he will bring relief to another's tears, but will not add his own. To the shipwrecked man he will give a hand; he will give shelter to the exile, and charity to those in need.

In Chapter 13 we will see a similar sentiment from Epictetus. In the meantime, Montesquieu's conclusions:

Montesquieu, *The Spirit of Laws* (1748)

Never were any principles more worthy of human nature, and more proper to form the good man, than those of the Stoics; and if I could for a moment cease to think that I am a Christian, I should not be able to hinder myself from ranking the destruction of the sect of Zeno among the misfortunes that have befallen the human race.

It carried to excess only those things in which there is true greatness – the contempt of pleasure and of pain.

It was this sect alone that made citizens; this alone that made great men; this alone great emperors....

While the Stoics looked upon riches, human grandeur, grief, disquietudes, and pleasures as vanity, they were entirely employed in laboring for the happiness of mankind, and in exercising the duties of society. It seems as if they regarded that sacred spirit, which they believed to dwell within them, as a kind of favorable providence watchful over the human race.

Born for society, they all believed that it was their destiny to labor for it; with so much the less fatigue, their rewards were all within themselves. Happy by their philosophy alone, it seemed as if only the happiness of others could increase theirs.

6. *Interdependence and service.* The Stoic regards human lives as interdependent, and finds in this a source of duty, affection, and solace.

Nor can anyone live happily who has only himself in view, who turns everything to his own advantage; you ought to live for the other fellow, if you want to live for yourself.

Seneca, *Epistles* 48.2

Why should I list everything that is to be done and to be avoided, when I can give you the duties of mankind in a rule of few words? All this that you see, including both the divine and the human, is one: we are limbs of one body. Nature made us kin, since she gave birth to us from the same substance and to the same ends. She put into us love of one another and made us social beings. She constructed fairness and justice; according to her

Seneca, *Epistles* 95.51–53 (quoting Terence, *The Self-Tormentor*)

dispensation, it is more wretched to harm than to be harmed. In obedience to her command, let our hands be ready where help is needed. Let that famous line be in your heart and in your mouth: "I am human, I consider nothing human foreign to me." Let us hold things in common: that is how we are made. Our society is just like an archway of stones, which would fall if they did not block each other. It is held up in the same way.

Epictetus, *Discourses* 2.5.25–26

What are you? A man. If you look at yourself in isolation, it is natural to live to old age, to be rich, to be healthy. But if you look at yourself as one person and as part of a given whole, for the sake of the whole your turn may come to be sick, or to run risks on a sea voyage, or to be in need, perhaps to be put to death.

This interdependence has significance for how we live and spend our time. The Stoics understand themselves to have a duty of service to others, including a duty to participate in public life. Cicero's rendition of the Stoic view:

Cicero, *On the Ends of Good and Evil* 3.20

Since we see that man is designed by nature to safeguard and protect his fellows, it follows from this natural disposition that the wise man should desire to engage in politics and government, and also to live in accordance with nature by taking to himself a wife and desiring to have children with her. Even the passion of love when pure is not thought incompatible with the character of the Stoic sage.

Seneca had a pithier version of what is expected from the Stoics – those in the sect of Zeno, as Montesquieu called them.

Seneca, *On Leisure* 2.2

Epicurus says: "The sage will not engage in public affairs unless he must." Zeno says: "The sage will engage in public affairs unless he cannot."

That translation is, again, a bit free – this time to keep the two halves of it parallel, which is irresistible. But what is meant by "public affairs"? Not just politics, but helping others on whatever scale is available, large or small.

> It is of course required of a man that he should benefit his fellow-men – many if he can; if not, a few; if not a few, those who are nearest; if not these, himself. For when he renders himself useful to others, he engages in public affairs.

Seneca, *On Leisure* 3.5

The Stoics also take a broad view of what it means to benefit others. Philosophizing counts. And they have a broad understanding, too, of the relevant "others" they are bound to serve. They did not view those in their immediate communities or their country as the only ones who matter. Everyone does.

> When asked what country you are from, do not say "I am Athenian" or "I am from Corinth." Say (like Socrates), "I am a citizen of the world."

Epictetus, *Discourses* 1.9.1

> For what is a man? A part of a state – first, of one that consists of gods and of men; then of the state to which you more immediately belong, which is a miniature of the universal state.

Epictetus, *Discourses* 2.5.26

> Let us grasp that there are two commonwealths – the one, a vast and truly common state, which embraces alike gods and men, in which we look neither to this corner of earth nor to that, but measure the bounds of our citizenship by the path of the sun; the other, the one to which we have been assigned by the accident of birth.... Some yield service to both commonwealths at the same time – to the greater and to the lesser – some only to the lesser, some only to the greater.

Seneca, *On Leisure* 4.1

Chapter Twelve

LEARNING

Stoics are students not just of Stoic doctrine but of the process of learning how to practice it. They view the philosophy as an approach to daily life, not an intellectual edifice to be enjoyed from outside or visited from time to time. This chapter thus offers comments on what in the study of Stoicism is realistic and what isn't, what helps and what doesn't, and where to look for encouragement.

Stoicism offers some exercises for those trying to follow its advice – review of each day and where one made philosophical mistakes or did well; imagining oneself being watched by an idealized figure, and asking what the watcher would think and say; and meditating on the principles of Stoicism until they sink in. The Stoics also offer views about the value of solitude and of social life, comparing the ways that either can help or hinder progress in wisdom. Above all, they stress that progress in the philosophy is not made by knowing its precepts. It is made by assimilating them, and by thinking and acting accordingly.

Stoicism is, among other things, a regimen for training the mind. If that sounds too hard, the Stoic would say it is because we aren't used to taking that task as seriously as we take the training of the body. Everyone knows that the path to becoming an accomplished athlete involves time and commitment. So does progress in Stoicism. Its methods are especially challenging because the mind is the trainer as well as the thing trained. It has to teach itself to do better. The Stoic looks at things from a point of view that differs from the automatic one, and seeks to resist the conventional reaction to whatever may happen. This all requires steady attention and energy, but it also gets easier with time.

We might think of Stoicism, as Seneca will suggest, as the equivalent of a demanding martial art. It takes practice. In return, the philosophy offers improvement in peace of mind, in fearlessness, in well-being, and in wisdom.

1. *Review*. The Stoics offer many techniques for improving the quality of one's thinking. In other chapters we have seen some of them, such as changes in perspective or anticipation of the worst that might happen. But Stoicism also offers meta-techniques – that is, techniques for getting better at the techniques. One of them is to set philosophical goals and keep track of progress in reaching them.

> If you wish not to be quick to anger, don't feed your habit; don't throw it fodder on which to grow. As a first step, keep quiet, and count the days on which you didn't get angry. "I used to get angry every day, then every other day, then every third, then every fourth." If you can quit for thirty days, make a sacrifice to God. For the habit is loosened at first, then totally destroyed.

Epictetus, *Discourses* 2.18.12

A similar suggestion is nightly review of how the day went from a Stoic standpoint.

> The mind should be summoned every day to render an accounting. Sextius used to do this. At the end of the day, when he had withdrawn to his nightly rest, he would interrogate his own mind: "Which of your wrongs did you correct today? Which fault did you resist? In what way are you better?" Anger will leave off and be more moderate, if it knows that it must each day come before a judge. Is there anything finer than this habit of

Seneca, *On Anger* 3.36.1–3

searching through the entire day? ... When the light has been removed and my wife, long aware of my habit, has become silent, I scan the whole of my day and retrace all my deeds and words.

Sextius was a Roman teacher of Stoic and Pythagorean philosophy who lived a generation before Seneca did. He founded a school in Rome that was later run by his son – the School of the Sextii – and that lasted from about 50 BC to 19 AD. We gather from Seneca's letters that he attended the school when he was young (see Chapter 8, Section 3). Seneca kindly supplied a model of the daily accounting to oneself suggested above:

Seneca, *On Anger* 3.36.4

See that you don't do that again; I'll pardon you this time. In that discussion you spoke too aggressively. After this, don't get into arguments with ignorant people. If they've never learned, they don't want to learn. You criticized that one fellow more candidly than you should have; as a result you didn't correct him, you just offended him. From here on, watch out – not so much that what you're saying is true, but that the person you're talking to can stand the truth.

This recommendation of daily review is sometimes described as Pythagorean.

Schopenhauer, *Our Relation to Ourselves* (1851)

The advice here given is on a par with a rule recommended by Pythagoras – to review, every night before going to sleep, what we have done during the day. To live at random, in the hurly-burly of business or pleasure, without ever reflecting upon the past – to go on, as it were, pulling cotton off the reel of life – is to have no clear idea of what we are about; and a man who lives in this state will have chaos in his emotions and certain confusion in his thoughts; as is soon manifest by the abrupt and fragmentary character of his conversation, which becomes a kind of mincemeat.

And the Stoics also will engage in a reverse sort of review: preparation for what is coming.

> Begin the morning by saying to yourself: today I will meet with the busybody, the ungrateful, and the arrogant; with the deceitful, the envious, and the unsocial. All these things result from their not knowing what is good and what is evil. But I have seen the nature of the good – that it is beautiful; and the nature of evil, and that it is ugly; and the nature of him who does wrong, and that he is akin to me – not because he is from the same blood and seed, but because he partakes of the same mind and the same small bit of divinity. I cannot be injured by any of them, because no one can involve me in anything ugly except myself. And how can I be angry with my kin, or hateful towards them?

Marcus Aurelius, *Meditations* 2.1

That passage may be studied with profit by academic administrators. Seneca had offered a similar suggestion:

> The wise man is calm and even-handed in dealing with error; he is not the enemy of the mistaken, but corrects them; and as he goes forth each day he will think: "I will meet many who have given themselves over to wine, many who are lustful, many ungrateful, many greedy, many who are driven by the madness of ambition." He will view all these things in as kindly a way as a physician views the sick.

Seneca, *On Anger* 2.10.6

2. *Watching*. Another Stoic exercise in adjusted perspective: adopting a doubleness of mind, and so observing oneself through the eyes of an imaginary other. Establishing an external point of view, and personifying it, is a way to see what you are doing more objectively and hold yourself to higher standards.

> We must single out some good man, and have him always in view, so that we may live as if he

Seneca, *Epistles* 11.8–10

were watching and do everything as if he saw it.... Choose the one whose life, whose speech, whose forthright countenance, all satisfy you; then show him always to yourself as your guardian and model. We need someone, I say, against whose example our own conduct can measure itself. You can't straighten what's crooked without a ruler.

Seneca, *Epistles* 25.5

It helps, no doubt, to have appointed a guardian for oneself, to have someone you can look to, someone you regard as taking part in your thoughts. The most noble thing, by far, is to live as if you were being seen by some good man who was always present, but I'm satisfied even with this – that you do whatever you do as if *someone* were watching. It's when we're alone that we are prompted to evil.

Epictetus described the dialogue one might have with such a watcher.

Epictetus, *Discourses* 1.30.1–3, 5–7

When you are going into the presence of some man in authority, remember that another is watching what is happening from above, and that it is not the man but the other you must satisfy. So the watcher inquires of you: "Exile, prison, bondage, death, disgrace – what did you call these in the lecture-hall?" "I called them 'indifferent.'" "So now what do you call them? Have those things changed at all?" "No." "Have you changed, then?" "No." ... Well then, go in confidently, remembering these things, and you'll see what it means to be a young person who has studied, among those who have not studied. By the gods, I expect you'll feel something like this: "Why do we make so many elaborate preparations for nothing? Is this what power means? The fancy entrance, the attendants, the bodyguards? Was it for this that I listened to so many lectures? These things were nothing, and I was preparing as if they were great."

3. *Meditation.* Sometimes Stoicism is helped by just contemplating it, and by reading and writing. It is both a way of life and a way of thought. Rehearsal of accurate thinking is how one practices Stoicism and how one improves at it.

It is clear to you, Lucilius, I know, that no one can live happily or even tolerably without the study of wisdom. Wisdom, when achieved, produces a happy life; wisdom only begun still makes life bearable. But this idea must be strengthened and driven deeper by daily study; it is harder to stick to the resolutions you have already made than to make noble new ones.

Seneca, *Epistles* 16.1

Good maxims, if you keep them often in mind, will be just as beneficial as good examples. Pythagoras says that our minds are altered when we enter a temple, see the images of the gods close at hand, and await the utterance of some oracle. And who will deny that even the most ignorant may be powerfully struck by certain sayings? Statements such as these, concise but weighty: "Nothing to excess." "No wealth can satisfy the covetous." "You must expect others to treat you as you treat them."

Seneca, *Epistles* 94.42–43

The character of those things you often think about will be the character of your understanding, for the mind is dyed by its thoughts. Dip it, therefore, in a succession of thoughts such as these: for instance, that where it is possible to live, it is also possible to live well.

Marcus Aurelius, *Meditations* 5.16

I must die; so must I also die regretting something? I must be put in chains; must I also be wailing about something? I must be banished; does

Epictetus, *Discourses* 1.1.22

anyone prevent me from leaving with a smile, cheerful and easy-going? "Reveal your secrets." I don't speak; this much is up to me. "Then I will put you in chains." Man, what are you saying? Me? You can chain my leg, but Zeus himself can't overcome my will. "I'll throw you in prison." My poor body, you mean. "I'll cut your head off." When did I ever tell you that my neck was the only one that could not be severed? These are the things philosophers should think about, should write down daily, should use as exercise.

4. *Places*. The Stoics do not always take identical views of the places one goes and the company one keeps, and how choices about them bear on philosophical progress. Perhaps the answers depend on the details. Seneca acknowledged that some locations are more suitable than others for the development of wisdom.

Seneca, *Epistles* 51.2–3

Just as some clothes suit the wise and honest man better than others – and though he does not dislike any particular color, he thinks some of them inappropriate for one who has adopted the simple life – so there are places the wise man (or the one aiming at wisdom) will avoid, as not conducive to good living. Thus if he is contemplating a retreat he will never choose Canopus, though Canopus will not prevent anyone from being virtuous; and certainly not Baiæ, which has become a den of vice.

Canopus was a city of the coast of Egypt; Baiæ was a town in the southwest part of modern-day Italy (near Naples). Both were ancient resort areas famous for debauchery. Notwithstanding the challenge presented by such places, the usual attitude of the Stoics is skepticism about the importance of being in one place rather than another. They regard life as lived in the mind more than at any physical site, and view the appetite for new locations as arising from the same source as the appetite for other new things: our sensibilities are too dull to appreciate what is around us already.

> "So when will I see Athens again, and the Acropolis?" Wretch, isn't it enough for you, what you look at every day? Could you have anything better or greater to see than the sun, the moon, the stars, the whole world, the sea?

Epictetus, *Discourses* 2.16.32

Compare Cicero's remark:

> Now, if we should be suddenly brought from a state of eternal darkness to see the light, how beautiful would the heavens seem! But our minds have become used to it from the daily practice and habituation of our eyes, nor do we take the trouble to search into the principles of what is always in view; as if the novelty, rather than the importance, of things ought to excite us to investigate their causes.

Cicero, *On the Nature of the Gods* 2.38

The Stoic is less interested in changes of scenery than in changes of the self, and regards the first as unlikely to be pleasing without the second.

> How can the sight of new countries give you pleasure? Getting to know cities and places? That agitation of yours turns out to be useless. Do you want to know why your running away doesn't help? You take yourself along. Your mental burden must be put down before any place will satisfy you.

Seneca, *Epistles* 28.2

Horace also gave expression to this idea: "they change their climate, not their disposition, who run beyond the sea." (Horace, *Epistles* 1.11.) Emerson offered a well-known expression of it, too.

> We owe to our first journeys the discovery that place is nothing. At home I dream that at Naples,

Emerson, *Self-Reliance* (1841)

at Rome, I can be intoxicated with beauty and lose my sadness. I pack my trunk, embrace my friends, embark on the sea, and at last wake up in Naples, and there beside me is the stern fact, the sad self, unrelenting, identical, that I fled from. I seek the Vatican, and the palaces. I affect to be intoxicated with sights and suggestions, but I am not intoxicated. My giant goes with me wherever I go.

And Plutarch used a similar example as an analogy to describe superficial changes of all kinds that don't help us.

Plutarch, *On Tranquility of Mind* 3 (466b–466c)

Like people at sea who are cowardly and seasick and think that they would get through this voyage more comfortably if they should transfer from their little boat to a ship, and then again from the ship to a man-of-war; but they accomplish nothing by the changes, since they carry their nausea and cowardice along with them; in the same way, changing one's way of life for its opposite will not relieve the mind of the things that cause it grief and distress. These are ignorance of affairs, thoughtlessness, the inability (and the not knowing how) to make proper use of what is at hand. These are the defects which, like a storm at sea, torment rich and poor alike, that afflict the married as well as the unmarried; because of these, men avoid public life, then find their life of quiet unbearable; because of these, men seek advancement at court, by which, when they have gained it, they are immediately bored.

5. *Solitude*. The Stoics view solitude as having similarly mixed attractions. On the value of it:

Seneca, *Epistles* 94.69–71

Solitude, in itself, does not teach integrity, nor does the countryside give lessons in moderation; but those vices whose object is show and display will subside where no witness or onlooker

remains. Who puts on the purple robe when he
has no one to show it to? Who serves a single dinner on a golden plate? ... No one is elegant just for
their own benefit, or even for a few close friends;
we set out the implements of our vices in proportion to the crowd there to see them. So it is: the
stimulus of all our extravagance is the complicit
admirer. You will cause us not to desire things if
you keep us from showing them off. Ambition and
luxury and lack of restraint all need a stage: you
will heal them if you are kept from view.

On the needlessness of solitude:

> They seek out retreats for themselves – places in
> the country, seashores, the mountains – and you
> too are accustomed to crave such things especially.
> All this is utterly amateurish, since it is possible to
> retreat into oneself any time you like.

Marcus Aurelius, *Meditations* 4.3

On the risks of it:

> They say that Crates – a disciple of that Stilpo I
> mentioned in an earlier letter – when he saw a
> young man walking by himself, asked him what
> he was doing there alone. "I am conversing with
> myself," he said. To which Crates replied, "Watch
> out, I beg of you, and listen carefully: you are con-
> versing with a bad man."... No ignorant person
> should be left alone. That is when they make bad
> plans and create future troubles, either for others
> or for themselves; it's when they organize their
> ignominious desires. Whatever the mind once
> concealed, whether from fear or from shame, it
> now reveals: it sharpens boldness, stimulates lust,
> goads anger.

Seneca, *Epistles* 10.1–2

Stilpo was a Greek philosopher born in the 4th century BC. As Seneca mentions, he was a teacher of Crates of
Thebes, a member of the Cynic school; Stilpo and Crates,

in turn, are both credited as teachers of Zeno of Citium, the founder of Stoicism. All three are heroes to the Stoics.

6. *Good and bad company*. Stoicism regards us as here to work with others. So while Stoics are very alert to the hazards of social life (as we saw in Chapter 7 and will see again in a moment), they also consider relations with others important and place a high value on friendship. They are just selective about it.

Seneca, *On Tranquility of Mind* 7.3

Nothing gives the mind so much pleasure as fond and faithful friendship.

Seneca, *Epistles* 7.8

Associate with those who will improve you. Welcome those whom you yourself can improve. The process is mutual; for people learn while they teach.

Seneca, *Epistles* 109.2

Skilled wrestlers are trained by practice. A musician is inspired by one of equal proficiency. The wise man also needs to have his virtues exercised; thus in the same way that he stirs himself, he is stirred by another wise man.

On the dangers of bad company:

Epictetus, *Discourses* 3.16.1–3

A man who frequently consorts with certain others, whether for conversation, for banquets, or just generally for good fellowship, must either become like them or else change them along his own lines. For if you put a charcoal that has gone out next to one that is burning, either the first will extinguish the second or the second will ignite the first. Since the danger is so great, we should enter very cautiously into social relations of this sort with laymen, and remember that it is impossible for the man who rubs up against someone covered with soot to avoid getting the benefit of some soot himself.

So until these wise thoughts have been fixed in you, and you have acquired some power to protect yourself, I advise you to be cautious about entering the arena with the uninitiated. Otherwise, whatever you have written down in the classroom will melt away day by day, like wax in the sun.

Epictetus, Discourses 3.16.9

Seneca thought it especially important to be cautious in choosing those to whom we listen.

Just as those who have been to a concert carry away in their heads the tunes and the charm of the songs – and just as they get in the way of thinking, and won't let you concentrate on serious things – so the talk of flatterers and those who praise depravity sticks in the ears long after it is heard. It is not easy to drive the agreeable sound out of your mind: it continues, and lasts, and comes back from time to time. You should therefore close your ears to evil sayings right from the start. Once they have gained an entrance and been admitted to our minds, they become more daring.

Seneca, Epistles 123.9

Seneca also suggested that the bad people we run across in life match potentials that exist inside us. The potentials are drawn out when we spend time with their representatives in the world.

Greed will cling to you so long as you are living with someone greedy and low; so will a swelled head, so long as you keep company with someone arrogant. You'll never be free of cruelty if you're sharing a tent with an executioner. The fellowship of adulterers will inflame your own lusts. If you want to be stripped of your vices, you must withdraw far from vicious exemplars. The greedy man, the seducer, the cruel one, the cheat – all capable of much harm, if they should be anywhere near you – are inside you.

Seneca, Epistles 104.20–21

7. *Multitudes.* A problem related to the company we keep is our relationship to the social world at large, as when one goes out in public. This is an important issue for the Stoic, because the philosophy calls for engagement with public affairs but also for resistance to popular judgments and contempt for them. The Stoic shouldn't avoid the crowd, then, but has to maintain a careful relationship to it. Epictetus takes a benevolent view of massed humanity, comparing it to pleasing masses of farm animals.

Epictetus, *Discourses*
4.4.26–27

If you find yourself in a crowd – say a contest, or a festival, or a holiday – try to enjoy it with the others. For what could be a more agreeable sight, if you love your fellow man, than a number of them? When we see herds of horses or oxen, we are pleased; when we see a fleet of many ships, we are delighted; when we see many men, who will find it distressing?

Seneca sought a moderate approach to the crowd. Sometimes this is found by alternation.

Seneca, *On Tranquility of Mind*
17.3

The two things must be combined and taken by turns: solitude and the multitude. The former will leave us with a longing for the society of others, the latter for our own, and one will be the remedy for the other. Solitude will cure our aversion to the crowd; the crowd, the boredom of solitude.

Seneca also suggested moderation when *in* the crowd. There he considered it best to find a middle way that allows participation in social life while neither succumbing to it nor hating it.

Seneca, *Epistles* 7.7–8

What do you think is going to happen to manners when they are under attack on all sides? You must either imitate or reject. Yet either way is to be avoided. Don't become like the bad because there

are many of them, nor hostile to the many because
they are unlike you.

The bold course is to remain dry and sober when
the crowd is drunk and vomiting. The alternative
is more moderate: not holding yourself aloof and
making yourself conspicuous – not mingling
with the crowd, either – but doing the same things,
just not in the same way.

Seneca, Epistles 18.4

8. *The assimilation of teachings.* Stoic philosophy is
meant to be absorbed rather than admired.

Wool takes on certain colors at once, while others
it will not absorb unless it has been repeatedly
soaked in them and boiled. In the same way, there
are other systems of thought that our minds, once
they have understood them, can immediately put
into practice. But the system of which I am speaking, unless it goes deep, and sits for a long time,
and has not just tinged the mind but dyed it, does
not fulfill its promises.

Seneca, Epistles 71.31

Students of Stoicism are therefore advised not to do a lot
of talking about it. Learning should be shown, not said.
Epictetus:

Never call yourself a philosopher, and don't talk
much among laymen about philosophical principles, but act according to them.... And if you
should come upon a discussion among laymen
about some philosophical principle, keep silent
for the most part; for there is great danger that
you will immediately vomit up what you have not
digested. And when someone says to you that you
know nothing, and you're not stung by the taunt,
know then that you are making headway. Sheep
don't throw up their grass to show the shepherd
how much they have eaten; after digesting the

Epictetus, Enchiridion 46

grass inside, they bear wool and milk outside. So for you, too: don't display your learning to the uninstructed: display the actions that result from the digestion of it.

Seneca, *Epistles* 84.7–8

Let our mind do this: let it hide all the things it has made use of, and exhibit only what it has produced. Even if you will bear some resemblance to someone you admire and whose influence lies deep within you, I want your resemblance to be that of a son, not a statue: a statue is a dead thing.

To illustrate this idea, Plutarch created a simile that has become well-known.

Plutarch, *On Listening to Lectures* 18 (48c–48d)

The mind is not like a bucket that requires filling, it is like wood that needs igniting – nothing more – to produce an impulse to discovery and a longing for the truth. Imagine that someone needing fire from his neighbors, and finding there a big blazing one, just stayed warming himself until the fire burned out. It's the same if someone who comes to another man to get his thinking does not realize that he ought to strike some light of his own and kindle his own ideas, but – delighted by what he is hearing – just sits there enchanted.

9. *Words.* Similarly, Stoics are wary of too much attachment to words. They regard progress in philosophy as measured by thought and action, not by a knowledge of precepts.

Epictetus, *Discourses* 2.9.14–17

If we don't also put the right conceptions into practice, we'll be nothing more than expositors of the opinions of others. Who among us right now is not able to discourse about good and evil, according to all the rules? "That among the things in existence, some are good, some bad, some indifferent; the good then are virtues, and things that participate in virtues; the bad are the opposites; the indifferent are wealth, health, reputation." Then if there is a loud noise while we are speaking, or if someone there laughs at us, we are thrown off the track. Philosopher, where are those things you were just talking about?

The Stoics thus warn against the risk of being beguiled by verbal formulations.

That is why we give children maxims to learn by heart ... because a child's mind can grasp them, when it can't yet handle more. But for a grown man, whose progress is definite, it is disgraceful to cling to gems of rhetoric, to prop himself up with the best-known and briefest sayings, to depend on his memory: for by now he should be relying on himself. He should make such maxims and not memorize them.

Seneca, *Epistles* 33.7

It is through speech and other such forms of instruction that one must progress toward perfection, and purify one's will, and correct the faculty that makes use of impressions. And instruction in those principles calls for a certain style of presentation, and a certain vividness and variety in the way they are expressed. So some students become captivated by these things and remain stuck there – one a captive of style, another of syllogisms, another of ambiguities, another in some other roadside inn of the same kind, and there they remain and waste away, as if among the Sirens.

Epictetus, *Discourses* 2.23.40–41

A wariness of words can also affect one's taste for certain kinds of philosophizing. The Stoics highlighted in this book were impatient with theory that didn't have a concrete payoff. But the right proportion of theory was a matter of debate not just between Stoics and others but between different Stoics. Early Stoicism sometimes had a reputation for clever paradoxes and conceptual refinements that the Romans did not find appealing. They thought the stakes of philosophy were too high for constant abstraction and excessive subtlety. Seneca ridiculed the idea of stirring people to heroic acts with syllogisms, including Stoic syllogisms.

Seneca, *Epistles* 82:23–24

It takes great weapons to slay great demons.... Those tiny darts of yours – are you hurling them even against death? Do you fend off a lion with a needle? They are sharp, these arguments you make; but there is nothing sharper than a blade of straw. Some things are made futile and useless by their very subtlety.

Seneca, *Epistles* 117.33

The mind is accustomed to amuse rather than to heal itself, to treat philosophy as a diversion when it is a remedy. I don't know what difference there may be between "wisdom" and "being wise." I do know that it makes no difference to me whether I know such things or not.... So why do you occupy me with the terminology of wisdom, rather than its results? Make me bolder, make me calmer, make me the equal of fortune, raise me above it.

In Seneca's view, the project of philosophy is to help people with their most serious problems.

Seneca, *Epistles* 48.7–8

Do you want to know what philosophy has to offer to the human race? Advice. Death calls one man, poverty stings another, another is tormented by wealth – someone else's or his own. This man shudders at misfortune, that one longs to escape from his own good fortune. This one, men mistreat; that one, the gods. Why are you devising those word games of yours? This is no time for playing around: you have been summoned to help the wretched. You have promised that you will carry aid to the shipwrecked, the captives, the sick, the needy, those whose heads are under the waiting axe. Where are you straying? What are you doing?

An allied suggestion attributed to Epictetus:

> What does it matter to me, says Epictetus, whether the universe is composed of atoms or uncompounded substances, or of fire and earth? Is it not sufficient to know the true nature of good and evil, and the proper bounds of our desires and aversions, and also of our impulses to act and not to act; and by making use of these as rules to order the affairs of our life, to bid those things that are beyond us farewell? It may very well be that these latter things are not to be comprehended by the human mind; and even if one assumes that they are perfectly comprehensible, what profit comes from comprehending them?

Epictetus, Fragment (Stobæus 2.1.31)

10. *Comparisons to physical development.* Earlier chapters have noted the interest of the Stoics in a recurring pattern of error: the tendency to overvalue what we can see at the expense of what we can't – money more than time, or the benefits of acquisition more than the hidden costs of it. Stoics look at philosophical progress the same way. If changing our habits of thought seems too hard, it is because we aren't used to bringing the kind of commitment to the task that we do to more tangible goals. So our writers compare the challenges of philosophy to the effort and hardship commonly endured for the sake of lesser causes.

> Armies have put up with deprivations of every kind; they have lived on the roots of plants, and have staved off hunger in ways too revolting to mention. All these things they have suffered for the sake of a kingdom – even more wonderful, for

Seneca, *Epistles* 17.7

the sake of someone else's kingdom! Who, then, will hesitate to put up with poverty in order to free his mind from madness?

The answer, of course, is that everyone will hesitate, but the Stoic position is that none should. A related line of argument compares the labor and training demanded by Stoicism with that needed for great physical achievements.

Seneca, *Epistles* 80.2

How many men train their bodies, and how few train their minds! What crowds flock to the wrestling show – it's fake, strictly for entertainment – and what solitude surrounds the good arts! How featherbrained are the athletes whose muscles and shoulders we admire!

Indeed, training the mind ought to seem easier than training the body.

Seneca, *Epistles* 80.3

While the body requires many things to be healthy, the mind grows by itself, nourishes itself, trains itself. A great deal of food and drink is necessary for athletes, and a lot of oil, not to mention a lot of work, but you can achieve virtue without equipment and free of charge.

A favorite comparison for the Stoic is the training undertaken by acrobats. How much harder than this can Stoicism be?

Seneca, *On Anger* 2.12.3–5

Nothing is so difficult, so far out of reach, that the human mind cannot conquer it and make it familiar with constant practice; no emotions are so fierce and independent that they cannot be tamed by training. Whatever the mind commands itself, it obtains.... People have learned to run on tightropes; to carry enormous burdens, scarcely within human capacity to support; to dive to immense depths and stay underneath the water with no chance to breathe. There are a thousand other instances in which persistence surmounts every obstacle, showing that nothing is difficult if the mind orders itself to endure it.

Acrobats face their difficult tasks without concern and risk their very lives in performing them, some doing somersaults over upturned swords, some walking on ropes set at a great height, some flying through the air like birds, where one false move is death. And they do all these things for miserably small pay – while we will not endure hardship for the sake of complete happiness?

Musonius Rufus, That One Should Disdain Hardships

11. *Dedication*. One should make no mistake: to practice Stoicism takes dedication. The Stoics don't view it as a hobby.

The study of philosophy is not to be postponed until you have leisure; everything else is to be neglected in order that we may attend to philosophy, for no amount of time is long enough for it, even though our lives be prolonged from childhood to the uttermost bounds of time allotted to man.

Seneca, Epistles 72.3

How can someone learn enough to oppose his vices, if he learns only in the time he can spare from his vices? None of us goes deep. We pluck only the tips: we think a little time spent on philosophy is enough, and more than enough, for men with things to do.

Seneca, Epistles 59.10

The last occupation of the preoccupied man is living – and there is nothing that is harder to learn. The world is filled with teachers of the other arts; boys learn some of them so well that even boys can teach them. Learning how to live takes a lifetime, and – what may surprise you more – it takes a lifetime to learn how to die.

Seneca, On the Shortness of Life 7.3

12. *Encouragement.* As these last sections show, sometimes Stoics say their philosophy is hard; sometimes they
say it is well within reach. They claim it takes a lifetime
to learn but that one can make progress immediately.
They are, in the end, demanding optimists. We have seen
the demands; let us end with the optimism.

Seneca, *Epistles* 50.5–6

To tell the truth, even the work is not that great,
if only – as I said – we get started molding and
reforming the mind before its crookedness can
harden. But I don't despair even of hard cases.
There is nothing that stubborn effort and close,
persistent attention will not overcome. Oak can
be straightened, however much it is bent. Heat
unfolds curved beams; those that grew in other
shapes are fashioned into whatever our uses
require. How much more easily may the mind be
shaped, pliable as it is, and more yielding than any
liquid!

Seneca, *On Anger* 2.13.1–2

We suffer from diseases that are curable, and our
very nature assists us – since we were born to follow the right path – if we are willing to be
improved. Nor is the road to the virtues steep and
rough, as some have thought: they are reached by
a level path. I do not come to give you false advice.
The way to the happy life is easy. Just take the first
step, with good auspices and the help of the gods
themselves. It is much more difficult to do what
you are doing now.

Seneca, *Epistles* 104.25–26

So often I meet people who think that whatever
they can't do, can't be done; who say that we are
always talking of things greater than human
nature can bear. But how much more favorable is
my own estimation of them! They too can do
these things, but they don't want to. And besides,
did these tasks ever fail anyone who tried to

achieve them? Was there anyone to whom they did not seem easier in the doing? Our lack of confidence is not the result of difficulty. The difficulty comes from our lack of confidence.

The combat is great, the achievement divine; for empire, for freedom, for happiness, for peace.

Epictetus, *Discourses* 2.18.28

Chapter Thirteen
STOICISM AND ITS CRITICS

This part of the book, as a kind of afterword, consists of three brief discussions. Each involves an attack made on Stoicism and a response to it.

1. *Heartlessness.* Our first criticism comes in response to this advice from Epictetus:

Epictetus, *Enchiridion* 16 — When you see someone weeping in sorrow, either because his child goes abroad or his property is lost, don't let yourself get carried away by the impression that he is suffering because of those external things. Hold this thought in mind: "what afflicts him is not what has happened, because it wouldn't affect someone else the same way; what afflicts him is his opinion about it." So far as words go, don't hesitate to sympathize with him, or even to groan with him if he groans. But take care not to groan inside as well.

That passage provoked this response from Joseph Addison much later:

Addison, *The Spectator* no. 397 (1712) — As the Stoic philosophers discard all passions in general, they will not allow a wise man so much as to pity the afflictions of another. If thou seest thy friend in trouble, says Epictetus, thou mayst put on a look of sorrow, and condole with him, but take care that thy sorrow be not real.... For my own part, I am of opinion, compassion does not only refine and civilize human nature, but has something in it more pleasing and agreeable than what can be met with in such an indolent happiness, such an indifference to mankind as that in which the Stoics placed their wisdom.

Addison's claim epitomizes a standard criticism of the Stoics – that their philosophy is heartless and at odds with compassion. The accomplished Stoic, if such a person ever did exist, might offer words of consolation but would feel nothing (it is said) for anyone else. The Stoic cannot care about others, or about the world, because that is a form of attachment to externals.

This is all a misunderstanding. The Stoics do not condemn feeling. In important ways they endorse it. Stoics value compassion, detest indolence, and are committed to service to mankind – the opposite of what Addison thinks they want. But the Stoic would unhook these commitments from inner distress over any given case. For why stop with that case? There is cause for such distress in every direction, and meanwhile it distracts from the big picture and from anything constructive one might do about it. So yes, the Stoics consider feelings of pity unhelpful to anyone; but their aim is to do the same things without such pity that others would do on account of it. This is explained in Chapter 11, Section 5. (Sometimes the Stoics suggest having a kind of pity for one's adversaries, but it wouldn't involve distress. See Chapter 7, Section 13.) Epictetus's way of putting the point might sound a bit harsh, but his conclusion isn't much different in substance from this gentler line from Epicurus:

> Let us share our friends' suffering not with grief but with thoughtful understanding.
>
> Epicurus, Vatican Sayings 66

Still, I would prefer not to defend the Stoics by saying that Addison didn't read enough of them. There is plenty to refute him in what the Romans said, but diligent searching might find language elsewhere that gives support to some variation on his case. We at least have seen that Stoicism need not entail any of his conclusions. Instead of dwelling further on comparisons of one quotation to another, I would rather use his criticism as a chance to think further about the place of feeling and compassion in Stoicism, or anyway in the variety of it this book offers.

As discussed in Chapter 9, what the Stoics wish to avoid are emotions or other states that interfere with the ability to see the world accurately – states of feeling, in other words, that get in the way of reason and arise from (or create) attachment to externals. Stoics have no difficulty with states that do not have those sources and effects. As a temporary convenience, I proposed in Chapter 9 to refer to the good or unobjectionable states as feelings as distinct from emotions. The difference between feeling and emotion is important – or the difference, however it might better be worded, between those states that oust reason and those that are no threat to it and so do not trouble the Stoics. It matters because states of feeling, as so defined, may well be necessary to motivate compassion and otherwise contribute to admirable character. Emotion probably isn't.

Let's consider more closely the intended effect of Stoicism on the inner life of the student, and especially on the emotions, by comparing it to the effects of time. Start with the case that Addison describes: a friend stricken by terrible loss. Suppose you lived a life long enough to experience such grieving friends 1,000 times, and imagine your likely reaction when approached by the next friend – number 1,001. Not everyone reacts to repeated experience the same way, so take the most appealing scenario. Your attitude might resemble that of a doctor – a very good one, let's say – who has had a long career of working with dying patients and their families. In the best doctor of that sort we would find kindness, warmth, and compassion. There would be feeling. But emotion would be unlikely. You would sympathize but you would not go through mourning of your own. You would have seen it all too many times for that.

So far these speculations involve no Stoicism. They are just observations about the way that long experience might affect the sensibilities of anyone. But the result of this thought experiment, if accepted, is a state of mind about the same as what the Stoics seek. The resemblance is natural. Time and experience are the teachers of life. They gradually bring about wisdom. Adam Smith said it this way:

Smith, *The Theory of Moral Sentiments* (1759)

> Time, the great and universal comforter, gradually composes the weak man to the same degree of tranquility which a regard to his own dignity and manhood teaches the wise man to assume in the beginning.

My claim here is the converse. If the Stoic says we are fettered to externals, or vice, or emotion, it may be as accurate to say we are fettered to our inexperience. Only the novice is inflated and grasping and fearful; but we are all novices. Life is regrettably short because it does not allow us enough trials to become as wise as we would wish. Stoic philosophy is a compensation – a substitute for time, or simulation of it. Stoicism means to offer the wisdom while skipping the repetition; it tries to get by contemplation some of the lessons, immunities, and other features of character we would acquire naturally if we lived long enough. The "wise man" of the Stoics thus resembles one who has had long experience of life – far longer, perhaps, than anyone is able to have in fact. Stoicism is the philosophy of a thousand trials.

The connection between Stoicism and the consequences of time can be extended. Think of the effect that repetition has on other emotions. What is frightening at first usually becomes nothing, or loses force, with long enough exposure. The source of the fear doesn't change; the mind does. Or imagine making a fortune and losing it a thousand times over, or loving and grieving a thousand times. You might not stop caring about these things, and might not want to. But you would probably gain a sense of equanimity about them and meet them with a certain detachment – with feeling but with reason, and thus without emotion. Little would likely be left of greed and vanity, either, after so much gain and loss. Experience is humbling. Instead you might have other types of joy – the calm kind that comes from appreciation and understanding.

To return to the point: the absence of emotion prescribed by the Stoics in response to a thing is also what we would expect naturally from long enough exposure to it. Feeling and compassion can survive and even grow with long repetition and experience. Emotion does not. The sifting between emotion and feeling that comes naturally with experience resembles what the Stoic aims to achieve by the practice of philosophy.

Connecting the Stoic disposition to the quality of character that arises from long experience is productive in several ways. First, it helps make the Stoic ideal less otherworldly. The long-experience view allows Stoicism to be viewed as an extension of the life we know – an effort to go farther down the road of being human, not to affect godliness in the way that we will see criticized by Dryden later in this chapter. Stoicism tries to give us what we would gain with more difficulty, but naturally enough, if we had more time.

Second, the experience-based view makes the goals of Stoicism more familiar and easier to understand. Everyone has had small experiences of inurement by experience and the difference between feeling and emotion that can result. We don't need a dozen lifetimes to get the idea of it. One can compare the first experience of grief with the tenth, or the first encounter with an amusement with the fiftieth, or the first kiss with the hundredth. These experiences need not lose their meaning or be had without feeling. We might say instead, in the most attractive case, that the feelings at stake mature and change. But even then such events do eventually lose their emotional charge and become no threat to reason. There are cases in which emotional inurement is harder to come by, of course. I only mean to say that the process of it, and the qualities of the Stoic "wise man," are familiar enough to most people on a modest scale.

Third, the long-experience view of Stoicism clarifies the Stoic ideal as admirable. In the personality formed by many trials we find the qualities of the finished Stoic represented in an attractive way. There is nothing ugly in the type of character produced by long experience, or at least nothing necessarily so. It *can* be unattractive; sometimes experience jades us and dulls our capacities. But there is nobility in it when joined with compassion. Stoicism demands this. It seeks to create not just the mind matured by many trials, but the best version of it – the doctor who has learned with the passage of much time to care well and energetically for the patient, not the doctor who is bored.

Fourth, viewing Stoicism as similar to long experience can help to solve some conundrums. Sometimes the general principles of the philosophy can seem tricky to apply to particular facts. Stoics discourage the emotion of anger, but what if you are the victim of some grotesque injustice? Isn't it then right to be angry – and maybe even important, since the anger will motivate efforts to stop the injustice from happening again? One can reason through that kind of problem with precepts that this book has discussed. You might say that the Stoic cares about justice and doesn't need anger to motivate a reply to a violation of it, etc. (See Chapter 9, Section 12.) But our current idea offers a shortcut. If you want to react to injustice like a Stoic, react like someone who knows it by long experience – not someone who has adapted to injustice and no longer cares, but perhaps someone whose life's work is the correction of it. Those sorts of people, in my own experience, tend to meet injustice with feeling but little emotion. Their equilibrium isn't upset by a fresh case of wrongdoing. They deal with it too often to respond that way. They are resolute, tough, and active in style; and (to return to our question) when the injustice afflicts someone else, they are highly compassionate. They have, for *these* purposes, become natural Stoics. The best lawyers can be like this.

We can end this part of the discussion by reversing our earlier thought experiment. You are grieving and can be consoled by either of two friends: one for whom your calamity is a new experience, and who is full of emotion about it on seeing your grief; or one who has seen it a thousand times, and so has warm and caring feeling but not emotion. I would take the second, but at any rate see no basis for admiring the first one more. The second one is the Stoic.

That is enough about heartlessness. By way of addendum, though, I wish to spend a few more words on the relationship between Stoicism and experience; for the discussion a moment ago mentioned some tradeoffs that deserve further comment. If experience erodes emotion, some might consider the erosion a loss, and then dread repetition precisely because emotions *don't* survive it. One can think of cases where those who have been through an experience many times may seem less wise with respect to it. They can't see it freshly; they barely notice it; they don't appreciate it. They have been corrupted by adaptation.

It might be fairest to say there are different types of wisdom, or sensibilities helpful on different occasions. There is the sensibility of the veteran who has seen it (whatever it is) too many times to be emotional but has other advantages: perspective, good judgment, and the ease and warmth that arise from long familiarity and knowledge. Those are great virtues. They are central to Stoicism. But they aren't the only ones, and aren't always the ones most wanted even by a Stoic. There is also the sensibility of the newcomer to a subject – one who has the advantages of the amateur, such as appreciation of what is at hand.

These claims about the effects of experience and inexperience can be restated in terms referenced earlier in the book. The Stoic seeks the most useful perspective on all occasions. I have emphasized here that, with respect to emotion and adversity, Stoics want the kind of wisdom that we associate with long experience. But in certain settings they seek, in effect, the attitude of the newcomer. A reminder from Chapter 12, Sec. 4:

> "When then shall I see Athens again and the Acropolis?" Epictetus, *Discourses*
> Wretch, are you not content with what you see daily? 2.16.32
> Have you anything better or greater to see than the sun,
> the moon, the stars, the whole earth, the sea?

From Chapter 5, Sec. 8:

> Don't imagine having things that you don't have. Rather, Marcus Aurelius,
> pick the best of the things that you do have and think of *Meditations* 7.27
> how much you would want them if you didn't have them.

In effect we can distinguish two kinds of mistakes. We fail to appreciate some things because they are too familiar. We overreact to others because they aren't familiar enough. In the first case we suffer because we can't see old things as a first-timer would. In the second we suffer because can't see new things as a long-timer would. The Stoic is more concerned with the second kind of mistake than the first, but understands them both and tries to move from one point of view to another as appropriate to the situation.

One can revisit many topics in this book and reinterpret them according to how much repetition (of a hypothetical kind) would be found in the ideal mindset for dealing with them. Acceptance and satisfaction, and therefore detachment from desire, can often be furthered by the newcomer's perspective – by learning to see familiar things as if they weren't familiar, and to touch them without callouses on our fingers. That same perspective can help us see that a convention is idiotic or unjust in ways too familiar to be commonly perceived. Emotion and adversity (and sometimes desires, too) call for the opposite view – that is, for an attitude toward the subjects of those states that would be found in someone with long experience of them. When considering whatever one loves or hates – when considering any reaction to anything – it is instructive to ask how much of it is owed to the number of times one has encountered the subject, whether it be many or few.

Stoicism should not be overestimated. Reflection cannot produce all the qualities of character and feeling that long experience does, nor can it reverse them, which may be harder still. But Stoicism should not be underestimated, either, because reflection can help with some of this. The point may be seen in settings that do not involve emotion as well as in those that do. When one has studied novelty and thought about it for a sufficiently long time that it loses charm and is less likely to cause you to do foolish things, that is Stoicism, and it is to the good. (Or replace "novelty" with "luxury" or "status" – all the same.) The alternative is to be taken in by novelty again and again until it is finally drained of its charm by many hard lessons about its unimportance, maybe late in life. The sage saves the trouble.

2. *Impossibility.*

Dryden, *Don Sebastian* (dedication) (1690)

The ruggedness of a Stoic is only a silly affectation of being a god, – to wind himself up by pulleys to an insensibility of suffering, and, at the same time, to give the lie to his own experience, by saying he suffers not, what he knows he feels. True philosophy is certainly of a more pliant nature, and more accommodated to human use.... A wise man will never attempt an impossibility; and such it is to strain himself beyond the nature of his being, either to become a deity, by being above suffering, or to debase himself into a stock or stone, by pretending not to feel it.

Dryden offers another familiar critique of Stoicism: that its teachings are impossible to carry out. To repeat the point that provokes the criticism, the Stoics say we should try to control what is up to us and avoid attachment to what is not. Our judgments, and our reactions to events, are up to us; the events themselves aren't. Stoics sometimes express the idea by depicting a "wise man" (or *sapiens*) who, by use of these principles, is free from desires and fears. No such wise man has ever been identified, and some dismiss Stoicism on this account as a philosophy that doesn't work.

As in the previous section of this chapter, we can use the criticism as a chance to think about a larger question it raises – here, about whether Stoicism might be valuable even if its teachings cannot be perfectly followed. But as before, a word should be said, first, about what the Stoic teachings really require. Stoics suffer and do not pretend otherwise, though they don't see any point in carrying on about it. What they try to do is understand the role of their own minds in the creation of their suffering, and then use that knowledge to reduce it. But the good Stoic, or in any event the type discussed in this book, takes a clear-eyed view of the human condition. Someone who likes Dryden's criticism should also like this passage about reacting to the death of a loved one:

> I well know that there are those whose wisdom is harsh rather than brave, who deny that the wise man will ever grieve. But these people, it seems to me, can never have run into this sort of misfortune; if they had, Fortune would have knocked their proud philosophy out of them and forced them to admit the truth even against their will.

Seneca, *Consolation to Polybius* 18.5–6

This might sound like just the sort of thing that should be said against the Stoics – a blast of realism that exposes the unworkable character of their philosophy. But in fact those are the words of Seneca, as found in Ch. 9, Sec. 6 of this book, where he offers a much more realistic vision than the one Dryden attacks. His words help correct the caricature of Stoicism as a theory that asks the impossible, or of the Stoic as someone who pretends not to feel anything. The reader who has arrived at this point in the book after reading the rest will already know that the Stoics were wiser than that.

Or at least some of them were. The passage from Seneca also shows, in fairness, that Stoicism doesn't always mean the same thing. The people he criticized there were probably other Stoics, and no doubt other Stoics would in turn have criticized him. As Seneca himself put it, "We Stoics are not subjects of a despot: each of us lays claim to his own freedom." (*Epistles* 33.4) The Stoic view of the emotions is very involved if one tries to view it as a whole and include what we know of the views of the Greeks. It is not done justice by this book (or by Dryden). Seneca's views above, and in Chapter 9, can indeed be viewed as lapses from Stoicism if the philosophy is defined in certain ways. As noted in the preface, I prefer to view the set of ideas in this book as a version of Stoicism rather than a mix of authentic and heretical claims. But the preface also noted my lack of excitement about such arguments, so for now I will just say that the framework offered by this book is not very open to Dryden's complaint.

Still, let's now acknowledge the truth in his criticism. A perfectly Stoic existence, even if it need not mean what Dryden thought, is no doubt impossible. It would presumably amount to never being attached to externals and to living a life of continuous virtue. The greatest Stoic teachers were the first to say that they hadn't managed this, though it was not their style to say it couldn't be done by anyone. The Stoics do urge their students and themselves to try to reach the Stoic ideal, and sometimes talk as though it is possible. They merely add that it has never been done in fact, or almost never.

Seneca, *On Tranquility of Mind* 7.4

Nor would I advise you that you should neither follow (nor take as a follower) anyone but a wise man. For where will you find that man – the one we have been seeking for so many centuries? In place of the best, let it be the least bad!

Seneca, *On the Constancy of the Wise Man* 7.1

There is no reason for you to say, Serenus, as your habit is, that this wise man of ours is nowhere to be found. He is not a fiction of us Stoics, a sort of phantom glory of human nature, nor is he a mere conception, the mighty semblance of a thing unreal; but a man such as we describe, we have displayed and will display again – though perhaps only seldom, and at intervals of many lifetimes for each example.

The Stoic that Seneca has in mind as an example is Stilpo, a Greek philosopher who had lived three hundred years earlier and left no writings; he in turn was a teacher of Zeno of Citium. The most famous basis for the assessment of Stilpo is an anecdote in which he loses his wife and children when his country is sacked, yet emerges calmly and says "I have all my goods with me." If Stilpo had been present in later Rome, he probably would have resembled Epictetus or some such figure, and would have joined him in denying his own perfection. And of course he would have been right. Anyone can seem perfect when we don't know too much about them. That is why the Stoic models, on the rare occasions when they offer them, are always from past generations.

Epictetus himself did not think a finished Stoic was any easier to find.

> Show me a Stoic, if you have one. Where, how? … As we   Epictetus, *Discourses*
> call a statue "Phidian" which has been fashioned according   2.19.21–25
> to the art of Phidias, in the same way, show me someone
> fashioned according to the doctrines which you prattle. Show me
> someone who is sick and happy, in danger and happy, dying and
> happy, exiled and happy, disgraced and happy. Show him – by the
> gods, I want to see a Stoic! So you don't have a completed one ready to
> show me – then show me the work in progress, the one leaning in that
> direction. Do me this kindness, don't begrudge an old man the sight
> of this spectacle, which up till now I have never seen!

So there are no perfect Stoics. This would be an important point if the "wise man," or sage, were a status one must reach or else fail entirely. The early Greek Stoics have sometimes been cited, fairly or otherwise, as taking something like that position. But the Romans did not, and sensibly so, for what would be the point of a philosophy (if ever there were one) that offers nothing without achievement of the impossible? The wise man of the Stoics is best considered a point of reference that is helpful even if out of reach. It is a convenient way to illustrate the meaning of perfect wisdom: imagine how someone in possession of it would think and act. That was Kant's view of the idea.

> The wise man of the Stoics is an ideal, that is to say, a human   Kant, *Critique of Pure*
> being existing only in thought and in complete confor-   *Reason* (1781)
> mity with the idea of wisdom. As the idea provides a rule,
> so the ideal serves as an archetype for the perfect and

complete determination of the copy. Thus the conduct of this wise and divine man serves us as a standard of action, with which we may compare and judge ourselves, which may help us to reform ourselves, although the perfection it demands can never be attained by us.

Kant's view is consistent with what the late Stoics said. We can compare it to Seneca's distinction between the ideals of Stoicism and the aims of it that are usually achievable. He understood the value of an ideal that might not be reachable.

Seneca, *Epistles* 95.44–45   It is necessary that we set up the highest good as the end toward which we struggle, and which our every deed and action has in view – just as sailors have to set their course by some constellation.

When speaking of actual progress in Stoicism, Seneca put students into three classes. The first and second have freedom from emotions and externals but differ in how securely they have made those gains. Then there is the third class, which seems to be as far as most can be expected to get.

Seneca, *Epistles* 75.14–15   The third class has got past many vices, and serious ones, but not past all of them. They have escaped avarice, but still feel anger. They are no longer troubled by lust, but still by ambition. They no longer covet, but they still fear. And even in their fear they are sufficiently resolute against certain things but give way to others. They despise death but dread pain. Let us reflect a moment on this last point. Things will be going well for us if we make it into this group. It takes great good fortune in terms of natural gifts, great and unceasing application to study, to attain the second level; but even this third condition is not to be despised. Think what a host of evils you see around you; see how no crime goes uncommitted, how far wickedness advances every day, how much wrongdoing occurs both in public and in private. You will see that we're doing pretty well if we're not among the worst.

By sometimes talking as though everyone should conform to the Stoic ideal, the Stoics no doubt set themselves up for some ridicule and received their share. We nevertheless should interpret Stoicism in a way that makes the best sense of it that fairly can be found. This includes choosing between the sometimes inconsistent teachings of the Stoics in ways that now enable the philosophy to best serve its purpose. The purpose of Stoicism is to help those who study it see the truth more accurately and engage in wiser thinking and living, not to reach an end point or else be judged to have wasted their time. The "wise man" is a help to that project. It is best understood as a pole star – a source of direction, not a destination.

3. *Hypocrisy.*

> From the testimony of friends as well as of foes, from the confessions of Epictetus and Seneca, as well as from the sneers of Lucian and the fierce invectives of Juvenal, it is plain that these teachers of virtue had all the vices of their neighbors, with the additional vice of hypocrisy.
>
> Macaulay, *Lord Bacon* (1837)

Some critics have claimed, with Macaulay, that Stoicism is a school of hypocrisy. Stoics claim to be free from vanity and greed and fear (the critic says), and they exhort others to join them, but are as immersed in those vices as anyone else. They advocate for virtue but are not virtuous.

Stoicism's reputation for hypocrisy arises mostly from its association with Seneca, and considering his case will be a way to address the issue generally. Seneca was a controversial player in the political life of his times. As noted in the preface, he served as a tutor and advisor to Nero, an emperor with an ugly reputation, and Seneca may have aided him in various immoral undertakings; Seneca's situation was, at the least, morally complex. Critics also are uneasy about Seneca's money. Seneca wrote that "No one is worthy of the gods except he who has disdained riches," yet he himself was immensely wealthy – the owner of many slaves, and evidently of villas in Italy, Egypt, and Spain. It is said, too, that he lent money to the colonial Britons that they did not want, then later recalled the loans abruptly and to ruinous effect.

I think it is more constructive to consider the example of Marcus Aurelius, a fellow Stoic whose reputation as a man and as a statesman is very favorable. But since Seneca has been the subject of so much discussion and suspicion, let me offer some comments on the use of him to disparage Stoicism, and on the problem of Stoic hypocrisy in general.

a. A great deal has been written about Seneca over the past 2,000 years, some of it sympathetic and some not. It is too extensive to be captured in this space. Most of what anyone thinks they know about him, though, is derived from the histories of Tacitus, Suetonius, and Cassius Dio, along with fragmentary comments from Seneca's contemporaries. The most prominent account of Seneca left from his lifetime was that of a bitter enemy, Publius Suillius Rufus, recounted in the *Annals* of Tacticus (13.42); but Suillius is described by Tacitus as highly disreputable in his own right.

Seneca himself left behind only his philosophical writings and plays. Beyond those works we know little of what he ever said to Nero (though see the interesting item at the end of Chapter 9, Section 10) or of how he thought about the harrowing ethical position he seems to have occupied. Sometimes good people work for bad ones. Seneca might have done it for the sake of the public, or for lesser reasons; he might have made Nero worse than he otherwise would have been, or better; he might have had a hand in trying to kill Nero, or maybe not (Nero certainly thought that he did). All of this ends in speculation, now and for the ancient historians. Seneca had been dead fifty years when Tacitus wrote his *Annals*. (Suetonius, who also wrote about Seneca, was a contemporary of Tacitus.) Cassius Dio wrote nearly a century later.

In view of the thin record, the grounds for skepticism about most judgments of Seneca are plain enough. For the sake of comparison, it has been aptly suggested that we imagine a figure from our own times being remembered and evaluated 2,000 years from now on the basis of contemporary accounts by an enemy and later writings of two or three historians who haven't been born yet. The historians don't have any recordings of the figure himself or access to more than a few people who ever saw or met him. By modern standards they have only a tiny set of records in written form. We have trouble understanding public figures from recent times who are studied by historians and psychologists without those disadvantages. Our wariness should greatly increase when we look into the distant past. All comments about Seneca's motives, inner life, and private conduct should be accompanied by an asterisk and notation that our odds of getting these things right cannot be very impressive.

Despite these limitations, there has been long and plentiful surmise about the sort of person Seneca was, much of it censorious and bearing no asterisk. Commentators have debated what he must have thought about his emperor, what he must have thought when he wrote his letters, what he must have thought when he killed himself. These speculations are unobjectionable if not taken too seriously. But judgments of hypocrisy require a detailed intimacy with the facts and characters involved that I do not think anyone can have now with respect to Seneca.

b. Then again, what difference would it make if we could? A bad man can write a good book. Seneca wasn't a religious figure trying to inspire by example. He was a philosopher trying to convince by reason. True, he does say that philosophers should be judged by how they live rather than what they say, so maybe he fails when judged by his own measure (or maybe he doesn't – see point 1 above); but the measure itself is ill-chosen. What a philosopher or psychologist writes should be judged on its merits. This is especially true of writings such as Seneca's, which mean to offer a useful way of thinking. It helps or it doesn't.

c. For all that, reconsider what Seneca actually said. It is too easy to fasten on to severe things he wrote without the qualifications that usually came afterwards. A moment ago I quoted a line from him about disdaining wealth. But now consider the longer passage from which it came, which also appeared in Chapter 6:

> No one is worthy of the gods except he who has dis-
> dained riches. I do not forbid you to possess them,
> but I want to bring you to the point at which you
> possess them without fear. There is only one way to achieve
> this: by persuading yourself that you can live happily without
> them, and by regarding them always as about to depart.

Seneca, *Epistles* 18.13

This reflects Seneca's approach to Stoicism generally. It is a philosophy of detachment from pleasures and aversions, not extermination of them. This is valuable to understand for its own sake, since otherwise the Stoics might seem to ask the ridiculous: no preferences or enjoyments allowed. It is also valuable to understand when judging claims that Stoics are hypocrites because some of them had money but said that nobody should. There admittedly can be something odd or distasteful when a philosopher argues for the unimportance of riches while surrounded by them. But if one insists on comparing what Seneca said to what he did, what he said should be remembered carefully. Maybe he managed the kind of detachment from his wealth that he advocates; maybe he gave large amounts of it away. Juvenal's Fifth Satire, written in the generation after Seneca died, mentions the generosity of Seneca as if everyone knew about it, and epigrams of Martial from the same era contain a similar reference. But again, what relationship Seneca had to his money is, in the end, something at which we can only guess.

Next, and relatedly, Seneca did not claim to be a particularly accomplished Stoic. His many criticisms of conventional behavior seem to have been directed largely at himself.

Seneca, *Epistles* 27.1   I'm not so shameless as to undertake to heal others while sick myself. It is rather as if we were lying in the same hospital room; I'm talking with you about our common illness, and sharing remedies. So listen to me as though I were talking to myself. I'm letting you into my private place, and am examining myself, using you as a foil.

Seneca sometimes showed exasperation with the complaints we are now considering, which were made during his life as well as later.

Seneca, *On the Happy Life* 18.1–2   "You speak one way, you live another." You creatures most spiteful, hostile to all the best men! This is the same taunt they threw at Plato, at Epicurus, at Zeno: for all of them were teaching not how they themselves lived, but how they ought to live. I am speaking of virtue, not of myself, and when I denounce vices, I denounce my own first of all. As soon as I can, I'll live as I should.

That last attitude is characteristic of Stoics. This book has shown many times over that their philosophy is founded on humility. Anyone who crows about being a Stoic isn't; progress in Stoicism may be measured in part by one's awareness of failure at it. A kindred offering from Marcus Aurelius:

This thought too will help you avoid empty self-es-
teem: you can no longer have lived your whole life,
or even your life since youth, as a philosopher. Rather
it has become obvious to many others, as well as to yourself,
that you are far removed from philosophy. You have become
confused, and getting a reputation as a philosopher is no longer
easy for you; your position in life is also at war with it. If you
have seen how matters truly lie, get rid of thoughts about how
you will seem to others. Be satisfied if you can live out the rest
of your life, whatever remains of it, with what wisdom your
nature provides.

Marcus Aurelius,
Meditations 8.1

d. Putting aside Seneca, the claim of hypocrisy also misunderstands
what Stoicism is *for* in the lives of most of those with an interest in it.
The claim views Stoicism as if it were a creed to which its adherents
try to make converts, or that they use as a basis for judgment of others.
That would leave the Stoic open to criticism for preaching one thing
but doing another. Such a vision arises understandably enough from
the writings in this book. In order to teach their ideas to others, the
Stoics had to offer them as instructions. But the practice of Stoicism
has nothing to do with telling others how to act or saying anything
else that might be contradicted by what one does. Stoicism, at least for
most who now study it, is a set of tools for thought, and a way of using
them, with which some find they can help themselves. It is something
to do, not something to say.

e. A productive last question one might ask about Stoicism is: compared to what? Suppose – plausibly, I think – that typical students of
Stoicism advance only slightly toward its goals. They end up with a
little less anxiety over what they can't control, and a little more
patience with irritation, indignity, and misfortune; a bit more resistance to convention in their thinking, and somewhat less desire or fear
directed at things undeserving of either, and so forth. In other words,
they make some modest progress. There are those who get more than
that from the philosophy, and some get less, but imagine that this
much were a common result. Those are paltry gains compared to the
attainment of sagehood, but considerable compared to a baseline

without them. They are considerable, too, compared to the results of other kinds of philosophical study (how much more does any philosophy do for its students?). It would be foolish to regard small improvements with contempt when it is so rare to find any other kind. So if Stoics seek great things but get only part way there, the discrepancy should not cause them to be thought of as hypocrites. They aimed high, fell short, and did well.

A NOTE ON THE TYPE

THE PRACTICING STOIC *has been set in Sabon Next, a type with a distinguished and complex history. Originally commissioned in the 1960s from the master typographer, designer, and calligrapher Jan Tschichold, Sabon is a contemporary interpretation of a roman type attributed to Claude Garamond and an italic attributed to Robert Granjon. It was named in honor of Jacques Sabon, a punchcutter who worked for the printer who created the specimen on which Tschichold based his design. Because the types were initially intended for machine composition on both Linotype and Monotype as well as for hand composition, the design was carefully drawn and modified to accommodate the limitations imposed by the various methods of composition. This process resulted in a widely popular type that was somewhat compromised by its lack of kerns, a feature that limited the appeal of the italic in particular. Sabon Next was drawn in 2002 by Jean François Porchez, who set out to harmonize Tschichold's type and the types that inspired it with the possibilities that the OpenType platform offered to the contemporary type designer. The result is an elegant, highly readable type with a complete range of characters (including a generous selection of ligatures, swash characters, and ornaments) that is beautifully suited to book work.*

DESIGN & COMPOSITION BY CARL W. SCARBROUGH

1970~2020
David R. Godine
Publisher
FIFTY YEARS